AN ARCHIPELAGO OF C

GLOBAL RESEARCH STUDIES

The Global Research Studies series is part of the Framing the Global project, an initiative of Indiana University Press and the Indiana University Center for the Study of Global Change, funded by the Andrew W. Mellon Foundation.

Hilary E. Kahn and Deborah Piston-Hatlen, series editors

ADVISORY COMMITTEE

Alfred C. Aman Jr.
Eduardo Brondizio
Maria Bucur
Bruce L. Jaffee
Patrick O'Meara
Radhika Parameswaran
Heidi Ross
Richard R. Wilk

# AN ARCHIPELAGO
# OF CARE

*Filipino Migrants and Global Networks*

Deirdre McKay

Indiana University Press

Bloomington and Indianapolis

This book is a publication of

Indiana University Press
Office of Scholarly Publishing
Herman B Wells Library 350
1320 East 10th Street
Bloomington, Indiana 47405 USA

iupress.indiana.edu

⊗ The paper used in this publication meets the minimum
requirements of the American National Standard for Information
Sciences—Permanence of Paper for Printed Library Materials, ANSI
Z39.48-1992.

Manufactured in the United States of America

Library of Congress Cataloging-in-Publication Data

Names: McKay, Deirdre, author.
Title: An archipelago of care : Filipino migrants and global networks /
    Deirdre McKay.
Description: Bloomington : Indiana University Press, [2016] | Series:
    Global research studies | Includes bibliographical references and
    index.
Identifiers: LCCN 2016041299 (print) | LCCN 2016044084 (ebook) |
    ISBN 9780253024671 (cloth : alk. paper) | ISBN 9780253024831
    (pbk. : alk. paper) | ISBN 9780253024985 (e-book)
Subjects: LCSH: Foreign workers, Filipino—Social networks—
    England—London. | Kankanay (Philippine people)—Social
    networks—England—London. | Household employees—Social
    networks—England—London. | Service industries workers—
    Social networks—England—London.
Classification: LCC HD8398.F55 M35 2016 (print) | LCC HD8398.F55
    (ebook) | DDC 331.5/440899921—dc23
LC record available at https://lccn.loc.gov/2016041299

1  2  3  4  5   22 21 20 19 18 17

# Contents

# Acknowledgments

MY THANKS TO my friends Biag and Labanet, who have generously shared their lives with me—both in London and in the Philippines. Keeping their real names confidential and blurring some of their identifying details are the least I can do to protect their privacy. While these same concerns preclude thanking all my other respondents by name here, they do not lessen the gratitude I feel to them for contributing to the project.

No book is an academic island; this one is especially well networked. As I developed the project, I had wonderful mentors in June Prill-Brett in Baguio City and Danny Miller in London. My research began with a visiting research associate position with Danny at University College London, part of my Senior Research Fellow role on the Footsteps project, an AHRC UK "Diasporas, Migrations, and Identities" theme initiative, led by Pnina Werbner (Keele University) and Mark Johnson (Goldsmiths). My work then received support from the Framing the Global initiative funded by the Mellon Foundation and Indiana University Press. As part of this amazing interdisciplinary collaboration, I benefitted from discussions with the other Fellows: Rachel Harvey, Prakash Kumar, Alex Perullo, Stephanie de Boer, Sean Metzger, Faranak Miraftab, Zsuzsa Gille, Tim Bartley, Deborah Cohen, Lessie-Jo Fraser, Katerina Teaiwa, Manuela Ciotti, and Anne Griffiths. Hilary Kahn and Deborah Piston-Hatlen gave great advice, as did project visitors Saskia Sassen and Gillian Hart. Finally, when it came to the nitty-gritty of polishing draft chapters, I owe thanks to my readers: Rachel Harvey, Marie-Andrée Jacob, Ben Smith, Lisa Lau, and Labanet.

Funds from the Framing the Global initiative enabled me to complete the bulk of the UK fieldwork. A small grant from the British Academy–supported Association of Southeast Asian Studies UK covered travel to the Philippines, while Keele University contributed travel costs for my final round of interviews in London.

The image on the cover is *Sa lilim ng plastic* (the shadow of plastic) by Baguio artist Jojet Lamberto Mondares. Jet's plastic bag collage shows a mother cradling her children. He created this piece in response to the landslide in Baguio City in 2011 plastic bags buried in a former landfill site made the slopes of the suburb built above it unstable. This same hillside suburb is where my respondents in chapter 6, "Back Home," have invested their London earnings.

# Note on Transliteration

To TRANSLITERATE MY respondents' comments from Filipino, Ilokano, and Kankanaey, I follow accepted linguistic conventions. Kankanaey, Ilokano, and Filipino terms appear in italics and are defined at first use. All translations are my own, with assistance from my respondents, and appear in square brackets within quotations. The exception to these conventions is the "text speak" slang—developed for SMS messaging and combining local languages with English—that my respondents also used to post comments on social media. I reproduce these comments verbatim, including keyboard errors, SMS "shortcuts," and spelling mistakes, and with translation for non-English terms. Similarly, where respondents spoke or wrote in Filipino English and I have transcribed or quoted their comments, their original grammar and syntax appears intact.

# AN ARCHIPELAGO OF CARE

# Introduction

## An Archipelago of Care

"To care, you have to CARE. It's that simple." Father Alabag brought his hand, palm flat, down on the table for emphasis. His gesture caused the table to shudder and coffee cups to clink. His wide-eyed expression held my attention as spilled coffee sloshed into the saucers. Recoiling from Father Alabag's intensity, Ros-al, Calangbay, and I drew back with gasps, our wooden chairs squeaking. Father Alabag had preached the sermon at his East London church that morning. In the evening, he would work as a caregiver for an elderly man with dementia. He spoke with eloquence about his inability to find steady work in London. He had arrived five years earlier on a tourist visa. He had overstayed, hoping to eventually find a permanent job and somehow convert his visa status. Now he felt stuck in London, unable to find a stable livelihood yet reluctant to go home—one of the United Kingdom's six hundred thousand or more undocumented migrants, working as a cash-in-hand caregiver.

Father Alabag was not only a caregiver, a priest, and an irregular migrant; he was also a community activist. I met him after church, introduced by his cousin Ros-al and her friend, Calangbay. I had invited all three of them to a café nearby to discuss their thoughts on Filipinos and care work in the United Kingdom. I wanted to know how Filipino migrants were able to sustain their reputations as caregivers in the London labor market. I'd hoped their answer would tell me what care was. Was it some special aptitude or technique? "No!" There was no special national Filipino aptitude for care—Father Alabag was adamant. So I'd asked, "What, then, gives Filipino migrants such a well-regarded aptitude for caring work? How do Filipino migrants support themselves in doing care?" And Father Alabag expanded on his initial idea:

> Care is care. Always the same . . . What you need to see is not how we care for our charges or employers, but how we bond with each other. It's our bonding that lets us care well. When we are cared for, we then can care for others. So it's our socials, our church services, our events that let us care. That's where we sustain ourselves. Me, I am also a caregiver—for an old man. So I can work each day, I need to take my good feelings—the bonding I have with my friends, my congregation here, family, even Facebook, like that. That's what lets me work . . . The bathing, cleaning, turning, talking with him, changing the sheets, laundry, toilet . . . all that I can do because I feel . . . I also have care; I

am cared about by my friends, my family. They look for me, listen, and give me advice; it's like that, you know?

It's not a special Filipino ability, to care . . . We Filipinos are just good at staying together, building unity among ourselves. But for us, us Kankanaeys—we're not just Filipinos but IPs [indigenous peoples]—and, for us, it's also an obligation to care for others. A spiritual obligation. Because we have this idea: *inayan*. It's like your karma.

Father Alabag was passionate about care. His strength of feeling, made evident in his wide eyes, raised voice, direct gaze, and in the rattle of the cups on the table, held attention. The power of this feeling was cocreated by the drawing back of his audience and by the way Ros-al's and Calangbay's responsive nods punctuated his speech. This flow of feeling from speaker to audience, back and forth in a relay, raised the energy with which Father Alabag spoke. His passion came from a personal, spiritual commitment to care, but also from frustrations he felt over his own failed plans. Father Alabag seemed anxious because, having overstayed his visitor's visa, he might no longer command respect from others in the United Kingdom's Filipino community. He wanted to be sure his analysis of his situation and work compelled our respect. Father Alabag went on to speak with conviction about both the business of global care and the roots of the capacity for compassionate care in Kankanaey culture, describing how he, himself, had traded on stereotypes about Filipino care to find work.

Father Alabag introduces the puzzle of sustaining global care. What is at stake in this puzzle is the future of care in aging societies, such as the United Kingdom, on the one hand, and economic development in peripheral areas in the global South, on the other. Care is risky: caring practices don't always deliver the affective experience of being cared about or for. But the care work of Filipino migrants like Father Alabag links the murky bottom end of the UK jobs market with social mobility for households in expanding economies on the other side of the world. Filipino migrants are recognized as delivering high quality, effective care—there is demand for their skills in the job market, even if they lack the formal right to work. It seems care workers and care skills are not easily substituted. Father Alabag answered my question, "What is care?" by directing me to sociality and networks. He was adamant that the Filipino capacity for care was the result of cultural practices and "bonding." His message was: "No care without culture."

Father Alabag's passion and precision about the cultural origins of care made me curious. He argued that cultural concepts, practices, and spaces created Filipinos' global capacity and reputation for care. He described care as a global field of reciprocity. Even if UK employers and UK society didn't quite reciprocate migrants' care, their friends, the spiritual realm, and family back home would take care of migrant care workers. Father Alabag identified the origins of care in social networks and unity. In these networks, the intensity of people's feelings of connection with each other sustained their capacity to give care.

To find this capacity to care, I looked to the workforce. Filipino migrants are famous for taking on caring work in a global labor market for caregivers, housekeepers, nannies, nurses, nursing home and home-care staff. Such is their global reputation that they can trade on their nationality as if it is a brand name.[1] When they leave the Philippines to take up such work, they are responding to government policies, economic forces, and their own desires for a better life for themselves and their families. Care work is often physically and emotionally demanding, and frequently exploitative, low paid, and lonely. Filipino migrant care workers, however, are reputed to be warm, caring, and resilient. Some of these much-vaunted caregivers work without formal authorization in their host countries. Nonetheless, they find ways to stay, sometimes for decades, while sending money back to the Philippines to support kin and build their future lives. Not only did all of them have to make tolerable lives, negotiate working conditions, and build the social networks enabling them to live and earn, the irregular migrants among them faced intense surveillance and greater precarity. For migrants without "papers," it would undoubtedly be more difficult to remain safe, keep sane, and keep going in London.

Previously, my research respondents in the Philippines had told me that nurses in the United Kingdom earned the best wages of all migrant workers and sent home the most money.[2] That had seemed straightforward information at the time, but listening to Father Alabag reframed their comments. The lucrative nursing work did not have to be done for the British National Health Service (NHS) in hospitals by migrants with formal nursing qualifications and proper work visas. Instead, care work could be predominantly informal work, not necessarily recorded as nursing at all, or even done by qualified nurses. Father Alabag suggested he was part of a sizeable informal economy of care employing irregular migrants in London. How does this space work? How do these migrants sustain themselves here? As Father Alabag directed me, I started to explore care's origins through the sites and spaces where migrants socialized and bonded.

I initially met Kankanaey-speaking Filipino migrants after church services and during events held in community centers across London. Migrants used these gatherings to build relationships with friends and roommates, fellow congregants, and neighbors. Eventually, more than half of my sixty-one interviewees would be irregular, working without authorization, while earning £250–£630 ($386–$974) per week as nannies, housekeepers, and care workers. These bonding activities—social events held Saturdays, after church on Sundays, or on the weekend evenings—happened almost every week. Those attending might spend £20–£50 ($31–$77) for travel and food, and even more for dress clothes and indigenous costumes—the "uniform"—for performances. Migrants felt that these events were vital to their lives in London. Sabel explained, "I thought I am here to work; I didn't know I would *need* to perform. But I do! You know, to attend these socials and dance, I can make friends, and bond with my fellow Filipinos. . . . It lets me adjust to life here." Migrants recognized that this intense socializing sustained them in a global world.

## Feeling the Global

In London, the daily life of an irregular migrant felt decidedly chancy, with few spaces of respite. Daily encounters were shaped by the ever-present threat of meeting the Transport Police or Border Force officials, being caught, and being deported. Migrants' vulnerability generated pervasive feelings of fear, exposure, and suspicion, often verging on paranoia. At the same time, Father Alabag introduced me to networks of migrants living lives saturated with closeness, faith, and intimate ties binding them to fellow Filipinos, their UK employers, and their families and friends back home. Migrants global networks countered the effects of regulation and surveillance. Their networks sustained migrants, making the care they exchanged for wages possible, thus migrants invested their spare time and earnings in extending and reshaping them. Being caught up in the intensity of migrants' feelings in these spaces myself showed me how affect worked. Affect was a powerful entry point to see how people coped with their precarity by living global lives. The flow of good feeling in these social spaces facilitated not only bonding but also the exchange of ideas, contacts, images, gifts, money, recognition, and respect for people, many of whom were working in the United Kingdom in contravention of its migration rules. These networked social spaces were not only British, but located migrants within a much wider, global field of Filipinos doing caring work.

Filipinos trade on their reputation in the UK labor market: "Filipino care workers are known for their resilience and have a compassionate and caring nature."[3] But this is a national-level stereotype, and Father Alabag was able to be far more specific about the cultural origins of his own capacity to care. For him, care work depended on the practices of bonding and the ethic of *inayan*. No one I met disagreed with Father Alabag's explanation of care and *inayan*. Bonding is a general Filipino English term for building closer social ties. *Inayan* is a Kankanaey word that connects an individual's fate to his or her obligations to others. *Inayan* is, as my respondents explained, the "deeper meaning" that shapes bonding activities. Kankanaey is the name of one of the Philippines' recognized indigenous or tribal groups and marks a vibrant regional culture originating in the central mountains of the north island, Luzon. *Inayan* is thus a regional concept, instead of an idea operating at a national scale that would be recognized as broadly Filipino. Most Filipinos would, however, affirm the connection *inayan* draws between a duty to care for others and the fate of the individual.[4] *Inayan* is what makes care work both an obligation and a possibility for Kankanaey migrants in the United Kingdom.

This book tracks how *inayan* works across a series of nodes—churches, social media, community centers, and migrants' houses in the United Kingdom and back home—to sustain the capacity to care. It describes an "archipelago of care"—a global network of nodes through which care circulates—giving migrants their sense of self. This archipelago of care makes migrants' work and way of living something they can consider worthwhile, profitable, and even a kind of emotional and social adventure, despite the risks and sacrifices involved. Using affect as an entry point to map this archipelago reveals the global to be a landscape of feeling. Migrants in London lived self-consciously global lives saturated with intense feelings—homesickness, anger, joy, frustration, love, and intimacy—that expressed affects circulating through nodes around the world.

## Affect

Affect is the primal energy flowing between people and attaching us to each other, our ideas, our institutions, and our relationships.[5] Affect is a field of communicable desire—positive or negative—underpinning people's emotions, behaviors, and actions. It is affect that makes the archipelago of care global in scope but particular to nodes and to forms of mediation. Affect is simultaneously a bodily capacity, a force, and an object of political action, but it is not easily reducible to people's accounts of their emotions or their dispositions.[6] Father Alabag's agitated outburst, above, is a case in point: an overflow of affect. As his audience did, people responded to flows of affect with feelings, but their emotions and orientations were not, in themselves, affect. Affective flows are mediated by encounters, events, images, tones, words, platforms, gestures, and expressions. Sometimes affect is evidently there, but it is not something people want to talk about. Or sometimes affect is evidently there, and people talk about it by attributing all sorts of emotions and motivations to others, based on their own projections. Affect produces disconnects as well as connections.

Affect can be a difficult concept to grasp when it cannot be felt or easily contextualized from words on a page. While affect seems abstract, it is not; it is visceral. I try to convey its impact through rich ethnographic data, using thick description and my respondents' personal histories to suggest to the reader the flows of feeling at play as well as revealing the underlying obligations and expectations giving these flows shape. Affect is easily confused with the social exchange of personal stories or shared narratives of emotions. But it is not that. People say one thing while they feel another or agree to a story of themselves that does not match their predominant experience. People do such things all the time. However, in moments of crisis, confrontation, or caring, people transmit and receive overwhelming affective flows. Being confronted on the Tube, holding the hand of a frail elder, viewing an evocative image or video online—there are pulses of energy circulating from one person to the next. This is affect, but it is difficult to figure out how to pursue a broader political economy analysis from the literature describing it. Affect theory has done that most often by focusing on public affect rather than private.[7] However, as Father Alabag suggests, this is, if not a false distinction, one that does not emerge without processes of purifying and performing public and private spheres. That distinction can likewise be undone by affective flows in practices of performance and connection. This is why political economy engages affect, but not always, and it does not entirely channel it or contain it. Affect turns up, elsewhere, in surprising ways and produces counterintuitive outcomes. We'll see those surprises in the following chapters.

My approach in this book takes migrant care as an archetypal example of the ways affect enables us to apprehend global processes. I could, of course, follow other artifacts of affect—feelings of anger, joy, sadness, and so forth—through the global. Care, however, requires close, reciprocal, positive affective connection to sustain it and is not reducible to specific emotions, even if the flow in any one caring relation is more or less one-way or unequal. Affect underpins care in ways that enable migrants to remain positive in the face of limited or no reciprocal care from their employers and host societies. These flows of affect, in turn, explain how care resists commodification and only some groups of workers are recognized as having the capacity to deliver it consistently and successfully.

I thus use affect to expand accounts of the global where people's agency and culture are muted or lost. The global is not simply an effect of processes and networks but an object itself—something people have feelings about. People desire, despise, seek out, or avoid the global, and they attribute experiences and ascribe meanings to it. For Filipino migrants, the global is about the hopes, possibilities, and potentials emerging from their connections with other people. People feel strongly about the global—they cathect to the idea—and the idea of the global itself. Affect is not simply individuated but shared or collective, working through flow and exchange, shaped by processes of mediation and attached to the global. So Filipino migrants who come to London already understand themselves as global because they have encountered the global through practices, projects, rituals, figures of speech, policies, and the like back in the Philippines. They know that their videos posted, comments made on Skype, photos, and messages will all carry affective charges, too, becoming artifacts revealing what this global is to their own networks.

## Knowing the Global

Much of our knowledge of the global has been produced through case studies of specific experiences of globalization. Scholars have focused on shifting sites of production for global markets and the making of these same markets, the reorganization of work and labor supply this entails, the mundane bureaucratic practices and public rituals supporting movements of people and changes in work, and the public debates on citizenship and global belonging shaping such changes. In the Philippines, research has explored investment, migration, and public ritual. Philip Kelly's *Landscapes of Globalization* examined the way local elites captured the idea of globalization and redirected foreign investment to consolidate their social and economic positions.[8] Steven McKay's *Satanic Mills or Silicon Islands* investigated the organization of Filipino workers in the global electronics industry.[9] Rhacel Parreñas's *Servants of Globalization* charted the experiences of Filipino migrants in the global labor force. My *Global Filipinos* explored the ways public ritual shaped the global desire of would-be migrants.[10] Studies such as these can be drawn together by thinking about the shifts and changes they describe in encounters with the everyday state or with global products and brands—situations in which economic actors and structures do things to people who are made over into the objects of their action. These micro-level or national studies of the global have enabled other researchers to undertake meta-analyses and generate broader theories. Meanwhile, broader conceptual work on the global has focused on the relationship between territory and subjectivity. Saskia Sassen has led the way with her seminal works, *Territory, Authority, Rights* and *Expulsions*.[11] Other scholars of the global have both curated selected empirical data and developed their own original analyses. The combined result is an account of the global as an imagined realm being shaped and reshaped by a real-world assemblage of regulatory structures, their slippages and bureaucratic demands, and popular or institutional resistances to them. Together these accounts offer a compelling vision of the global. But this scholarly work tends to leave out some vital parts of the global story. It needs to be supplemented by something else, something more intimate and familiar, to provide the fullest possible understanding of the global. This something else is affect. Affect offers us an entry point to the global where the global itself is not just an institutional superobject or an artifact of a globalized popular culture but something more.

Affect's intimate, cultural ties have frequently been elided from accounts of the global, not because they are unimportant, but because they are difficult to apprehend. Affect leaves behind far too few artifacts for secondary academic analysis. Affect, emotions, and intimacies are challenging, and are often too subjective, obscure, and language-based to be easily accessible to global research. Affect is difficult to represent, let alone quantify, and seems somehow less urgent and relevant to policy, but affect plays a significant role in the manipulations of identities, markets, and value comprising globalization. Neglecting affect means that accounts of the global seem to hinge on the ubiquity of a universal,

Western-style individuated subject. Global affect requires a different sort of methodology: an approach attuned to the different—and differentiating—shape taken by personhood in a globalizing world.

For Filipinos, as with the rest of us, there are at least two versions of the global. One global is a space of free movement in which people may achieve economic security and be respected and recognized for their merits and talents. This global imaginary is one of round-the-world connections, increasing material security, and easy movement. The global here means not only flows of money but also flows of migrants between nation-states, according respect and success to people who demonstrate a global awareness and build global personal connections. Affectively, their global has an expansive, positive valence—it is something to be excited about, to share, and to struggle for. This global is where people expect to find their future, forging intimate connections with different people and places—falling in love with strangers. Yet other people consider the ways in which the global and its connections open spaces, routes, and links for terrorism, epidemics, and economic crises, thus creating global fear, global surveillance, and paranoid or neurotic global citizens. This other global, in contrast, is one of a diminished, fearful humanity with a negative affective valence—it is something to struggle against, repress, or undo. Not everyone would identify with one consistent affective orientation toward the global; people tend to vacillate between positive and negative affective attachments, depending on which affective valence they encounter in the moment. Either global attachment offers people a way to know their subjectivity—their sense of being and feeling as selves in the world—being simultaneously local selves and also worldwide and expansive in felt and shared experiences.

Affect can thus be added to Arjun Appadurai's (1990) famous five dimensions of cultural flows: ethnoscapes, mediascapes, technoscapes, financescapes, and ideoscapes. Flows of affect are foundational to and deeply intertwined within the operations of technology, the mediation of media and mediatization of its content, the movement of money and value, the spread and exchange of ideas, and the production and reinvention of ethnic identities. Tracking flows of affect is a way of mapping the constitutive outside of the usual account of globalization.[12] Because it is embodied, connected, and shared, affect makes the global intimately social and spatial—but also particular and different. The Anglocentric and (post) imperial West tends to produce a dominant understanding of the global that homogenizes and flattens peoples' subjectivities instead of seeing the global as emerging in diverse forms through intercultural, multilingual spaces. But affect moves through particular networks and nodes, so the global does just that too.[13] Affect thus offers a useful way to combine the accounts that frame the global as a particular reconfiguration of political economy and territory with those accounts describing how specific experiences of globalization produce new forms of subjectivity. To track how affect flows, then, requires concepts that can explain the particular circumstances of Filipino migrants in London.

## Global Particulars

Accounts of people's changing relations to territory and government are a key feature of scholarship on the global. Expulsions, as theorized by Sassen, explain recent history in the United Kingdom. Sassen observes how a political economy of expulsion has displaced people who enjoyed middle-class livelihoods and state services and protection in the prosperous years after the Second World War in the global North. These former middle classes are increasingly being ejected into social spaces of precarity and exposure, or being terrified into apparent complacency by the threat of that expulsion. In the United Kingdom, postwar restructuring and then globalization saw people's traditional economic practices—ways of sustaining selves and families—largely absorbed by capitalism. Here, the state first encouraged people to depend on government services and benefits to improve productivity but is now withdrawing these supports. Large sections of British society find themselves abandoned to the market, without the government support and protection they had anticipated. This new political economy of expulsion emerged from the 1980s, not only with the globalization of the nation's economy but also with the appropriation of more and more value by a small elite. The previously reasonably secure and relatively prosperous—those who once enjoyed postwar entitlements to a good but simple life—are now exposed to the depredations of capital in an intensified and advanced form. These people resent the exigencies of globalization at the same time as they feel forced to accede to its demands, and this has shaped the way they feel about themselves and their place in the world.

The anthropologist Henrietta Moore describes their subjectivity as "still life." Still life is a kind of affective paralysis in which, with no pleasurable future or security on the horizon, people withdraw, defer, and disconnect, expressing only self-interest and apathy. In still life subjectivities, Sassen's "expulsed" people feel themselves largely individuated and isolated in their private crises, feeling they are losing status and hope or trapped in welfare dependency, unemployment, ill health, and the breakdown of intimate relationships and social connections. They feel and see themselves as powerless to connect with others, to act. Instead they dwell in the negative moment of the global, having lost industry, jobs, pride, intimate connections, and their imagined future. Expulsions and still life describe the experiences of the expanding underclasses in the United Kingdom and elsewhere in the West. Expulsions also shadow the increasingly precarious sense of middle-class entitlement, but they do not tell the entire global story.

On the other side of the world, states in Asia were never so consolidated as to expel middle-class citizens from any accustomed prosperity or dependency. The last three decades have instead seen the emerging economies of Asia producing expanding middle classes of hopeful, ambitious, and well-networked citizens not accustomed to or dependent on state welfare provision. Caught up in a rising tide of prosperity generated by financial globalization, they have enjoyed consumerism and a new kind of political influence. Asian societies have supported developmentalist states keen to harness national resources—natural and human—to the expansion of homegrown Asian capitalism. Unlike rapidly industrializing China or India, the Philippines has been a latecomer, riding on the coattails of this boom. Instead of widespread industrialization at home, much of this economic expansion has come from the export of Filipino migrant workers. Migration has become the route to social mobility, opening the way to becoming globally middle-class.

Beyond the new, urban Asian middle class, parts of rural Asia still have a fourth-world, indigenous, and nonstate periphery. This is true of the Philippines, and this indigenous, nonstate space is where Kankanaey speakers have their ancestral territory. Beyond the reach of effective government and at the edges of mainstream Filipino culture since decolonization, Kankanaey people cultivate tradition, ritual, and indigenous ethics—*inayan* among them. Their location does not impede their desire for the global. Culture enables them to both sustain themselves in migration and resist and defer further assimilation of their territory by the Philippine government and the national elite. At home, migrants' remittances support their assertions of regional autonomy in the face of predatory attempts to develop their homelands. Abroad, Kankanaey migrants carry with them the strategies and ethics needed to reproduce and extend this kind of nonstate space. Not yet expulsed or stuck in still life, they go global with an optimism born of real potential to change their lives and those of their families back home. Kankanaey people have not suffered ejection from a state on which they had depended, but instead created a space in which to avoid a state from which they wish to remain largely autonomous. They create and inhabit the reciprocal space of the expulsions we find in the West: a global shatter zone.

Historically, a shatter zone was a space where people took refuge from, avoided, deferred, and repressed the projects of making a nation-state.[14] Shatter zones were both geographically inaccessible and diverse in their cultural and ethnic makeup.[15] Shatter zones thus coincided with the peripheries of state projects, such as mountainous uplands, remote islands, or inaccessible coasts. These spaces were inhabited by people who eventually became more familiar as ethnic minorities or indigenes, but who still live on the periphery of mainstream national cultures. In Southeast Asia, James Scott described the mountainous territory of Kankanaey speakers—the Philippine Cordillera Central region of Northern Luzon—as an exemplary shatter zone. The Philippine Cordillera is a region: it comprises a geographical area marked off from adjacent areas by important cultural features. Such features include ethics such as *inayan* and forms of ritual and reciprocity we will see later in the book.[16] Originating from what remains a shatter zone means Kankanaey-speaking Filipinos are state subjects only in the most superficial sense, having lived largely beyond the frontier of effective state governance.[17] Rather than finding power in force of arms or governmental authority, they tend to think of power as lying in relationships—in the potential to build new relationships of exchange with coequals.[18] So they seek freedom in a dynamic balance of mutual obligation in which they juxtapose kin group and consociate ties. The Philippine state, where it appears on the Cordillera, is uneasily grafted on top of these extended kin and neighborhood relations or captured by them.[19] Kankanaey people arrive in the United Kingdom as past masters at avoiding, placating, buying off, and evading governance, and also in building networks and consolidating friendships.

In London, Kankanaey migrants find a new kind of shatter zone. In London's inner city they also find that everyday governance has comparatively little effective purchase on much of what people do in their day-to-day lives. Attempts to manage and regulate migration falter, while rules and policies touch down on daily life in an unpredictable and contradictory way, if they make their presence felt at all. In the chaotic boroughs of East London, recently arrived migrants from around the world jostle for jobs in the informal economy and the cheapest of housing. They encounter employers who are staving off their own expulsion from the middle class by paying cash-in-hand casual workers the lowest possible wages. Their employers feel increasingly squeezed by the long-hours culture of work and very high costs of living, including housing costs. Employers find opportunities to bend labor laws in the "light-touch" regulatory frameworks, employing "self-employed" cleaners, housekeepers, and caregivers. Many employers don't ask to see passports or check visas; they operate on a "don't ask, don't tell" policy. Migrants' cash-in-hand work may be piecemeal and unstable, but it can also be comparatively lucrative. Though migrants' lives can be chaotic and precarious, sending money home is worth the risk of being caught and deported.

Migrants' lives combine London with the Philippine Cordillera to make a new global shatter zone space. This space reflects fundamental global shifts within the relationship between controlling land and governmental power. There are now other structures and relationships of power more important or more effective than direct control over land.[20] The shatter zone shows how the corollary is also the case: resistance to imperial power now emerges in new virtual and networked, non-land-based guises here. The global shatter zone resists state power and emerges within, beneath, and outside nation states. It is a space that states can no longer afford to govern or regulate effectively but depend on to generate value. The global shatter zone is a not a single territory but a dispersed, networked space, linking together sites on the global periphery with informal economies and migrant spaces elsewhere. London's global shatter zone is made by migrants who are irregular and transient, circulating between host and sending countries. Where the global shatter zone emerges on East London's streets, much of what happens is now governed from afar and only loosely—but sometimes spectacularly—regulated by the UK government. We find the shatter zone in the land of "beds in sheds"—illegal conversions of back garden sheds into makeshift housing—where irregular migrants vanish into communities of conationals and informal work. Here the government's best estimate of the resident population comes not from the Census but from the water demand on the sewerage system at night.

Living in London's global shatter zone incorporates Kankanaey migrants into an expansive network of coethnics in similar spaces in Canada, Australia, the United States, and even Singapore, Hong Kong, Dubai, and beyond. Flowing between the nodes of this network, the movement of affect, people, and information extends and transforms the shatter zone space. Filipino migrants' much vaunted ability to care emerges from within churches, social organizations and events, shared houses, social media, and the like, which comprise the shatter zone space at the same time as they connect it to the formal markets, legitimate economies, and host nationals of migrants' receiving nations.

## Mapping Affective Nodes

Exploring these particular physical and digital sites in the global network—which I call affective nodes—will show how flows of affect enable migrants to care. I show how the specificities of encounters and exchanges in these sites generate the affective flows sustaining migrants and shape migration. Tracking affect through these nodes challenges three prevalent assumptions about global labor migration and irregularity. The first assumption is that governments must be concerned about managing the increasingly mobile global poor. The second is that irregular migrants wish to find routes to become citizens and taxpayers, regularizing their presence in host nations. The third assumption is that migration takes shape through the visa categories that governments deploy to manage it. When these assumptions are unpacked in light of the complexities of social networks and affect flows, we can see why almost everyone—migrant workers, their employers, fellow migrants, families at home, British taxpayers, and UK government agencies—has an interest in having irregular migrants perform care work.

Chapter 1, "In London," outlines the social, regulatory, and economic context in which migrants work. It shows how the United Kingdom's shatter zone fits into its national economy and geography. Each subsequent chapter describes an affective node within the global shatter zone inhabited by Kankanaey migrants. The first chapters describe the broader Kankanaey community in London through interviews with a few key respondents. The later chapters explore individual migrants' lives in more intimate detail, following respondents into their domestic spaces in the United Kingdom and in the Philippines.

Chapter 2, "At Church," examines how church congregations mediate relationships among migrants, bringing together irregular migrants with visa holders, host nationals, and employers. Here concepts of *inayan* and debt are inflected with religion and sociality to shape and sustain migrants' capacity to care. Chapter 3, "On Facebook," investigates how migrants represent themselves and negotiate belonging through social media. It explores migrants' profile images, tagging strategies, commonly exchanged memes, practices of community surveillance, and representations of employers. It shows how migrants experience their global connections as underpinning their caring capacities. Chapter 4, "In the Community Center," examines the space in which face-to-face social events and civil society meetings are held. This space is where migrants negotiate—and manipulate—surveillance and belonging, and where forms of citizenship proliferate. Chapter 5, "Our House," follows migrants home. It examines the dynamics of crowded rental houses filled with boxes of *karbut* (finds from car boot sales) to be shipped home to show how materiality is a vital conduit for affect. Chapter 6, "Back Home," looks at investment and another kind of materiality—infrastructure—in the Philippines. Evaluating migrants' return and retirement strategies reveals how remittances shape the urban landscape and capture government officials with bribes. Chapter 7, "In Transit," describes the spaces of "hiding in plain sight" in London for an irregular migrant. Being on the move allows her to sustain herself in her work, manage relations with her supportive employers, assist her housemates, and cultivate her own hopes for a brighter future on her return home. Finally the conclusion, "Care's Archipelago," explains the persistence—and even expansion—of these informal economies of care as an element of the global.

Together, these chapters describe how an archipelago of care made of affective nodes is a particular but global space and locates a global self-awareness. It is through this archipelago of care that intimate connections—like the affective flow across the coffee table, above—shape the more familiar structures of a global political economy. Affective nodes channel the care transforming peoples' ideas of self, state, and freedom, connecting them through a dynamic, shared culture mediated by digital technologies. Mapping nodes in an archipelago of care does more, though: it reveals the power of affect to reconfigure the global. It does so explaining how informal economies of care emerge and why particular migrants move to work within them.

The Kankanaey networks my respondents inhabit are at once both global and particular, not merely local. Though the global shatter zone they inhabit emerges and works through particularities, it is important to see that the shape of this space is also generalizable. I unpack these Filipino and British particularities to show how the global can be framed through affective flows. But, equally, a version of this book could be written—with some differences, of course—of other migrant groups, affective nodes, the global shatter zone and similar kinds of care work in global cities such as Sydney or Toronto. Indeed, it is being written, as you read, in the comment threads and chat screens of migrants' social media exchanges.

## Notes

1. Lusis and Kelly, 2006.
2. McKay, 2005.
3. Representatives of the United Kingdom–based Filipino service organization Kanlungan, personal communication, 2009.
4. My respondents noted that the Tagalog term *kapwa*—togetherness, with a deeper meaning of recognizing the self as dependent on the other—resonates and overlaps with *inayan*.
5. McKay, 2014.
6. Anderson, 2014.
7. Anderson, 2014; McKay, 2014.
8. Kelly, 2000.
9. McKay, 2006.
10. Parreñas, 2001; McKay, 2012.
11. Sassen, 2006 and 2014.
12. Pain, 2009, p. 468.
13. Harvey, 2014.
14. Van Schendel, 2002; Scott, 2009.
15. Ibid., p. 8.
16. Ibid., p. 16.
17. Reid, 1993; Scott, 2009, p. 16; Kelly and Reid, 1998.
18. Kelly and Reid, 1998.
19. Abinales and Amoroso, 2005.
20. Ashcroft, 2001, p. 147; Allen, 2002.

# 1  In London

In London, I met Labanet and Biag through Father Alabag. He introduced the young couple to me at his church. Labanet was his distant cousin by marriage—fourth or fifth, he thought. Biag was her husband. Biag and Labanet had arrived in the United Kingdom in the mid-2000s on tourist visas. They, too, had overstayed when their visas expired. They ostensibly came to London to visit distant cousins who had settled in the United Kingdom after gaining citizenship, having entered on work visas in the 1980s. The real purpose of their visit was to work while avoiding an unpleasant situation back in the Philippines. Having worked for two years in London's informal economy, they claimed asylum after the police apprehended Biag. Both before and after becoming irregular, they depended on community support. On arrival in London, Biag and Labanet had turned to their church in order to find a place to stay. Conyap, one of the long-time-settled migrants in the congregation, rented them a room in her house. Labanet found a regular part-time nanny/housekeeper job through Gumtree.com, supplementing this with a rolling roster of part-time casual work: dishwashing, cleaning, babysitting, caregiving, acting as a companion for an older person, and housekeeping. Biag wasn't so lucky. He found odd jobs as a handyman, often through the English members of the congregation. Eventually, one of their fellow non-Filipino congregants offered Biag and Labanet a house to rent. They were able to move out of Conyap's house and into a small, three-bedroom terraced property. They finally had a space of their own and, in turn, they became key actors in wider Kankanaey networks. Tracing these networks shows what the global means in their London-based lives.

This chapter outlines how this economic niche migrants have found in London emerged. It brings together the recent history of the United Kingdom's formal economy of care, the United Kingdom's Filipino community, and the particularities of the Filipino approach to the global to show how London's shatter zone was created by movements of people and shifts in government policy.

## Methods and Ethics

Labanet, Biag, and Father Alabag were just three of the migrants I encountered in over five years of ethnographic fieldwork (2009–2014). During this period I interviewed sixty-one migrants, conducting one or more follow-up interviews with more than a dozen of them. I also interviewed activists and church congregants and engaged in participant observation among Kankanaey migrants in London, in the Philippines, and on social media. This long-term ethnographic approach tracked fundamental changes in people's feelings as they lived global lives. The evidence for my arguments here comes from participant observations, interview quotes, text from online chats and e-mail exchanges, reports in the media, material objects, and government documents I collected both in the United Kingdom and in the Philippines, which was then triangulated with other respondents and textual sources. My analysis sought to identify how strategies of affective connection and exchange work—or don't—through these social spaces.

My analytical approach to my data was to identify sites of affective intensity, whether negative or positive, which persisted over the long term. I thus sought out sites in which relationships among my respondents were most volatile and under strain, as well as most close and affectionate. I tried to interview and observe people who seemed grumpy as well as those who were elated, seeking out breaking as well as bonding in relationships. This meant many of the stories and observations I collected were highly charged. Because confidentiality, anonymity, and informed consent are key aspects of research ethics, I often cannot reveal as much detail as I have collected. When people have asked me not to use certain materials or details, I have kept those confidential. Trying to ensure that everyone I'd interviewed or had involved in participant observation understood my research approach given that my work was global—spanning multiple sites and relationships simultaneously, including digital fora—took time.

I obtained informed consent from all those who participated in interviews and asked for consent to follow a smaller group of individual respondents' social media profiles directly. When I have used quotations from those profiles, I have asked for specific consent. I often relied on respondents to help me translate their Kankanaey "text-speak" (from mobile phone shortcuts) into English. When I viewed comments made on a respondent's social media profile and available to "friends of friends," I obtained consent to use them from the profile owner. I also joined and followed publicly accessible social media groups and blogs set up by migrants' churches and nongovernmental organizations (NGOs) or activist groups. Following a smaller group of respondents for the more intimate spaces of the second part of the book allowed for informed consent to be negotiated on an ongoing basis. While anonymity can never be perfectly guaranteed in such a study, I have tried to obscure identifying details and locations where they are not relevant to my arguments.

For all my respondents, I have assigned Kankanaey or Filipino pseudonyms. These are first names, but not respondents' own "native" or government-registered names. The hometowns of Biag and Labanet and the area in which they are building in Baguio are likewise made-up names, but Baguio City appears under its own name, as does the Kankanaey ethnic group. I have obscured the identity of churches and denominations in London, and have given generic names to the various NGOs visiting the several spaces I have combined as "the community center." I asked my respondents to approve the use of my original photographs, screen shots, and downloads from their Facebook posts before having them digitally altered. While these measures will likely not prevent some readers from speculating on the actual identities of the churches and NGOs involved, it will give my respondents the plausible deniability I offered them.

For several of the leading figures in this book, I selected people who have left the United Kingdom. For others, I have created composite characters from the details of two or more respondents. In a community where older—over the age of fifty-five—working migrants and younger, student visa-holding migrants moved through quickly, time has meant people have moved on or changed status, and we are no longer in close contact. Father Alabag, as a visa overstayer, did several years of domiciliary care for an elderly man with dementia, cash in hand. When this gentleman died, Father Alabag was unable to find another employer who would hire him without a visa. His work with his church congregation was also informal and temporary, and it would not sustain him. He had been depending on his niece and her family for food and lodging, but he was aware that the situation had become a strain on his niece's family. He eventually decided to return to the Philippines. Whatever difficulties back in the Philippines his sojourn in London had helped him avoid had receded. He left hoping to pick up his old life back home. But he was also part of a much broader extended-kin network. He is now a respected elder in the Philippines. His position in the church enabled him to introduce new arrivals to other Filipinos in his congregation and to help his younger relatives settle in to life in London. He was instrumental in finding respondents for my study and encouraging me in the work, but he was not present, physically, for much of it.

Other characters, representing those who remain in the United Kingdom, combine details and quotes from respondents who shared similar demographic characteristics—say, female, over fifty-five, and permanently settled in the United Kingdom, but planning to retire back home; or female, under forty-five, irregular, working as a housekeeper and caregiver for an older person. The combination of details should obscure any single individual identity. Following a similar strategy, I have opted not to include high-profile activists and public figures by name or profile. I admire their work in advocacy and public education, but their public visibility means the anonymity of my respondents could be easily compromised.

After 2012–13, I wound down my broader interviews and participant observations. I continued to maintain close research contact only with Biag—whom I had known since a research visit to the Philippines in 1992—and his wife,

Labanet, Father Alabag's distant cousin. I asked them to be my key respondents not only because of their cultural self-awareness but also because of their stable relationship and strong network ties. Neither students nor retirement-aged, they had not churned through London but had stayed as irregular workers for five years (Biag) and more than nine years (Labanet). Labanet was a high-earning, professional woman who was extremely competent in managing her finances and relationships. She served as a great example of the possibilities of migrant success glimpsed by others.

I found doing long-term research, much of it carried out while Biag and Labanet were separated by distance, both rewarding and challenging. Our research relationship required a great deal of clear communication and trust. I had spent several years interviewing both Biag and Labanet and joining in their London activities before renewing my acquaintance with their family in the Philippines. I owe much of my insight on the work of affect to Labanet's willingness to discuss my ideas in regular voice calls as well as her comments on the first draft of the manuscript, translations, and regular updates via web chat. As the book goes to press, we have attenuated our communication and I am unsure where she is living.

Because of the sensitive nature of some respondents' visa statuses, a further caveat is necessary. At no point in the research did I view or authenticate anyone's passport, so any comments I make on individuals' visas or visa statuses should be treated as unverified and indirect reports. The time elapsed between my interviews and publication will hopefully obscure identifying detail what is now recent history. For Kankanaey readers who may have met me during the research and know some of my respondents, thus have their own opinions of their "papers," I rely on their discretion and deeper knowledge of *inayan*.

To show how the global is personal and how affect works, I use Labanet and Biag's stories in detail. Of all my interviewees, Labanet was the most successful undocumented worker I met in London. By 2012 she was earning just under £37,000 ($57,238) per year, tax free. In that year, the average UK worker earned £25,000 ($38,674), before taxes. Formal economy workers with similar after-tax earnings included a senior hospital nurse—a team leader—or a midlevel university professor, such as a senior lecturer, roughly equivalent to a new associate professor in the United States. Labanet had given up her own college-level teaching job in the Philippines to become a nanny/housekeeper in London, trading a decline in status for much greater earning power. After four or five interviews, Labanet and I finally started talking about her investment plans and it opened up into a discussion of our comparative earnings. After taxes, there wasn't much of a difference. We ended up laughing together with relief. Labanet decided she would foot the bill for every second coffee, if I didn't have research funds for my travel to visit her. But, as she pointed out, she did live in London: housing was hideously expensive and transportation both costly and a daily necessity. I explained that her life there intrigued me because she was such a good money manager and labor-market strategist. She seemed the antithesis of the stereotypical Filipina caregiver. Labanet agreed but suggested simple categories of success or exploitation did not really fit her situation.

Labanet thought about herself, her work, and her migration in terms of the global. She told me about confessing her status to one employer who responded, "We're willing to gamble." She felt that this employer, for whom she worked long-term, "really cared" for her welfare and valued her contribution to her household. One day, she took the employer's two daughters on an excursion, picking up McDonald's Happy Meals as a treat. When the older girl opened the McDonald's box, she looked at the French fries and asked Labanet, "What's this? Worms?" She asked Labanet for rice and fish. This family had recently moved to London from the United Arab Emirates (UAE) for the Dutch-English father's banking job. In the UAE they'd had a Filipino nanny who cooked them rice and fish. The mother, Malaysian-English, had herself grown up with Filipino nannies in Singapore. Labanet joked, "Us Filipinos? See, we're more a global brand than McDonald's!" Not only had Labanet remembered this as an experience of global branding, but she linked it to the way other employers spoke about hiring irregular migrants as expressing a caring kind of globalism. Labanet introduced me to Agnep, her cousin, so she could share her own example of this phenomeon. Agnep explained, "My employers care about me, even if I have no papers. 'Agnep,' they say, 'you care; you make our lives run smoothly and thus also the UK economy. You are one in a million here in London; it's a global world and the old rules for migration don't make sense anymore.'" Talking with Labanet, the global wasn't an abstract idea my research imposed on her, but part of the vocabulary of her migration experience. She shared my curiosity about the way affective connections brought this global into being, why these jobs for irregular migrants had opened up in London, who the employers were, and how she and her friends were able to sustain themselves.

## London's Informal Economy of Care

As elsewhere, Filipino migrants in Britain are disproportionately found in care work, work as cheaper labor, and have a reputation for being compliant and uncomplaining.[1] They do care work in London work for two broad kinds of employers: the new globally mobile elite and those left in the lurch by the withdrawal of the welfare state. It seemed that for every migrant who worked as a nanny/housekeeper for an elite household in West London, I met a caregiver for an elderly resident of one of the less salubrious inner-zone residential areas. Migrants moved between the two kinds of jobs and employers, often combining them in a portfolio of part-time work.

The first kind of employer included members of the global city's hyper-mobile, international upper middle class, or those aspiring to it. They were likely to be redeployed to Asia or the United States or retrenched on short notice. Not having much job security in London, or necessarily a long-term plan to remain in the city, they wanted flexibility in their commitments. But their mobility was a secondary concern, trumped only by their hours of work. This type of employer worked incredibly long days, often for the UK offices of large multinationals or in other well-paying, high-status jobs with similar long-hours cultures. To support them in caring for children and organizing household logistics, they sought workers who could extend their own hours on even shorter notice. Their ideal worker would be someone without immediate, in-person family commitments of her own, someone who did not require the usual period of notice for termination, days off, holidays, or sick leave. As one working mother from this group explained of a nanny, "This is someone who comes to your house bringing no problems, loves your child nearly as much as you do, looks after them probably better than you do, tidies up, and leaves, i.e., the best friend you could possibly have. I would have SOLD my best friend for a visa that allowed my daughter's brilliant . . . nanny to remain in the UK."[2]

The second kind of employer encompassed older adults desperately determined to stay in their family homes but who were living largely alone in inner London. In most cases their adult children and young grandchildren had been forced to the outer suburbs or commuter belt by the price of housing and the failures of state schools. These retirees, becoming frail, had assets above the threshold needed to qualify for state assistance and refused to enter a "care home" (nursing home) or similar facility. Conditions in most care facilities for older people were reported to be terrible, and the costs were most often met by the sale of the family home, the only asset parents had to pass on to their children. A week in a residential care home in London cost £625 ($967) in 2013, with a cost of £825 ($1276) if nursing was included.[3] In 2010 the average agency rates for domiciliary care—home visits by a care worker—in London were between £13.77 ($21.30) and £14.46 ($22.37) per hour, depending on the time of day and week for visits.[4] The Filipino irregular care workers I interviewed charged between £10 and £12 ($15.47–$18.56) per hour. Domiciliary care workers in the formal sector, however, were typically paid a lower wage, usually around £7.50 ($11.60) per hour, and working conditions were exploitative.[5] The standards of care delivered by agency workers were often low, visits rushed and little emotional support offered. For older people facing this situation, a Filipino private caregiver was a lifeline to personalized care for a dignified and peaceful final few years. A private caregiver meant that an older person had the help needed on call or on hand, around the clock. With the introduction of personal care budgets for older people who qualified, government support could be directed to hiring private caregivers. Filipino migrants could take this work even if undocumented, as long as they could show a valid visa permitting work (not necessarily their own.) This second kind of employer also needed a flexible worker without other commitments who could make something of the modest wages on offer.

In these two London examples, we have the two faces of the late-twentieth-century crises in colonial capitalism and its concurrent crisis of care. The now-familiar form of the British welfare state introduced after the Second World War is proving unsustainable. The immediate postwar years were lean ones and jobs growth focused on "men's work"—employment that paid family salaries—and the state provided benefits to those not in work. Eventually the United Kingdom reconfigured labor markets, benefits, and family relations to enable women to enter the formal workforce, with the two-breadwinner household becoming increasingly common in the middle classes. To encourage further labor force participation and raise productivity in what had become a service-oriented economy, caring work was increasingly contracted out from the middle-class household and undervalued by the mid-1990s. The United Kingdom's middle-class households and their corporate and public sector employers soon grew to depend on comparatively cheap caring labor. Government subsidies through the benefit system supported their use of childcare workers and formal childcare facilities for the young, while older people depended on state support for nursing homes, care agencies offering home visits (domiciliary care), or private in-home care workers. Because work done in private homes is difficult to regulate and citizens are reluctant to police their elderly neighbors or the family down the road, work in the home care sector has been comparatively lightly regulated.

Today, the low wages paid to caregivers do not even enable lower working-class nationals to live a comfortable, if basic, life. At the bottom of the labor market, people who cannot find any other work and have little security in their own housing, employment, or personal lives are pushed toward care work. The government tops up low-paid workers after-tax earnings with tax credits, having set up a complex system of social benefits to address low pay and poverty. Workers on low pay easily become mired in these regulations, finding that they have little incentive to take on additional hours of work. They are often months in arrears with complex and seemingly arbitrary repayments and overpayments of their cash benefits. Their sense of alienation and hopeless frustration can undermine their ability to care either for themselves or for others, stuck in "still life." Migrants, however, can make something out of these low wages. If they work without authorization, they can avoid paying taxes and national insurance, stay out of the benefits system entirely, and reduce their living costs by sharing housing. From this social location, irregular migrants can cope quite well. They can see a future beyond their immediate work. So migrants may tolerate exploitative working conditions because they can accumulate productive assets elsewhere.

For several years, the United Kingdom did offer a route to regularizing undocumented workers. From 1998 until 2012, the United Kingdom regularized irregular migrants under a fourteen-year-long stay concession.[6] In 1998, the Long Residence Concession was issued, via chapter 18 of the Immigration Directorates' Instructions, allowing applicants, in the absence of countervailing factors, to be granted settlement (or Indefinite Leave to Remain, ILR) on the basis of either ten years (lawful) or fourteen years total residence. Since reforms in 2012, the long-stay concession is now available after twenty years of residence, and migrants be in the country legally for virtually all that time. The fourteen-year-long stay concession meant that migrants working without formal authorization who were not caught by immigration authorities could eventually attain permanent, legal status. Irregularity could be a route to citizenship.

For irregular migrants who were apprehended, making a claim for asylum was another avenue to extend their stay. Under international law, anyone has the right to apply for asylum in countries signatory to the 1951 Refugee Convention and to remain in that country until the authorities have assessed their claim. In the United Kingdom, asylum seekers can apply for permission to work if they have waited longer than twelve months for an initial decision on their claim. Asylum seekers can also apply for permission to work if they have had their claims refused but have appealed. They can work only if they have not received a response to their appeal after twelve months and the delay in decision-making is not considered their responsibility. But those asylum seekers who do receive permission to work may not become self-employed. Asylum seekers are restricted to occupations on the Shortage Occupation List published by UK Visas and Immigration.[7] This list provides salary thresholds for each approved category of employment. Restrictions on employment and salary thresholds for jobs are intended to prevent employers from hiring migrant workers at lower wages rather than paying settled migrants or nationals the going rates. These regulations prevent the asylum system from being used to access the labor market and thus protect resident workers from having their wages undercut by migrants.

With an expanding number of migrants and a declining budget in the early 2000s, the workings of the asylum system became chaotic. Decisions were long delayed and Case Officers overburdened. A few Filipino migrants I met had made successful claims for protected status (a subcategory of asylum), settling in the United Kingdom at least temporarily. Others became part of the much larger group of migrants who filed unsuccessful claims and subsequently disappeared from their contact addresses. Doing so, they joined what's called the "migration refusal pool"—people whose application for temporary or permanent leave to remain had been refused but whose whereabouts were unknown to the authorities. In 2008, there were 174,000 cases of apparently unsuccessful applicants remaining in the United Kingdom after being directed to leave, and the number continued to grow.[8] In 2012, the Home Office outsourced the task of locating these people and assessing their cases to the private company Capita. Capita worked through a backlog of 248,000 cases, finding that 121,000 people could not be contacted because their addresses were either false or no longer current. Because the asylum system was so overburdened, some asylum applications filed before the end of 2007 were deemed "legacy cases" and placed in an "active archive" for later resolution.[9]

The contradictions in this situation show the interdependence that has been created by globalization. To maintain the last vestiges of the welfare state and sustain the working/middle-class comfort people consider to be part of the social contract, the United Kingdom needs migrant labor in the care sector. Likewise, to develop peripheral places where under- and unemployment prevail, the Philippines wishes its nationals to have access to the global labor market. Where these needs intersect, value can be extracted. This is if the United Kingdom tolerates informal care work by irregular migrants. Dealing with informal care work and irregularity among these migrants has not been a pressing social policy issue.

While the government may claim to be a victim of these global flows of people, it is actually a beneficiary.[10] Most British nationals could not live on the wages paid for care work in London if they were working in the formal economy. Many London employers could not afford to pay citizens a living wage with the required taxes and benefits included on top. By tolerating irregular work, at least in practice, the United Kingdom minimizes demand for supported childcare places, childcare tax breaks, additional hospital admissions, publicly funded nursing home places, and local council support for domiciliary care or health care, reducing costs to government. Meanwhile the government of the Philippines deplores sending workers into markets where their rights may not be respected, but it needs the remittances. After three decades of global labor migration, Filipinos know that government approvals can mean little—and formal employment contracts are not always enforceable—so formal economy work, facilitated by the correct visa, does not always offer better protection from exploitation by employers. Having authorization to work is no guarantee against exploitation.

## Migration's Impacts?

The impact of irregular migrants on the UK labor market is unclear. If the labor market is split into formal and informal work, the first kind of work is visible and taxed, and the other is invisible and untaxed. The available data on care work come from the murky bottom end of the labor market, reporting poorly paid formal work often done by workers on zero-hour contracts. Informal care work performed by irregular migrants is invisible and untaxed, so no data is available. Even resident workers rarely declare income from cash-in-hand and casual care work to the authorities as they are required to do, and it is difficult to audit their benefits claims or tax returns. This situation means irregular migrants can often find work where there is already strong demand for informal workers. Irregular migrants also do formal work. They borrow others' documents or purchase counterfeits and take jobs where they pay taxes and make National Insurance contributions, even though they are not able to claim benefits. Overall, migrants pay in more than they take out from the benefits system, at least as far as their contributions to the formal economy are measured accurately. Irregular migrants undoubtedly contribute to British society and the UK's economy.

Of course, it is migrants with permission to work who work in the formal economy that generate more robust data. Yet even these migrants have a complicated impact on the United Kingdom's formal labor market. A large influx of migrants depresses wages slightly in low-wage sectors and migrants arriving in the United Kingdom from outside the European Union are associated with fewer jobs for citizens.[11] The United Kingdom's Migration Advisory Committee reports, "A ballpark estimate is that an extra 100 non-EU working-age migrants are initially associated with 23 fewer native people employed for the period from 1995 to 2010."[12] This statistic gives only a partial picture. It is difficult for the government to find reliable data, to discern long-term trends from the noise within it, and to define who should be counted as a migrant. That said, care work—whether in domiciliary care, housekeeping, child care, or, increasingly, nursing—is one such low-wage sector, with the jobs considered un- or semiskilled work. In 2009, the UK Low Pay Commission found that new migrants with the right to work did depress wages in the domiciliary care sector in London, to the detriment of settled migrants and UK citizens.[13] Nobody, however, can say definitively what the effects of irregular migrants are on the informal economy of care.

The number of people doing informal work in the United Kingdom is unknown, as are the number of jobs they occupy. Best estimates placed the value of the United Kingdom's informal economy in 2012 at £150 ($232) billion, or 10 percent of the United Kingdom's Gross Domestic Product.[14] Concerns about these "hidden" jobs being taken by irregular migrants are difficult to articulate because the data don't exist. This is compounded by the fact nobody knows exactly how many irregular migrants there may be. However, the data do show that there are more overstayers than there are people in the migration refusal pool. Estimates range from six hundred thousand to eight hundred thousand at the low end to one to two million irregular migrants at the upper end, with the expectation that these people are living mostly in London and the Southeast of the United Kingdom, where the jobs are.[15]

In London, migration, low wages, and the informal in economy intersect. There's no shortage of care-sector workers or skills, per se, among UK citizens or EU migrants, only reluctance to work for low wages in precarious conditions in an expensive city. There is an enormous affective drain on workers delivering care in such circumstances. In the United Kingdom, some scholars have described a "migrant ethic of care," suggesting that migrants are more humane and less alienated than the United Kingdom's own citizens and thus offer better care for others.[16] There has also been debate in the UK media about the extent to which citizen workers have the wrong disposition when it comes to providing care work to strangers. People available to staff the care sector in the United Kingdom see no future in taking these jobs.[17]

Public debate in the United Kingdom shows that people know migration policy and labor market reforms have worked to disadvantage the working class: "The difference is that an 'immigrant' can repatriate money that is worth a great deal at home; help his family, plan for a house, etc. None of this is possible for the working class who are disenfranchised by education and property and ownership."[18] Those who have care-work jobs in the formal economy describe publicly, how they struggle socially and financially. As one anonymous care worker attending a local Jobs Centre to claim benefits recounted, "It's impossible. You're trapped. . . . Sometimes, with care work, the hours are zero hours, so you don't know this week if you would get 16 hours [the number of hours you must work under to claim JSA [Job Seeker's Allowance]. You may get 10 or 11 hours and then you have to come here and sign on to make it up to the 16 hours. It's impossible. You're trapped and there's no way out."[19] Already experiencing themselves as abject objects of state policy and with strained or broken family relationships, people on the margins of the working class often do not feel nurtured or valued. Instead, they feel contempt. The policies of austerity in the post-2008 United Kingdom have made them into objects of derision—shirkers who refuse to work.

Meanwhile, seeing the opportunities offered by an aging society, private equity firms have been buying up inner-city nursing homes. They have often purchased them for the land value and relocated the nursing home services to the suburbs and the countryside. In less accessible and often less salubrious facilities, private equity owners maximize their profits by sweating the labor. They pay the lowest possible wages to minimally qualified staff and offer poor working conditions. Domiciliary care workers find similar conditions, as agencies employing them squeeze wages and hours to make competitive bids to local government who must cut the costs of the bill for social care.[20] Thus the formal care sector also seeks out migrant workers. Agency employers are sometimes so desperate for capable workers that they are not too particular about their papers.

Irregularity can work to a migrant's advantage in this particular situation. Taking on formal work means they are tied to one employer by their work visa. Without contracts binding them to employers, taxes owed to the government, or the complexities of benefits regulations, they may actually have more power to negotiate wages and conditions or to withdraw their labor and move. Irregular migrants' UK employment trajectories typically combine a variety of private, informal work in caring roles, moving from nanny/housekeeper to eldercare to pet care and back to housekeeping, either during the week or over their sojourn. Though they may live precarious lives in the United Kingdom, these migrants are heroes to their countries, influential in families and in local politics. With luck, they can return home to successful businesses and investments. Seeing a much brighter future ahead of them can make them more reliable workers and better able to deliver care.

Exploring in-depth how irregular Filipino migrants navigate this terrain shifts the usual story told about Filipino migrants and globalization.

## Filipinos in London

The widely accepted account of Filipino migration describes female domestic workers who are exploited in their global workplaces. Their care is displaced from their families in the Philippines and redirected to their employers.[21] These migrant workers are created and exported by the Philippine state. As a feminized and unskilled migrant workforce, they are part of a national development strategy.[22] Through complex bureaucratic structures and discursive practices evolving across sending and receiving states, individuals entering this workforce become compliant and self-disciplining laboring subjects in their host countries.[23] The regulatory frameworks shaping their migration tend to negate workers' individual rights. This curtails their ability to challenge working conditions. Workers' everyday resistance is further circumscribed by their internalized ideas of the good foreigner or good Filipino worker.[24] Both the mechanisms of labor export and these internalized ideas of compliance enable broader structures of race, gender, and class to be reproduced in migrants' work and relationships within their employers' households. This whole apparatus thus produces Filipino migrants who take on the work of sustaining households—typically by absorbing aspects of the domestic and emotional labor of middle-class women—in more affluent countries. Filipinas find themselves in an ethnically marked global occupational niche combining housekeeping with childcare and eldercare. This niche not only requires displays of emotional closeness, but also personal services, and it includes tasks such as cleaning, pet care, running errands, and so forth. In these jobs, much of the work lies beyond effective government regulation, being governed by informal agreements with employers. On entering this global work space, women's migration creates an affective drain, sucking caring energy out of the Philippines and delivering it to families in the global North.[25]

This account of migration for care work has also underpinned a popular discourse on migrant Filipinas themselves. They are discussed as naïve, economically deprived, semi-educated "maids to order," willing to endure harsh working conditions and unjust legal regimes in order to remit a few meager dollars back home, and struggling as mothers separated from children left behind. Lauded as natural caregivers and known for kindness and generosity in their work, they are globalization's martyrs. It is rare that Filipina migrants are represented as canny middle-class professionals with global strategies. But that is exactly how Labanet sees herself. Though to some extent Labanet might agree with this bare bones of this account, her own biography nuances it in particular and powerful ways. Labanet enjoys comparatively high earnings, has made lucrative investments, and has high status in her social networks. When examining the flows of affect sustaining her care, we will see she is sustained by affect flowing through global networks of Filipino friends.

Exact figures on the number of Filipinos in the United Kingdom are not available, but there are some useful estimates. In 2012, the Philippines Commission on Filipinos Overseas reported 218,777 Filipinos in the United Kingdom. Among these there were (approximately) 25,000 irregular migrants alongside 160,881 permanent residents and 32,896 temporary migrants.[26] The United Kingdom Home Office data on foreign-born UK residents listed the Philippines as the tenth-largest source of migrants from outside the European Economic Area for 2012–13. The Home Office reported there were 106,000 Filipinos recorded in the United Kingdom in that year. Of this number 54,000 (43 percent) had migrated primarily for economic reasons, 6,000 (5 percent) for study, 30,000 (24 percent) for family reunification, and 26,000 (21 percent) as dependents.[27] Filipino community groups estimated that the true number of Filipinos in the United Kingdom would be closer to 300,000, and that about 60 percent of this UK Filipino community would either be in the country on a temporary visa for work, study, or travel, or would be irregular.[28] The figures suggest the United Kingdom's Filipino community is characterized by both high rates of labor force participation and high numbers of temporary migrants—students or short-term contract workers. However, if the community's own estimate of about 300,000 people is not seriously inflated, a significant proportion—about one-third—of the community no longer has a recognized right to reside or work in the United Kingdom. Even the presumably conservative government figures, both UK and Philippine, combine to suggest that a fifth of the community is irregular.

The majority of Filipino migrants are employed. They are typically nurses, domestic workers, housekeepers, nannies, care facility staff, and private caregivers, though highly skilled professionals work as engineers, managers, and academics. Formal sector work—nursing, engineering, care facility staff, and so forth—requires a formal authorization to work. However, informal work in the caring occupations can accommodate migrants both with and without current work or student visas, and those with Indefinite Leave to Remain (ILR or permanent residency), or citizenship. Those doing care work without appropriate work visas are frequently Filipino graduates of nursing or caregiving courses.

An individual's migration category and thus economic status is rarely fixed for long, until they become a permanent resident. Someone who might have arrived on a student visa or a temporary work permit could become eligible to settle in the United Kingdom and work through marriage to a settled migrant or UK national. Or they could make a successful ILR application, should their salary and record of work meet the requirements. Starting in April 2016, non-EU migrants must earn at least £35,000 per year to obtain ILR and may apply only after six years on a work visa. Because salaries for most jobs taken by Filipino migrants are not that high, they might do neither and, instead, allow their visas to lapse. By becoming irregular, they would be joining people on student or tourist visas who similarly fail to exit the country when their visas expire. People's extended kin and place-based ties cut across all these visa categories. Thus the family visitor of a legitimate holder of a temporary five-year skilled-worker visa can overstay, becoming a casual, cash-in-hand housekeeper in West London. When the distant cousin of a long-settled citizen nurse turns up, having overstayed a tourist visa to look for work, of course family and friends provide support and recommendations to employers. They are considering their own investments and relatives' interests in the Philippines. Neighbors at home become roommates in London, even if one is a nurse on a temporary work permit and the other has overstayed a tourist visa to work as a housekeeper.

My sixty-one Filipino interviewees thus spanned several migration categories. Those with ILR or UK citizenship and their spouses and dependents did not have any limits on their stay in the country, received tax credits, and were not restricted from applying for benefits—in UK immigration jargon, they enjoyed "recourse to public funds." Interviewees in all the other categories had valid visas or other documents that entitled them to be in the country for a defined period of time but they could not claim access to any public funds. These interviewees were (1) those with a work visa, (2) those on a student visa, (3) those who entered with a tourist visa, (4) those on a spousal visa, (5) people who had claimed asylum or protected status and whose application was being processed, (6) those who had been granted protected status, and (7) those without any valid visa— irregular migrants. Only a very few of my respondents or their acquaintances had claimed asylum. Those who had, and who were willing to discuss it with me, had all lodged their asylum claims after being stopped by the authorities. They had overstayed their original visas to take up informal employment or continue their informal work. They were overstayers first, though several had backgrounds and personal histories making their claims for protection plausible. People in all these visa categories were intimately jumbled up together, sharing the same houses, community halls, and church events, the same friendship groups and the same families.[29]

## *Why Irregularity?*

Filipinos saw the United Kingdom's lightly regulated space of care work as an opportunity for those without access to the "papers" required for formal work. There has been a longstanding practice, dating back to at least the 1970s, of Filipino migrants evading detection by immigration authorities: becoming "T&T" (from the Filipino, *tago at tago*, meaning hiding and hiding).[30] This euphemism for irregularity originated among Filipinos in the United States. T&T described people who entered the country on a student or tourist visa and then stayed on to work under the table while trying to regularize their status. They sought either to marry a citizen or to have a child who would be born a US citizen. Filipino T&T strategies persisted with expanding labor migration. As of December 2012, the Philippine government estimated that there were 1.3 million irregular Filipino migrants overseas.[31] Thus Filipinos who are drawn to the United Kingdom are already familiar with irregularity as a migration strategy. There is money to be earned and London has a large informal economy, so it has been relatively easy to avoid apprehension by the authorities. Stories of T&T migrants who had found steady work and supportive employers have circulated back to the Philippines. Migrants who had regularized their stay appeared to be enjoying prosperous, middle-class lives as citizens of the United Kingdom. Filipinos pursuing irregular strategies saw the UK's long stay concession as both an insurance policy and a possible route to settlement, depending on the visa with which they had arrived. Both Father Alabag and Agnep, above, had planned to apply for permanent residency (ILR) on this basis until the regulations were changed in 2012. When Labanet and Biag arrived in London, they intended to overstay and work in the informal economy with this concession in mind.

Irregular migrants were a vital part of the United Kingdom's Filipino community. Though doing precarious work, they were potentially earning high wages. Other migrants depended on these unreported earnings circulating through the community. Settled migrants covered their own rent or paid off their mortgages by renting rooms to work-visa holders, students, and irregular migrants. Visa holders supported irregular relatives by helping them find employment in return for help with their own rent and, occasionally, study expenses. Students relied on these same networks for recommendations for employment and cheap, shared housing. Irregular migrants themselves needed to borrow others' passports in order to present documents to be recorded by their employers. Asylum seekers needed to show they had somewhere to stay and friends who were supposedly supporting them as they worked under the table while their claim was processed. People in each visa category needed compatriots in the others to survive.

Irregular migrants comprised a small but significant group—twenty-four of sixty-one—of my interviewees. All my irregular interviewees had overstayed their original visas and were doing casual, cash-in-hand private caregiver work. Of my thirty-seven interviewees who did have the right to work, sixteen were still on valid student visas at the time of the interview and twenty-one were converting or had already converted their work visas to ILR or citizenship. Only two of those twenty-one settled migrants had initially come to the United Kingdom on domestic worker visas. Another four had arrived on spousal visas. My twenty-four irregular respondents had arrived on visas that had expired by the time of our first interview. Eight had entered the United Kingdom as tourists, thirteen as students, and three had been on family visit visas. I was not able to determine exactly how many had eventually submitted an asylum claim, but gossip suggested some had done so to extend their stay. My interviewees' visa statuses definitely changed over the duration of my research. A number of the students I initially interviewed had their visas expire, but they remained employed in London. By the end of my intensive fieldwork interviews, in 2012–13, approximately thirty-nine of my respondents were irregular. While irregularity was already familiar to my respondents as a migration strategy, most had only decided to pursue it themselves in response to particular shifts in UK migration and labor market policy.

First, the United Kingdom had dropped embarkation controls in 1998, so the government no longer recorded who left the country. The lack of exit controls made it easy for irregular migrants to leave only when they were ready. Overstayers knew they could vanish from the records and nobody would stop them at the airport on their way home. At the same time, the UK health and care sectors expanded international recruitment of overseas nurses and nursing home staff. The National Health Service (NHS), care facility managers, and staffing agencies targeted Filipino nurses already working outside the Philippines. Though these workers entered the United Kingdom on temporary work visas, it was comparatively easy for them to make successful applications for ILR after five years of work. However, when the United Kingdom opened the borders to workers from the rest of the European Union in 2003, migration regulations changed.

The government introduced new regulations effectively restricting care work and nursing as routes to permanent residency for all non-European Economic Area (EEA) nationals in 2003. In 2009, they launched a further set of reforms to skilled-worker migration schemes designed to open up more work in the care sector for UK citizens and EEA migrants. These changes to work visas made it increasingly difficult for employers, including care facilities and the National Health Service, to hire workers from outside Europe. This was to ensure European migrants and local workers could find work. The cumulative effect of these reforms was to reduce the number of care jobs open to overseas staff from a third of the open positions in the care sector to about a fifth.[32] Nurses were also affected. In 2006, the government removed general nursing jobs from the Shortage Occupation List. At the same time, it extended the period of time required to qualify for ILR from four to five years of employment. Migrants now had to meet an income threshold to qualify for settlement, but migrant nurses' pay often left them below that threshold, even after five years of work. Work visas for care workers were subject to yet another set of new restrictions in 2011. Non-European applicants for work visas in the care sector were now required to have: an approved sponsor with a demonstrated labor market need; two years' experience; a qualification recognized as equivalent to the United Kingdom's National Qualifications Framework Level 4; and supervisory responsibilities. Compared to the 1970s–2003 period, Filipinos' access to work visas, if not "closed," was now severely restricted.

Migrants already working in the United Kingdom found deteriorating working conditions created further barriers to eventual settlement. Following complaints from employers over raising wages for skilled care workers (senior carers or senior care assistants) in the social care sector to £8.80 ($14.29) an hour, the government lowered the qualifying wage rate to £7.80 ($12.67) an hour. These rates were still higher than the 2009 national minimum wage of £5.80 ($9.42). However, employers funded by local government, in particular, had to seek the best value possible, meaning the lowest possible salary bill. Care workers already on temporary work permits did not receive the required pay rise from some employers. Nurses, like other public sector workers, had pay rises restricted as part of the government's austerity program. Thus after five years of work in the United Kingdom, migrants found they were no longer able to earn the salary needed for a successful ILR application. Many Filipinos reported having applications denied.

During the same period, the United Kingdom began encouraging foreign students to study in the country, bringing money from overseas sources into the publicly funded tertiary education system. Migrants holding student visas were permitted to work a limited number of hours per week, initially twenty hours. New training courses quickly developed to offer UK-recognized care work qualifications. These were through twenty hours per week of paid work and twenty hours of practical learning, often via an online study component. Such programs offered a workaround for the restrictions on migrants doing care work. Migrants could still engage in care work, but now while officially studying. Offered by tertiary education institutions, including technical colleges and universities, these courses served as new income streams for institutions whose core funding from the government was effectively reduced. From the Philippines, these programs looked as if they would qualify student migrants to apply for senior carer/senior care assistant positions and thus for post-study employment and eventual settlement in the United Kingdom. But the problem of low wages and the income requirements for residency applications persisted. Some Filipinos reported that their employers had offered to provide them with false reports of income so they could qualify for residency while continuing to pay them significantly lower wages.

The numbers of Filipinos arriving on short-term work visas for care work and health care continued to expand. However, migrants no longer had access to the assured routes to settlement and family reunification that had been open to Filipino health care professionals who had arrived earlier.[33] Filipino migrants already in the country on temporary work permits and those en route to the United Kingdom—a process taking some months, if not several years—had their expectations frustrated. At best, they would work but no longer see the expected return on their investments of time and savings or be able to settle or reunite their families. At worst, many would now struggle to repay the debts they had incurred in order to migrate. These reforms created resentment and frustration among migrants, making irregular work more prevalent.

With their access to the now well-known routes to permanent residency restricted, Filipinos on temporary work or study visas increasingly overstayed to enter the informal economy of care work. Still more Filipinos heard that such work was possible and came on tourist or student visas to try their luck. They were looking for employers seeking private care directly and prepared to risk working without authorization. Labanet among them, these migrants arrived well-networked and astute, not duped by globalization so much as prepared to master it to their own ends.

## Mapping a Shatter Zone

This chapter has located Filipino migrants within the regulatory apparatus governing migration and work in the United Kingdom. I have outlined several reasons why regulation has a comparatively inconsistent purchase on migrants' daily lives and why irregular migrants are tolerated. There are other factors I've not explored. At a time of budgetary constraint, middle-aged Filipino housekeepers in private homes may be visa overstayers, but they are not high-priority terrorist threats. Another contributor may be the social position and high-profile work undertaken by their elite employers. However, offering an exhaustive explanation of the regulatory production of irregularity in the United Kingdom is not my goal here. Though my respondents' experiences and motivations were shaped by these regulations, they were neither reducible to nor exhausted by them. Instead, my respondents created spaces for socializing, celebration, and mutual care, channeling global affect to sustain themselves. Their social networks and the flows of affect in them are my focus. The chapters ahead thus do not compare national policy regimes or state bureaucracies; other scholars have done much excellent work in both these areas.[34] Likewise, I try not to frame my respondents only through their work in employers' households or in relation to their nuclear sending families. Instead I foreground migrants' other global networks: the ones drawing together friends, neighbors, and more distant kin to connect them with employers.[35] I show how Kankanaey culture enables them to secure long-term employment and sponsorship relations with host nationals and produce the global shatter zone.

Focusing on migrants' social networks beyond the workplace—without ignoring exploitation within it—these chapters explore the cultural richness of Filipino migrant lives.[36] Such networks are themselves a particular kind of research object when compared to nation-states or nuclear families. They are diffuse, dynamic, and multiple, changing quite quickly over time. They are not constructed or fixed through legal regulation, unlike, say, marriage, tenancy relations, or employment contracts. The networks I study are thus largely invisible to the bureaucratic practice regulating migration. Friends, congregations, and housemates are not formally appended to individuals as sites of obligation or exchange in UK law, but they are in Kankanaey culture. These networks are created on an ongoing basis through affinity, exchange, and the sharing of good feelings. They are about mutuality of support and understanding and mutual exposure. Other than being there and joining in the feeling oneself, evidence of these networks is archived largely in memory and through the artifacts made in social exchange: in text messages, letters, gifts, photographs, and, increasingly, on social media. Because of their properties and origins, these networks tend to be fissiparous and sometimes fleeting, yet sustain the capacity to care. In Labanet's words, echoing those of Sabel, earlier, "I came to work. I didn't know that I'd need my native dress for dancing every weekend. But that's how it goes! How I find my friends, find my work. Me, I have a project back home. I can go back to something, so I can stay sane here, as if hope is all I have. Here, my hope is in my friends."

## Notes

1. Manalansan, 2010.
2. Bartley, 2015.
3. www.payingforcare.org (last accessed October 10, 2015).
4. www.payingforcare.org (last accessed October 10, 2015).
5. UNISON. UNISON reports that care workers were paid between £6.08 and £8.00 per hour. As of 2016, the national living wage was set by the government at £7.20 per hour. Firms in this sector have been prosecuted for paying below statutory minimum wage.

6. Levinson, 2005.

7. The United Kingdom's Shortage Occupation List is updated periodically. For an example, see https://www.gov.uk/government/uploads/system/uploads/attachment_data/file/423800/shortage_occupation_list_april_2015.pdf.

8. Anon., 2015a.

9. Vine, 2012.

10. Sassen, 1991.

11. Nickell and Saleheen, 2008.

12. Jowit, 2014.

13. Cangiano, Shutes, Spencer, and Leeson, 2009.

14. Schneider and Williams, 2013.

15. Migrationwatch UK.

16. See Datta et al., 2010.

17. Moore, 2011.

18. From the comments thread on Jowit, 2014.

19. http://falseeconomy.org.uk/cuts/testimony/low-paid-work-to-benefits-to-low-paid-work-to-benefits (last accessed September 15, 2014).

20. UNISON.

21. Constable, 1997; Parreñas, 2001; Stasiulis and Bakan, 2005; Tyner, 2004.

22. Parreñas, 2001; Pertierra, 1992; Stasiulis and Bakan 2005; Gibson, Law, and McKay, 2001.

23. Rodriguez, 2010.

24. Constable, 1997; Parreñas, 2001.

25. There is debate over whether the geometry created by exported care workers is a "chain" or a "diamond," but the debate largely elides the importance of varied colonial histories and different cultural contexts. See Raghuram, Madge, and Noxolo, 2009; Ragurham, Henry, and Bornat, 2010; Raguhuram, 2012.

26. Stock estimates as of December 2012 from the Commission on Filipinos Overseas, available at http://www.cfo.gov.ph/images/stories/pdf/StockEstimate2012.pdf.

27. See Cooper, Campbell, Patel, and Simmons, 2014. Figures are from page 11, Table 3: Largest country of birth groups, by immigration category, EEA and non-EEA, 2012–13.

28. Kanlungan, pers. comm. 2009. These figures were published by Kanlungan in Jamima Fagta's (2012) briefing note, Some Facts about the Filipino Community in the UK, November 25, 2012, available at http://www.kanlungan.org.uk/some-facts-about-the-filipino-community-in-the-uk/ (last accessed May 12, 2015).

29. Pattacini and Zenou, 2012.

30. Tan, 2012.

31. Commission on Filipinos Overseas, Stock Estimates for 2012, available at http://www.cfo.gov.ph/images/stories/pdf/StockEstimate2012.pdf (last accessed September 12, 2014).

32. Travis, 2009.

33. See Jamima Fagta, "Some Facts about the Filipino Community in the UK," November 25, 2012, available at http://www.kanlungan.org.uk/some-facts-about-the-filipino-community-in-the-uk/ (last accessed May 12, 2015).

34. For European migration regimes, see Andersson, 2014, and Feldman, 2012; for the Philippines, Rodriguez, 2010. For Filipino labor migration, see Constable, 1997, 1999, and 2014; Faier, 2009, Pratt, 2012; and Parreñas, 2001, 2005, and 2011.

35. See Raghuram, Henry, and Bornat, 2010, for South Asian professional migrants in the United Kingdom.

36. Johnson et al., 2010.

# 2 At Church

IN CHURCH, MIGRANTS learned about debt and faith. They found that meeting Christian obligations to care coincided with *inayan*. Being together, working on shared tasks, singing, dancing, contributing talents, and being recognized as equal children of God in church services consoled migrants and renewed their energy. Affective flows here were mediated by ritual, physical practices. Singing in harmony, kneeling in unison, lining up to receive communion, sipping consecrated wine from a cup still warm from fellow congregants' lips, exchanging the peace—these actions opened up connections among congregants. Church was a space where Filipino migrants and local English citizens met on an equal footing. "Where would we be without church every week?" Labanet observed. "We'd be lost! In church, I feel I belong."

When Labanet and Biag first came to London, they found their way to the redbrick East London church where Father Alabag preached. Biag joined the church choir. On my first visit to his church, he and I recognized each other. We had met twenty years before in his home village. Biag's rich baritone could be heard distinctly as the choir moved down the church's central aisle. Biag's wife, Labanet, sat with her cousins and housemates at the back—she'd slipped in late. She'd returned from babysitting in West London on the night bus and had overslept. Labanet lent her mellow alto to the harmony of "Amazing Grace." The space swelled with raised voices. Labanet and her companions swayed in unison in their pew, standing shoulder to shoulder. In the middle of another swaying pew and moving with them, I felt the warmth of shoulders pressed against my arms carrying a charge that felt like calm and unity across the congregation. After the sound trailed away, we exchanged the peace. Congregants left their pews and shook hands, looking each other in the eye to say, "Peace be with you." At the back of the church, as worship ended, Biag and the choir broke into "Amazing Grace" again. The congregation joined in at the chorus, revisiting this moment of shared feeling; nobody wanted to let go. Church offered migrants sanctuary, expanding and renewing their networks, while reaffirming their Christian faith. For Labanet and Biag, church brought Christian faith and *inayan* together in ritual practice and daily conduct.

## Faith and Culture

The Filipino members of this church congregation were not typical Filipinos. Most Filipinos, 80 percent, are Catholic, while the remaining 20 percent of the population is Muslim, *Iglesia ni Cristo*, and a variety of other Protestant denominations.[1] In this church, Filipino congregants came from the mountains of the archipelago's northern island, Luzon, and spoke Kankanaey as their first language. They had grown up in indigenous communities as syncretic Christians. While they identified as members of a worldwide church, they regularly observed so-called pagan traditions. They brought elements of their Kankanaey culture into their worship, singing hymns in Kankanaey and celebrating feast days by playing gongs. Their origins made their church-based networks in the United Kingdom ethnic and regional.

Speakers of other Filipino languages (Tagalog, Cebuano, Ilokano, etc.) are typically Roman Catholic and belong to the Philippine cultural mainstream, so Kankanaey-speaking Protestant migrants were different. They had separate congregation, household, and friendship groups, and their congregations functioned in an encapsulated way within the broader community of Filipinos in the United Kingdom. While Kankanaey people had friends, colleagues, and acquaintances in that broader community, they rarely shared houses or attended the same church. They did join fellow Filipinos for charitable activities organized by UK-based Filipino NGOs. UK Filipino networks thus remained broadly regional.

Labanet came from Gameng, Biag from Katangoan, both municipalities north of Baguio City. While their cousin, Father Alabag, had relatives in Gameng, he grew up in a mining town slightly to the south. Their pagan traditions originated in agricultural rituals from the Kankanaey *ili* (village)—rituals still observed in both Gameng and Katangoan. These rituals marked life-course events and key points in the farming year. In the Philippines, their ritual practice would involve the ritual sacrifice of animals and redistribution of meat to kin and neighbors. In the United Kingdom, the same rituals were marked with big ethnic performances in church halls, combined with huge spreads of donated food for all. Sometimes songs and dances were incorporated into the church services themselves. Non-Kankanaey congregants were invited to attend after church events, sharing in the food and joining the dancing and singing. Ritual, sharing, and strategic openness were all elements of *inayan*.

*Inayan* originally described the relationships between the Kankanaey human/ social world and the supernatural world concerned with natural resources. People did not own resources unless they had mixed in their labor, but not all of nature was available for ownership. To cultivate successfully, Kankanaey ancestors had performed rituals to ask the unseen forest keepers permission to cultivate. Transgressions of the forest keepers' taboos were met with punishment. Being rice cultivators, the most important Kankanaey ritual sought the permission of the water spirit. Each year villagers had to *apoy* (sacrifice a chicken) or else *inayan*—the rule—would be violated. Without a proper sacrifice the water spirit would take the water away, cursing their village with drought. Later, when rice fields were rebuilt with the skills and materials provided by the descendants of the original builders, sacrifices were also made to the ancestors. Transgressing the traditions of the ancestors who had made the original *apoy* to the spirits of place became *inayan*, too. The scope of transgression included relationships with other descendants of the same ancestors. So *inayan* came to apply not only to relationships with the supernatural but also to those with other people. Migration then extended *inayan* to cover conduct toward fellow congregants and employers.

My respondents described *inayan* as similar to karma but carrying a Christian overlay of universal brotherhood. For them, *inayan* marked a deep sense of self, and one's future, bound up in one's ability to care for others and to have care refracted back across all one's personal relationships. *Inayan* is not limited to kin, community, nation, or ethnic groups, but is rather a global ethic with global obligations. *Inayan* underpins the global, spiritual potency of Kankanaey culture.

A Kankanaey environmental activist explained, "*Inayan* is . . . [a] version of the Golden Rule: 'Do not do unto others what you don't want others [to] do unto you.' This is a complex system of taboos that discourages acts which cause harm to anybody or anything. It is full with values—as in respect for other people and nature, justice, sharing of resources with others, helping one another, etc. It is more or less similar to the . . . philosophy of karma."[2]

A Kankanaey indigenous rights advocate argued: "*Inayan* is a value and practice of Kankanaey, it's related to *ayew*. *Ayew* means do not waste food, things, money, or your life. And *inayan* means do not do bad or evil things to others and to the earth."

In London, Father Alabag found *inayan* shaped his care work:

First, it's a job. But to do that job, you must care. You must form an attachment to the person. To see them as a person. Yes, you get paid. But you also give them recognition, respect . . . treat them as you would your own relative. That is giving care. And that is why, when they will die, you are the one crying. Sometimes even more than their own children. They will be the ones comforting you. Because you really form an attachment.

For me, when the old man died, at the funeral . . . I cried. The family requested we all, all the carers—attend. I went. My companions, the other carers, were expecting some give-aways. They expected the family would give them extra money. *Inayan*. I was shocked. We were paid already per hour, why would they give more? This was just about honoring the dead. Giving the proper respect for him. So the family did not give money to them and they were disappointed. Not me. It was good just to pay my last respects to the old man.

Us Filipinos are flexible . . . with kinship. Yes, relatives are important. But there are also many honorary relatives—aunties and uncles and . . . Just maybe anybody could become like family. Well, not just anyone, but if you're close, if you spend a lot of time together. Adopting, fostering . . . We can also join other families too—you can double up. The more, the merrier! That's how it was, with my employer's father, the old man. So, the employers, they really got to know the carers, to rely on them. You know, the son would to discuss to me how their father is and what is his condition. . . . And after the funeral, they didn't say just "good-bye"—they made sure they got my cell phone.

Primarily, our attitude to caregiving comes from our [Kankanaey] culture. We respect the elders—the *ap-apo*—they are our advisors and leaders. That is our practice—how we are brought up—to respect our elders, our parents. Second, there is the Christian teaching: honor thy father and thy mother. It's the same thing. So it is doubled. And when we are far from our family, we can honor our elders there, as if they are our own. *Inayan*. If we do otherwise, it will come back to us, to our families . . . as bad events.

Are we self-effacing? No, I don't like that. That's not right. It is more "*pasiensyamo na lang . . .*" [just hold your patience] or *kimkim* . . . in Ilokano. We just hold our feeling and it fills us up. See, we have compassion, yes, for our fellow human beings? That's us being Filipinos, of course. We think: we're all people, after all. And *inayan*, that someone would have that care and patience with us, when we are old, or with our families, in their time.

*Inayan* entails a corporate social responsibility. Punishments for transgressions are directed not to an offending individual but distributed across an extended kin group. The reach of *inayan* likewise extends beyond the boundaries of this corporate group to the global.

For example, when Oedma overstayed in London, she was working as a private caregiver for an elderly woman she had met through her church. When her former husband, the father of her children, became ill with cancer, Oedma chose to remain in London. She felt caught between the expectation that she would attend the funeral and her obligation to her employer. She prayed about it. But what more might happen if she were to abandon her employer before her death? Not only would she return to the Philippines to be a dependent on her adult children, she would expose herself and her family members to a similar threat of abandonment in extreme old age. It was not only a sense of the obligations of Christian marriage or charity that influenced her decision, but also a gut feeling that her future would be shaped by her ties to her employer as much as to her wider family.[3] For her, *inayan* and *alayan* (help, sacrifice, or assistance) were inextricably intertwined with both Christian faith and pagan tradition. Those who did not sacrifice their own interests to help their fellows would be punished by fate. Oedma reflected, "The Bible tells us . . . that you are your brother's keeper. . . . Like that. And that's also where we have our obligation to care. *Inayan* if we do not. What more would happen to our mother and father, our brother, our children, even us, if we did not care?"

Kin relations—extended well beyond the nuclear family—are key to the way *inayan* works. Kankanaey people recognize kin to the descendants of common great-great-grandfathers and sometimes beyond: "to the third degree of consanguinity and affinity," as Labanet explained.[4] They maintain kin relations in this bilateral system through reciprocal exchanges of goods, labor, and money. People forget kin who do not reciprocate and incorporate other people into their kin network as fictive kin. Back home, these exchanges mark alliances among villagers and common membership in state-defined units—the Barangay and, above it, the Municipality. In the United Kingdom, church networks replaced these alliances. What happened in church—who among the Kankanaey congregants attended each week, who sat with whom—took its shape from ongoing reciprocal exchanges.

Visa status created distinct but interdependent groups of migrants in the church. People with the right to remain in the United Kingdom—either as citizens, permanent residents, or on temporary work visas—could take public and visible roles in the congregation. They read the lesson, acted as leaders, and appeared in official photographs. People who had no authorization for their stay tried to hide from the authorities but also conceal their status from others. They kept a low profile. Long-settled migrants were embarrassed by the propensity of newer arrivals to break their visa conditions. They feared this gave the community a bad reputation. They worried about children left behind in the Philippines. Newer arrivals found the established migrants complacent, a bit stingy, and out of touch. The positive affect flowing through church services was thus sometimes disrupted by ructions between congregants. People refused to share a pew and sometimes exchanged harsh words. On one occasion the tension erupted into physical violence, with one congregant slapping another's face during the after church coffee gathering.

In church, people brokered relationships leading to housing, employment, and other kinds of support. Conyap, a British citizen, paid the mortgage on her terraced East London house by renting rooms to other migrants. Biag and Labanet met her at church and became her tenants. They fell out with Conyap when she made disparaging comments about leaving their children behind in the Philippines. "*Inayan*, that she would be the one commenting. She has not lived in the Philippines for more than twenty-five years!" said Labanet. Labanet and Conyap rarely spoke in church and avoided each other. Conyap felt new migrants did not know how to honor their debts to older migrants who had "paved the way" for their work in the United Kingdom and offered them hospitality, helping them out with accommodations when they were desperate: "*Inayan*, they don't know what it is to be grateful for help. They just expect."

Linking *inayan* and Christian faith to debt, Conyap argued church's affective flow depended on proper reciprocity. *Inayan* governs balanced and reciprocal exchanges not just characterized by financial debt, but also by broader obligations. Debt and borrowing featured prominently in the priests' sermons and in migrants' social lives.

## Debt and Cutting Networks

For all Filipinos, debt—*utang*—is a practical problem and an important strategy for building relationships and sustaining a sense of self. In church people borrow and lend money, but also exchange support and care. The Filipino concept of *utang na loob* (internal debt or debt of gratitude) is fundamental to church networks, my respondents' conception *inayan*, and Christian care.[5] While there may be no *bayad* (payment) or *kapalit* (exchange) made for support received or gifts given in church-based networks, the idea of internal/constitutive debt depends on affect. Receiving flows of positive feeling obliged people to share, to turn up, to support, to perform, to make community within and around their church, and to extend this ethos more widely.

Take Adamey's story: Adamey worked as a nanny on a tourist visa in Austria. She had been able to convert her visa in order to work as a nurse in a homeopathic neurological hospital. After returning to the Philippines in 1997, she married and had two children. She came to the United Kingdom as a senior care assistant in 2000. Her husband and children joined her in 2006, and the whole family now has citizenship. She had recently moved into private care work. Adamey explained, "If you didn't have your church, it would be like . . . living in a foreign place. . . . For us Filipinos, we expect people from our church to be close. So, if you are sick or have a problem, they are the first people to approach you, to assist you, you would feel close to them, as if you should go with them—it's like that!" I asked, "Is that a kind of *utang na loob* [debt of gratitude]?" Adamey continued:

> Yes, of course. Like that, exactly! This *utang na loob*, it's like we share it with our employers here. Even if they aren't Christians like us. For me, my employer is Jewish. What I observe is that Jewish families stay in touch. They are like us, they appreciate our practices. My sister was working for a Jewish family in Toronto and the old lady is very old—dementia. When she left, the family petitioned for my mother-in-law to replace my sister as live-in caregiver. But the old lady deteriorated before she could arrive and went to a care home, then she died. So my mother-in-law spent $50,000 HK plus-plus [approximately £3,700 or $5,800] to get to Canada. And the family, they helped her when she arrived. We're just thankful she is there and can find another work, we hope. My sister was invited to the funeral and is close to the daughter of the woman who died. She also went to the bat mitzvah of the granddaughter. So I am happy to work for a Jewish employer here.
>
> What I understand is that Jews are . . . their culture is the origins of our Christian faith. That's where the Bible and our practices come from. So they are like the *manong* [older brother] of Christianity. Even if they do not accept Jesus, we are close . . . I can respect their practices, their festivals. As a people, they have suffered so much, yet they still have a strong culture. I can accept that my work should comply to Jewish practices. It's a way of giving respect. And the work really means you must care what they want, how they feel and think . . . and believe. You can respect their beliefs without sharing them.

Those who just do their tasks and complete their forms are just doing the job, not caring. They don't have a spiritual awareness and, without it, I think they will suffer with this job. For this job, you really must keep yourself healthy and centered—emotionally, physically, spiritually. For me, I do that in church. So it is very important to me to go to church, to participate in my community. My employer is Jewish, but they know my care, for me, it comes through my Christian church, too.

Migrants could find many competing faith-based networks to join. Both at home and in the diaspora Filipinos have converted to a variety of new denominations. Many of these "new churches" preach some version of a prosperity gospel.[6] For Kankanaey migrants, in contrast to traditional reciprocity with kin and community, the new churches offer an alternate form of family—*kapatiran* or brotherhood—based on congregational support. Converting to a new faith allowed people to withdraw from extended family or village networks and traditional exchange obligations. The new Protestant denominations I encountered in London included the Philippine-based *Iglesia ni Cristo* (INC), the Pentecostal London Worship Circle—with a "mother church" in Baguio City—and the Australian Hillsong. The INC and Hillsong were actively recruiting new members among Filipinos in London. There were several other denominations advertising in the London Filipino community papers, but I met no members of their congregations during my research. A focus on prosperity and indebtedness was a key theme in the affective work of building networks through church. Migrants sometimes borrowed funds to remit home, though their UK churches did not always sanction debt. Churches rarely questioned how migrants found money to make their regular tithes and weekly offerings. Some churches had no particular teaching on borrowing and lending and did not describe God as a creditor and his congregation as debtors. Others churches, like the Filipino Protestant (INC), forbade congregants from borrowing or lending money. This church taught them that their primary debt was to God, who had loaned them their lives. The prohibition on credit was one my INC respondents struggled with. They observed it mainly in the breach—as a desirable ideal they would enact in their own lives once their finances and families at home were "stable."

Religious teachings on debt and the appropriate forms for transacting with the spiritual realm featured in a wide variety of postcolonial Filipino spiritual practices.[7] In teaching that INC members' lives were merely borrowed from God, their church both reinforced and subtly transformed the same Kankanaey understanding of relations with the spiritual realm as reciprocal transactions.[8] Before Spanish colonization, Filipino societies were shaped by variations on debt bondage and social relations were constructed around notions of exchange. Colonial conversion to Christianity transmuted these exchanges with patrons, ancestors, and spirits into those with the Christian God and the Catholic Church.[9] More recently many Filipinos have not been entirely satisfied with Catholicism as the appropriate path to propitiate a God who will guarantee prosperity.[10] Thus my respondents noted a great deal of important variation in the ways churches approached economic exchange as an aspect of faith and worship. Within and between denominations, my respondents debated whether one could truly engage God in an exchange relationship. If you prayed for something, should God give it to you? If he didn't, did this mean you had committed some offence you had yet to remedy? Should you try a different form of asking, through ritual or sacrifice?

For everyone, the key Biblical text was John 15:4–5: "If you remain in me and my words remain in you, you may ask what you will and you shall get it. It is to the glory of my Father that you should bear much fruit, and then you will be my disciples." Each denomination interpreted this quote—"the vine and the branches"—differently. Interviewees across multiple congregations quoted this verse to me as a way of grounding accounts of debates on prosperity and debt. Did the fruit mean material wealth? Did asking for what you wanted actually get you a specific blessing from God? If you did not receive what you had asked for, should you join a different church with new practices or rituals to make you a better person and thus improve your access to God's blessings? Some people were dismissive of the churches that preached a prosperity gospel as being led by demagogues. Others were intrigued, particularly by the kind of economic benefits church brotherhood may offer. If you owed your life to God, would he give you additional blessings to help you pay him back?

Changing their faith offered my respondents a means to extricate their sense of self from the reciprocity demanded by extended family networks. By joining new, more limited, and, most importantly, self-chosen families of churches, they could save money. As James Weiner writes, "The task confronting humans is not to sustain human relationships . . . [but] to place a limit on relationship."[11] This insight resonated particularly strongly with people who found that migration meant more demands from kin. Migrants typically discovered that they had far more relatives than they had previously recognized. Some of these kin connections were beneficial—assisting with finding jobs abroad and investing in property or business at home. People renewed other kin relations only to make predatory extractions.[12] The anthropologist Marilyn Strathern describes how, in these circumstances, relationships are "cut." Cutting describes how one phenomenon stops the flow of others, operationalizing apparently limitless concepts like faith and family to produce social effects.[13] The kind of cutting behind religious conversion is not only about severing ties but also about conjugation—the breakdown and repackaging or reassembly of network components. Conjugation is precisely what happened, via affect, in the fallout from congregational disagreements.

Conyap, as a traditional Kankanaey Protestant, was critical of the ways the new churches set themselves up in the United Kingdom's Filipino community. She saw these churches as little more than scams run by unscrupulous pastors.

Their leaders enriched themselves at the expense of their migrant congregations, promising that donations to the church would result in abundance to be delivered by God. These new churches cut people off from the rest of the community and from their families at home in the Philippines. By family, Conyap meant the Kankanaey extended-kin network that converts "forgot"; she was not suggesting that migrant converts were neglecting their duties to support their own parents and children left at home. The new churches accomplished this forgetting of kinship responsibilities by redirecting members' surplus earnings into local religious networks and events. Conyap told me her story of joining in a church-led community event marking Father's Day at a London park. Conyap was conserving her money. She had only brought a donation of food and enough money for transportation to the picnic. During the prayers led by the Protestant pastor, his wife circulated a donation bag. But Conyap had no cash to offer. In a subsequent set of prayers, the names of the fathers of all those present were commended to God, except Conyap's. All the other people there were from her municipality back in the Philippines and would have noticed that her surname was not read out. This was *inayan*; it was a karmic wrong to exclude someone from the blessings of faith because of money. The whole group subsequently prayed for the prosperity of the woman who had made the biggest cash donation, in a blatant prayers-for-money exchange.

Conyap did believe this was truly Christian. She thought this church was a spiritual pyramid scheme through which donations from the faithful had enabled the pastor to have a nice house, three cars, and a wife, who now worked nursing shifts only once a week. "We're so busy with the congregation," Conyap mimicked the pastor's wife for me, "we don't have time to work." In her own voice, Conyap imagined speaking back, "That's because you are taking their money, while they remain living in bad housing and desperate for steady work." Addressing me, she said, "That is not what Christ taught."

Conyap was also dismissive of the new church ideas of God having "a program" for migrants. She recounted the story of a young woman she had met, a new arrival in the United Kingdom, who had joined this church while in Hong Kong. She had explained to Conyap at length how God had "a program for me" and helped her travel to London. Conyap discovered she was an overstayer who had arrived on a tourist visa. She was living hand-to-mouth, dependent on her fellow church members for housing and the occasional recommendation for casual work. She was working, as an unpaid volunteer, in the house of her pastor. "That's not God's plan for anyone," Conyap exclaimed. "That's a disaster in your life. You are stuck here, hiding and illegal, not earning anything, not using the education your parents sacrificed for. You just depend to your church. You cannot help your family. You should better just go home." Conyap held this church culpable for luring this woman into a form of servitude.

Chayapan and Geya both affirmed Conyap's view of conversion. They had seen that people who had converted while abroad tended to distance themselves from their families, forgetting their obligations and causing a great deal of pain at home. Converts redirected their earnings to tithes to their new churches. They no longer remitted little extras to be distributed to their extended kin by their spouses, parents, and children in the Philippines. Chayapan suggested that converts might be forgetting almost unconsciously, because the weekly services and friends in the congregation were their most effective sources of emotional support, practical advice, and contacts for employment. But to forget obligations back home, no matter what their struggles, violated *inayan*. It was usually the care from extended family that helped a would-be migrant complete his or her education, marry, and establish a household, so failing to remember kin revealed selfishness and moral weakness, generating bad karma.

Geya, a community worker with fifteen years of experience among Filipino migrants in London, thought migrants often converted to cope with some kind of family conflict or breakdown. Changing churches resulted from the failure of long-distance marital relationships or from strain between siblings, usually as a result of a dispute over land, inheritance, or the allowances sent home for children left under the care of their relatives. In such situations, humiliated migrants found it difficult to face cousins and village-mates who were also members of their congregation. They felt as if their family and village were watching them and judging them through the eyes of the UK church members. It was, Geya told me, as if distressed migrants narrowed their whole social world to only the members of their new church in an attempt to become "a new person."

Conversion, Geya, Chayapan, and Conyap all agreed, saw migrants withdraw from almost all of their previous place-based or extended-kin networks to focus on church activities. New churches had big events, frequently demanded that members attend two or more weekly services, required additional bible study, and expected volunteer work as well as participation in festivals, socials, and sports events. In return, joining a new church offered a different kind of family relationship, with members addressing each other as sister and brother, socializing intensely, and providing each other with reciprocal gifts of food and goods that traditionally sustained Filipino kin relations.

Daguon M., a convert to one of these new churches, explained her decision to convert from being a "renewed" traditional Protestant to a member of a Pentecostal denomination. Her reasons combined spiritual affinity and settlement strategy. Hers was among the first "founding families"—meaning nuclear families—of the London congregation for a denomination with a mother church in Baguio City. Daguon's church activities kept her focused on her life in the United Kingdom, where she was a new citizen. She contrasted herself to some of her friends who remained traditional Protestants. These friends constantly thought about returning home and invested there. Daguon's tithing and charitable activities meant she did not invest in land at home, nor did she plan to retire there. All she was currently providing was a small allowance for her aging parents. Now, unlike the first few years of her life in the United Kingdom, as a Pentecostal she no longer offered money to her siblings or nieces and nephews, or for community-wide festivals at home. She said, "I am happy I no longer have to observe our pagan practices. This way, now, I can be free—free to move about here in the UK. I am not tied, like before."

Chayapan was dismissive of this kind of freedom. First, she observed, the traditional Protestant and Catholic churches were where Filipinos met and interacted with other UK citizens, particularly people they considered "white English." Filipino-only denominations were not sites of integration for new migrants at all. Chayapan didn't think her own Protestant church fostered deep and meaningful intercultural socializing, but that just having the Filipinos contribute as wardens, reading the lessons, offering coffee and tea, attending social nights, and supporting the theatre troupe in fundraising was a good start. The new churches, she observed, were almost exclusively Filipino, with the occasional (typically silent and awkward) exception of a boyfriend of a Filipina worshipper. Chayapan identified possible economic and networking benefits to worshipping in a mixed congregation of migrants and local citizens and gave me an example. Last year, Ros-al, one of her Gameng village-mates, had arrived on a student visa. Ros-al had been looking for part-time work when she joined a Protestant congregation in South Kensington. She requested spiritual guidance from the priest. Hearing about her situation, he published her name and mobile phone number in the parish newsletter along with her suggested hourly rate for cleaning and a brief description of her circumstances. This led Ros-al to a part-time housekeeping job for another newly arrived family of medical professionals in the congregation. She then picked up casual hourly cleaning work for several more elderly English congregants.

Chayapan described how forms of social debt figured in the community dynamics of conversion. She recounted how she had been pressured by her own upline (line manager) in her housekeeping job to attend an INC service. She described how the church members tried to "catch" her by offering her food and inviting her to training workshops and a weekend trip. She interpreted these overtures as attempts to activate her *utang na loob* (internal debt or social obligation). This would bind her to the congregation through reciprocal expectations, obliging her to convert. She was uncomfortable because this was not about understanding the abstract tenets of her faith. Instead, it was an attempt to place her in a social position where she would lose face and appear ungrateful if she withdrew from the relationship without reciprocating with her time and interest. Chayapan did so, nonetheless, because, as she told me, "I didn't need that kind of support any more. My job is stable. My upline can't influence my employer against me because of church. I already have my own church and it is the same as that of my employer [Protestant]. So what can my upline really do? My employer will support me staying in her church, after all. I have my shared apartment. I'm ok. But if I had needed money or work, or just a Filipino friend to talk with, I would have been easily caught."

This church recruited members not so much by offering spiritual knowledge and insight but by offering Christian brotherhood—*kapatiran*—and extending networks of employment and support. To refuse this invitation was, for Chayapan, to cut her network with her upline. Likewise, Chayapan eventually cut off her relationship with Daguon M., who had been her high school classmate.

Debt and faith marked fissures in the Kanakanaey-speaking Filipino community. Who was authentically Kankanaey? "As if they want to be something else already," Chayapan said of new church converts. People in the new church congregations were skeptical about transplanting syncretic pagan practices to London, thinking them improper in any kind of Christian faith. Daguon M. observed, "Why do they want to keep doing that ritual even here in London? They claim to be Christians, but they do not truly believe, it seems."

## Borrowing and Lending

In traditional Protestant congregations, Kankanaey people organized money-*ogbo*—This practice saw lending circles circulate interest-free loans through a closed group recruited through after church social events. Those who had papers (valid work visas, Indefinite Leave to Remain, or citizenship) could also borrow from banks, credit unions, or payday lenders. When desperate, however, everyone turned to community moneylenders. Moneylenders would lend at 3 percent per month to cousins and other near relatives, and 5 percent or 10 percent to more distant kin or acquaintances. Labanet would sometimes loan out some of her earnings at 3 percent or 5 percent to make a bit more money each month. People repaid each other after church.

After church, more established migrants also greeted new arrivals, giving gifts of cash—*supot*—to kin and covillagers. These gifts were exchanged between household groups. *Records of supot* would be texted or e-mailed home to be added to the books of debts and obligations kept by family elders. Such obligations resulted not only from previous exchanges but also from extended kin ties. When Labnay, one of Biag's neighbors from Gameng, arrived in London in mid-2009 and attended her first church service, she received about £500 ($771). Biag and Labanet gave her £40 ($62). This amount paid her rent and transportation costs as she waited for her Tourism Management course to begin and sought work. In order to migrate on a student visa, Labnay had borrowed most of the amount she had needed to show the UK Border Agency (UKBA). These funds were returned to her relatives to minimize the interest payable. Church gave her *supot* funds and job recommendations instead, so she was soon able to remit money to her family at home.

Communities at home understood migrants' gifts, repayments, remittances, redistributions, development assistance, charitable donations, and emergency aid channeled through church as discharging an obligation created by migrants' departures. Ghassan Hage has generalized migration itself as incurring a new kind of foundational debt migrants must repay.[14] Yet no matter how much migrants send back home, it is never enough. Migrants find that both the scope of this social debt and the size of their networks continue to expand, accelerated by their apparent success overseas.[15]

Church connections and ethics benefitted employers, too. Parts of migrants' exchanges with their employers were fairly simple and social. Some employers sent their own gifts to the Philippines for employee's family members alongside employee's regular boxes of gifts. In return, employees gave employers Christmas and birthday gifts, and these were reciprocated. Employers also made personal donations to employees' family emergencies and donations community relief funds through church. Through church networks, their employees could find them substitute caregivers and babysitters at short notice. Church thus enabled migrants to forge new connections, using *inayan* as a kind of social insurance policy, and to fold these networks back into their work. For irregular migrants, the ethics of exchange and obligation structuring indebtedness between employers and employees were more complex. Where a migrant had accepted work around study on a student visa, and the employer had changed their hours and caused them to miss classes, the employer became indebted to the worker.

Ros-al G. was working as a part-time housekeeper while studying hotel management when her employer asked her to switch to full-time work. Ros-al stopped attending her college, commuting instead to her employers' home six days per week. Her college cut off her student Oystercard (a prepaid card enabling the user to access public transportation) for nonattendance. The Transport Police apprehended her on the Tube and turned her over to the UKBA for breaking the terms of her visa. She was held in immigration detention and deported to the Philippines. As this was happening, Ros-al contacted Chayapan, a senior member of her church congregation who had papers. Chayapan packed up Ros-al's possessions and shipped them back to her. She also phoned Ros-al's employer: "At first, she said 'Well, what do you want me to do?' so I explained that Ros-al had put herself at risk really just to help her out, this employer. And that Ros-al was now struggling, because she hadn't prepared any money yet to go home. So she relented, then. She got Ros-al's details and sent her £500 [$771] termination payment by Western Union. So Ros-al had some money. And then I gave the employer two recommendations for a new nanny. She was also hard up, without a nanny for her kids." While her employer felt obligated to Ros-al, she did not wish to be identified—and possibly fined—for employing Ros-al outside the terms of her visa. But she recognized that she had some responsibility for Ros-al's situation. Chayapan thought she recognized *inayan* being violated, which meant something worse might happen to the employer if the employer didn't help Ros-al. The employer then agreed to send Ros-al six weeks' salary via bank transfer to help her resettle at home and to pay off the debts she had incurred to secure her initial visa to study. The employer's motivation for doing this was not simply karma but also the possibility of finding another housekeeper—this time someone with authorization to work—through Chayapan's church-based networks.

## Faith in the Shatter Zone

In this chapter, we have seen how church shapes flows of affect through norms for exchange and debt. When migrants settle in the United Kingdom, they may change churches and cut their networks. Translating their Filipino extended-kin network into a UK-style nuclear family, depends on a process of purification—deciding who their friends and intimates will be, against traditional Kankanaey kin obligations. If traditional Kankanaey people find their personhood dispersed among networks of other persons, new church members, in contrast, tend to be much more bounded individuals, set in nuclear families.[16] In church, neither their working conditions nor government regulations are necessarily at the forefront of migrants' minds. The everyday questions people ask themselves here are, what does kinship mean? What are the limits to community? Who am I? What ties sustain me? What is God's program for me and how do I enact it? As a migrant, what should I expect from and give to my family? God? My church? Churches reach out to migrants to deal with these concerns directly.

At Labanet and Biag's church, migrants hear a positive message of diversity and inclusion, valuing them for their contributions to UK society. As their priest explained to the congregants:

> We are very fortunate to be a church congregation where a large number of us are immigrants. Secondly, as we celebrate this we need also to be sensitive to the situation of immigrants in our midst. None of us here is rich, but some of us are much poorer than others. Many are here as migrant workers, sometime working without papers and receiving very low incomes, sometime much lower than the minimum wage. What little some earn is sent back to their home countries. So in all our church activities we need to be sensitive to not asking people for money they cannot afford. If we are to be a church where none are excluded, we need to relaxed about money while at the same time recognizing how much we benefit from other ways in which people are more than generous, not least in donating their food, time and labor. And the final thing I want to say and to emphasize very strongly is that if we are to be a church for all we must be a church where immigrants, not least those whose immigration

status is not settled (including overstayers), feel welcome and safe. . . . We are not an arm of the government and certainly not here to do their work for them on immigration issues. The church is a place where, whatever our immigration status, we should feel safe and supported and I hope we can do more in this church to strengthen our support for immigrants. Jesus had a preference for the excluded—let us be sure to follow his example as we support and celebrate the presence of immigrants here in this church and in our wider community.

This church gave migrants clear messages about belonging and Christian congregational care in the shatter zone. Their congregation is separate from government and people in it are not responsible for migration regulations. What is established here, instead, is belonging based on a set of norms shaping interactions with others, blending *inayan* with Christian care across the boundaries created by visas, ethnic backgrounds, and nationalities. In the affective flows created through rituals of worship, singing together, exchanging the peace, and sharing food in church, ties are forged between migrants and other congregants. The church consoles those living in the space beyond the state, assuaging migrants'—and other congregants'—guilt about breaking rules, focusing instead on the flow of positive feeling in Christian care and charity.

The affective work of church ritual assuages anxieties and extends caring networks. This work does not stop when the service ends. Migrants carry the flow of feeling with them, in its ethos and expectations, out into the world and their work week. It thus emerged in other sites, including social media. A popular Facebook meme claimed, "Your most powerful testimony is how you treat others after the church service is over." Fely U. posted this meme to her Facebook profile. To this, someone identified as Agnep wrote, "*ha, Fely ..wen tet-ewa..*[Yes, I know] am just reminded of someone:-):-)" Fely's one-word reply: "Trueness!"

This Facebook meme illustrates *inayan*: there are standards here for reciprocating care for others performed and enforced by public shaming, however indirect. And the affective charge behind this shame carried a panoptical effect—who was watching and who was gossiping, about what behaviors, what events? The text accompanying these memes expressed intense sadness and frustration with relationships. This post garnered forty-eight likes and twenty comments in fourteen hours, with responses posted by Fely's relatives and school friends across in thirteen countries. It was not clear what rupture in which relationship had upset Fely. Those who cared for her online didn't necessarily feel the need to know the details. Instead, they offered care and comfort, responding with consoling words.

One such response had a positive, placating charge to it. Oedma R. wrote, "Sad to say that sometimes having a taste of a good salary changes one's personality that we become insensitive of others feelings. Lets be contented and thankful that we are lucky enough to be in this country and have each respective jobs. I pray for them Lord to open their hearts! Amen." My respondents felt that a global, open community, including non-Filipino members of their church congregation were watching them.

Considering church as an affective node also reveals how affect gives rise to London's global shatter zone. In this space, Filipino migrants are not sustained by the British state, but by London's position as an outpost of Filipino exchange economies and faith networks. These migrants are neither traditional indigenes nor classically self-actualizing neoliberal subjects, but a neo-tribal Christian hybrid. In church rituals, flows of affect link them to each other and to non-Filipino congregants. Care emerges through the brotherly love and support of worshippers, the after-church social rituals of tea, coffee, and conversation, and through the more prosaic practices of giving *supot*, hiring handymen (like Biag), or renting out houses—and liking posts on Facebook.

## Notes

1. Cannell, 2006.
2. From discussion on "Katangoan" in Transition Facebook Group, May 12, 2012.
3. See also Liebelt, 2011.
4. Eggan, 1960.
5. Aguilar, 1998.
6. Coleman, 2006; Wiegele, 2005.
7. Aguilar, 1998; Cannell, 2006; Rafael, 1988.
8. Aguilar, 1998; Cannell, 2006; Scott, 1983.
9. Aguilar, 1998; Rafael 1988.
10. Wiegele, 2005.
11. Weiner, 1993, p. 292, cited in Strathern, 1996, p. 529.
12. See http://www.filipinouk.co.uk/forum/showthread.php/8894-Ungrateful-so-called-family -in-Philippines!!/page2, last accessed July 2, 2013.
13. Strathern, 1996, p. 522. See also Derrida, 1992.
14. Hage, 2002.
15. McKay, 2007b and 2012.
16. Strathern, 1988.

Fig. 1 Labanet shopping in London—perfecting her performance of prosthetic citizenship. Posted to Facebook.

Fig. 2 Labanet taking a nap while babysitting Kittay's baby on her day off. Posted to Facebook.

Fig. 3 Biag with his children in Baguio City.

Fig. 4 Labanet and Biag's daughter pulling cabbages in Gameng, with much grumbling.

Fig. 5 Labanet and her charges in Trafalgar Square. Posted to Facebook.

Fig. 6 Biag and Labanet socializing after a church service.

Fig. 7 Biag dancing to celebrate a Kankanaey festival at the community center.

Fig. 8 Labanet and Oedma at Essex Street on their day off, updating their social media profiles and reading posts.

Fig. 9 Second-hand clothing from the *karbut* drying on the clothesline at Essex Street.

Fig. 10 Author (left) and friends attend a Kankanaey festival in Katangoan.

# 3   On Facebook

MY RESPONDENTS USED Facebook to negotiate global belonging, exchanging digital images and comments on the social media site. Because of the semipublic way these images and comments are archived, they were rich data for exploring affect.

Filipino Facebook is a visual space. Filipinos have been among the early adopters of mobile phones, digital cameras, camera phones, and phones with video capacity. These technologies have become much more accessible in the last decade, largely because of migration and remittances. For migrants, displaying images brings together aspects of an extended self usually separated in space and time, such as images from home and abroad. Facebook both amplifies and complicates the possibilities of exchange and display, juxtaposition and comment, cultural production and self-shaping, giving images their social meanings. The politics of images makes Facebook yet another space in which networks are cut and conjugated. But migrants' Facebook is not only "Facebook." It also incorporates data from other platforms because of the interplay between them.

Facebook sits within polymedia: "an emerging environment of communicative opportunities that functions as an 'integrated structure' within which each individual medium is defined in relational terms in the context of all other media."[1] Exchanges between people cross polymedia's platforms. For instance, Labanet and her friends in the United Kingdom lived their daily lives on Skype, but also documented those Skype sessions for Facebook, making public evidence of what were more private conversations. Adamey, Labanet, and their cousin Daguon all posted a series of daily Skypeshots to Facebook albums. These albums consisted of webcam photos of their children and other relatives collected into a time series. Their photos showed the children growing, the seasons changing, the décor and furnishings in their home in the Philippines being modified and improved with things they had sent back from the United Kingdom, and recorded birthday greetings and displays of the kids' homemade Mother's Day cards, among other slices of daily life. Facebook thus made public and archived selected parts of Skype.

Polymedia encompassed text messages, voice calls, and various social media platforms—not only Facebook and Skype, which predominated among my respondents, but (previously) Friendster and, now, What's App and Snapchat (for younger family members and younger migrants)—along with their various chat applications, conventional e-mail (Yahoo and Gmail), videos posted to YouTube and Facebook, and letters sent in the mail. Polymedia could be extended, too, to include the boxes of goods sent home from London! Sometimes CDs containing video recordings of important events were mixed in with boxes of groceries and gifts. Importantly, not everyone at home had equitable access to all these media platforms. Bandwidth, particularly in sending communities in the rural Philippines, was frequently too limited to Skype. There was a lot of contention at peak times of the day. Not everyone in the Philippines had a smartphone, though most aspired to own one. Moreover, the cost of home broadband remained out of reach for many households in rural areas. So what Labanet's kids could do from their house in the city with Skype could not be done in the villages where Labanet and Biag's extended families lived. But most of Labanet's peers and siblings had access to Facebook, and they could log on at times of lower demand to view status updates and make or comment on new posts as well as send e-mail messages and chat. They also left video and chat messages on Skype.

All this meant that Facebook, because of the way the platform archived material and enabled users to access, share, and recall it, became the obvious platform for my research. Facebook enabled users to make sensitive posts private or to delete comments. Because the posts I would see as a Facebook "friend" were already ones published to friends or to the rest of the platform, respondents were mostly comfortable with my online research presence.

## Life Online

People's choices among these platforms for different kinds of topics or levels of intimacy reflected moral, emotional, and social concerns. On Facebook, migrants shared evidence of their positive affect and intimate connections with home and family. Disagreements, distance, and disciplinary conversations did not feature on Facebook, but they did happen over Skype, e-mail, or chat, sometimes triggered by comments and posts (or noncomments and nonposts) on Facebook. Different respondents had different polymedia preferences and patterns of use. While Facebook offered me an opportunity to capture a cross section of the wider networks and community, more individual communication strategies shaped vital affective flows. Much of the affect captured on Facebook also flowed across other platforms. We can see this in the way polymedia saturated Labanet's daily life in London.

While Labanet logged in and out of Facebook, she could live on Skype, all day. She travelled across London logged in to Skype through a new 4G mobile phone. She logged in at home through her laptop, morning and evening. If possible, she kept Skype open and tucked her phone discreetly into her pocket at work. On the other side of the world, in Baguio City, the desktop computer in her children's home was likewise connected to Skype. Most of the time this computer was hooked up to a wall-hung plasma TV monitor. This monitor had been discarded by one of Biag's London employers. Biag shipped it home for use in their still-under-construction house. Labanet and her kids would leave their cameras and audio feeds open in parallel as often as they could. Their voice contacts were continual, if annoyingly intermittent during the Philippines' typhoon season. Thus sometimes when she was at work, Labanet was talking to her kids through her pocket. She waited until it was appropriate, though: "We talk—me and my kids—when I'm cleaning. Or maybe running errands. And when the kids I care for are at school. But not when I am babysitting or helping [her charges] with their homework, no. Those times I mute it, so my kids won't be hearing. But yes, when I'm in the street, of course. If they are there, they like to hear the noise of the cars passing. So they know London is such a big city."

Polymedia allowed for a life lived in parallel, and Labanet was someone who found this comforting. She enthused:

> Talking, seeing—it's almost like we're living together but apart. Texts, I don't send so much now. Not to my kids. I just leave chat messages or video messages. You know, when they are not there—for them to find, later. The more they receive from me—that they see my face, hear my voice, the better it is for them. The more it's like I'm really there. And it might get better still. You know Google glasses, yes? That I would buy, when it gets inexpensive. So I could do my cleaning work here, but watch my kids sleeping and getting ready for school through the webcam at the same time . . . and talk to them on the Skype. You know, advising them at their breakfast about their school that day.

Other people might have found the potentially constant surveillance and demand to interact draining. With text and e-mail messaging, users can choose when to turn their phones on or open their e-mail accounts. Migrants like Labanet, however, experienced that periodicity as an affective disconnect. Labanet had discovered that the constant flow of presence, potential interaction, and emotional availability across an open channel was something she had wanted but didn't know how to describe—until she found Skype.[2] Working in precarious conditions far away from loved ones, she felt that this kind of mediated connection made her exist more fully in her life at home. It offered her a compelling way to locate a true version of herself. It may have been a kind of fake version of "living with," but Labanet had not seen her children in person since 2007. The necessarily limited affective flow the open channel carried back and forth gave her a vital sense of intimacy. But using Skype in this way was only possible between London and Baguio City.

Beyond Baguio, out in the provinces, people relied on Facebook for broader, networked conversations and performances. So, too, did Labanet, to stay in touch with them. In rural areas, Facebook has been a revelation in its reframing and expansion of community networks and users' sense of self. Labanet's cousin, Chayapan R., a teacher working in a state school near Gameng, posted the following as a status update:

> Feeling wonderful
>
> Being here on FB is not somewhat like being an addict. But it is how we—family and friends—link with each other. In school, our head used to give us points for community linkages which most of the time I always failed. It is because I am inactive to community activities—Barangay Day, Peoples' Day. For those times that I was so antagonistic [to community activities], I'm very sorry. Anyhow, I still do belong. Going back to FB, hmmm . . . Interesting! On FB I can see my family and friends around the world. I can easily ask help from them in all aspects which sometimes people outside FB can't provide (and they usually grant my favors, thank you so much). I see different places and read sensible quotes (which I could share with my colleagues and students), meet unknown relatives and new friends, shop online (which others don't know how [to do]? Ha ha). FB makes me grow professionally. It lets us extend help with each other. And, most of all, to lean on in times of problems and loneliness. This is how I do community linkages. FB, so great, so powerful. This is one of the communities where I belong. Make it your community too.

Labanet responded by commenting (in Kankanaey), "*Hehe wen met a* [Ha, ha, but yes of course]." Responding to English in Kankanaey, Labanet knew her response would be seen and "liked" not only at home but also by her own "friends" networks around the world as a statement of her cultural identity.

This story shows us the particularities of Facebook. There is not simply one definitive Facebook; this version of it was distinctively Kankanaey.[3] Facebook's ability to act as archive of and conduit for culture made it popular with global Kankanaey networks. Different groups of Kankanaey Facebook users engaged in a wide variety of interactions through the site, not all of which simply reflected their offline interactions. Instead, their use of the site was inevitably transforming everyday life.[4]

On Facebook, the online actions of "friends" reveal some "friend" relationships to be simply tokens of recognition over time. Other "friend" relationships are virtual markers for long-term relations offline involving the mutual exchange of gifts, favors, opinion, affect, and support. But online interactions also build connections that extended beyond Facebook, transforming "friends" into friends. Users often feel a need to continually track activity on the site in order to learn of evolving network connections and disconnections in their social worlds, generating a compulsion to visibility among users because the site gives them new ways to display and manipulate images and text—and thus relationships—online. All this was true for Kankanaey users, but Kankanaey Facebook became an important public archive of cutting and conjugating networks, mapping affective connects, and disconnects.

My respondents' use of Facebook created new ways for them to feel themselves as big and expansive, or as small and excluded, in relation to others. Facebook made visible the negotiations of intimacy and exchange shadowed by abandonment, withdrawal, and insecurity. It revealed gaps opening up around individuals in their affective connections. Confronted with a gap—and knowing others could see it on Facebook—impelled some migrants to cut themselves off from networks in which they had previously experienced closeness or care. My respondents' feelings about themselves on Facebook resulted from affective flows carried by images that gave them a sense of immediacy and connection. Their feelings were largely about image politics.

Images on Facebook enable users to review and communicate past experiences with others, create shared and playful narratives, express affection, and create their own art. These positive aspects of image sharing attracted users and maintained their interest. However, sharing images also lead to confusion, distress, humiliation, and alienation. A single digital image can act in a wide variety of these modes simultaneously. Research has identified six ways in which digital images work within broader online communications. Some images amplify—in the same way as emoticons, cartoon characters, and so on—accompanying text.[5] Images can narrate—telling a story in themselves. People also use images to express or heighten awareness of feelings. Some images bind a local subculture by acting as a kind of shorthand inaccessible to outsiders. Images can invite others to interact, initiating a kind of image-exchange conversation. Lastly, images work as objects or instruments when people send others pictures of objects they owned or of objects having, for them, a symbolic importance. All of these modes—and more—occurred in my respondents' image exchanges.[6] I found certain genres of image and practices of engaging images, carried specific affective charges. People's feelings about themselves through Facebook arose through the timing of comments and genres of images people posted. Prompt responses to posted comments and prompt postings of visual documentation of current activities sustained and renewed feelings of trust and intimacy across distance. People noted who shared, who commented first, who liked instead of commented, and who commented late or not at all, all of which were seen as indications of care, comfort, or discomfort. Likewise, the genre of images shared, "liked," or commented on was another vital part of Facebook's channeling of affect.

Pictures of daily domestic life featured most prominently in migrants' posts to Facebook from East London. Popular posts incorporated photos of activities in employers' homes, at church, in the community center, in their rented flats, at basketball games, and on the street. Almost all of these images showed migrants in the company of kin, friends, or wards. Though some of the images were doubtlessly intended to tell stories about cosmopolitan spaces and sophistication, such as showing off new clothes (particularly things such as winter boots and coats, not seen at home), the bulk of the postings were similar to the items sent home by migrants: relentlessly intimate and domestic, speaking of sustaining the texture of everyday interpersonal interactions. Photos on Facebook made these domestic settings global by incorporating non-Filipino viewers and networks beyond East London into users' intimate daily lives and social worlds. Facebook sustained global friendships. To make this very point, Labanet reposted a popular meme about friends: "Good friends care for each other, close friends understand each other, but true friends stay forever, beyond words, beyond distance, beyond time."

Comments on Facebook posts captured the challenges of living lives across distance. For instance, Labanet's comments on Sylvia's birthday wish for her daughters addressed the guilt of absent parents. Sylvia posted a studio photograph of her two daughters to her Facebook timeline to mark her daughters' birthdays. Sylvia was working in a care home in the UK Midlands, supporting her husband and their two girls in Baguio City. The post read, "It's just a few hours to count 19 years ago today when I held you in my arms for the first time [name] . . . now you've grown, I hope you will do better in your studies, that's my only wish today. . . . and my darling princess [name], you're turning 12 and really I miss you being the young girl I left 7 years ago . . . oh how time flies I wish I could hold it back . . . to both of you HAPPY HAPPY BIRTHDAY! Mama loves and misses you dearly." Labanet, Sylvia's cousin, "liked" this photo and, in the comments thread, posted her own greeting to her young cousins: "Happy birthday guys. Am sure ur mama will gonna send budget for that." Here, as a "friend," Labanet addressed anticipated criticism of Sylvia's absence by highlighting the economic value of the mother's work in the United Kingdom.

In another Facebook exchange, Labanet acknowledged that the challenges of being separated from family shaped her own sojourn in the United Kingdom.

> Adamey S.: . . . goin' home at last . . . missin' my little [name] so much!!! aye sa!!! ajak upay kaya man abroad..hehe. [Oh my!! I just realized I can't manage to stay abroad ha ha]
>
> Domia N.: Nu awanen choice ket makaya . . . medjo makatok ta lng bassit ngem ti impt ket agsubli metlng sanity..hehe..rigat talaga . . . [You can if there will be no choice. You can go a bit crazy but what is important is you can save your sanity. It's hard though]
>
> Basig: Truliii dyta mng. Adamey. hihi [That's very true older sister Adamey, hah hah]
>
> Oedma G.: Tetewa ay naligat ngem kasapulan met hehe...[That's true it's hard, but we also need to, hah hah]
>
> Labanet: You check Adamey no na gain sanity na hehe [check on Adamey if she gained her sanity again]

Oedma G.: Labanet na gain mo sanitym hehe . . . [Labanet, did you gain your sanity, hah hah?]

Labanet: Hehe it's ur fault Ademay ta ur presenting sanity sunga ta check tko. Oedma my fren, nostalgic sometimes that proves I'm normal and I'm still sane [Hee, hee, it's your fault Adamey that you're discussing sanity so we're checking on you. Oedma, my friend, being—nostalgic sometimes—that proves I'm normal and I'm still sane]

In this joking conversation, Labanet explained that the nostalgia she felt for her time with her children when they were small was evidence of her sanity. These two exchanges show that Labanet considered herself to be good mother and knew, too, what good long-distance mothering looked like, on Facebook.[7] She used Facebook to support and, if necessary, defend her "friends."

## Posting Photos Shapes Selves

Facebook is a site of revelations. Sometimes the intimate knowledge "friends" revealed to each other in person allowed them to interpret Facebook posts in particular ways. Labanet's responses to images posted by her "friends" indicated the depth of connection between them. For example, after Typhoon Yolanda struck the Philippines in 2013, Domia S. posted a photograph of herself standing in a coat and hat, on a high street, collecting donations for the British Red Cross.

Braving the freezing cold, I've done my bit to help my countrymen who was devastated by typhoon Haiyan with the help of BRITISH RED CROSS . . . It feels GOOD to know that there are SAMARITANS willing to give for those in need. It seemed at first that nobody would give then a coin was dropped . . . followed by more coins and occasionally some bills! And top tip if you do some charity work . . . look them in the eye and give them your sweetest smile . . . they won't resist to drop that much needed money even if its a penny . . . it all counts! And don't forget to say THANK YOU!—feeling overwhelmed.

Labanet congratulated Domia on her fund-raising by liking the post and adding a comment: "Thank YOU!" She later told me that she envied Domia—who had recently been granted Indefinite Leave to Remain—the ability to publicly perform her commitment to the Philippines in the streets of the United Kingdom by doing things Labanet felt she couldn't do without papers: "Now, I would be scared that they might ask to see my papers. But she is fearless . . . Yes, I guess she is not going to be found out doing that, though! She is celebrating her papers—she's acting like she's British already."

Labanet was able to find other ways to establish her civic virtue on Facebook. She raised funds for former classmates in the Philippines who were ill and required expensive hospital treatment, including a former classmate who required dialysis. In 2012, she posted a "certification" from this classmate—a JPEG of a typed, signed letter—acknowledging receipt of PHP 23,000 ($494 or £322), enough to cover more than two weeks of dialysis at PHP 10,000 per week. Her activities garnered "likes" and praise from across her networks, from family and friends in both the Philippines and in the United Kingdom.

Labanet also posted images showing her as a good citizen of the United Kingdom. Some were photos of church events—visiting a mosque and joining in a pilgrimage to a historic site. Others showed her taking English children around the iconic sites of London. For a while, her profile photograph was one of her in Trafalgar Square, with the two children for whom she was nannying tucked between the paws of one of the large bronze lions under Nelson's Column. By appending the sites and attitudes in these images to herself, she was practicing prosthetic citizenship. Posting these photos implied she was good enough—and certainly no different from—Filipinos who were formally UK citizens and suggested she was—or would soon be—a formal citizen herself.

> For me, it's as if I should be a permanent here already. This is what our lawyer will argue to the UKBA, so I'm the one to show it on Facebook. I contribute here and back in the Philippines. Here, I care for those English elderly at church. I cook sometimes for our events and send some home with them. I give them tea after church. I do some visiting and help them find a worker to shovel the snow or fix their broken taps. And I work hard for my employers, too. Besides . . . I participate to the activities that integrate us as immigrants to UK society—the interfaith visits, the outreach to migrants, the programs for the church. I'm supporting the collection of money also when there's a death in our community, sending the body back. And when someone has crisis and must go home. And I take care of my family back home, too, also doing my charity work. I do all the things that make me a good person here. They don't have to ask; they can see it, from my Facebook, too.

Just as virtue in the United Kingdom was attached to the individual by the image, so, too, were cultural ties to the Philippines. Thus, while Labanet's Facebook profile was indexed by the photograph of her in Trafalgar Square, "friends" of hers were indexed by black-and-white photos of their shared ancestors.

Profile images are intended to be faces on Facebook. When they are not the face Facebook anticipates but something—or someone—else, it breaks the implicit rules of the site. Yet some of my respondents were—online—their ancestors. For them Facebook was not a site of a networked individualism so much as a venue in which to express and recompose forms of Filipino extended personhood persisting from the precolonial era.[8] Appropriating ancestors' images was all about the affective power of displaying faces to others. This affective relay was strong, with respondents convinced they could "read" facial expressions carrying affective charges across time. Adopting the familiar faces of ancestors as profile photographs indexed feelings of closeness to indigenous culture, history, and particular family genealogies. Facebook enabled the ancestors to watch over people now living far from their village of origin. Indexing their profiles this way showed how people used Kankanaey Facebook to express and transform culture. Migrants would respond to a crisis at home or a disconnect in one of their close personal relationships by changing their profile picture to an ancestral one. This change not only asserted identity, it also expressed judgment by bringing to bear *inayan*. Because *inayan* works by honoring the ancestors and their traditions with the correct rituals and conduct, no matter where one is in the world, seeing their images suddenly suggested that a transgression had occurred. Ancestor's photos reminded a Kankanaey Facebook public that ritual and reciprocity still mattered and debts still had to be paid.

Facebook also worked against these ties, creating a record of cutting networks. Facebook could exclude individuals from these same exchange relations, kin, or community groups while also documenting new affiliations with churches or host nationals instead. We can see this in material made visible on Facebook via tagging and comments, focusing on the social meanings of tagging practices. Image posting and tagging gave clear messages about care and belonging—messages with affective impacts.

## Vacant Tags

There were two distinctive tagging practices used by my respondents on Facebook. They tagged to name people in images and to share images across Facebook "friend" relationships. Both practices involved adding the names of people who were not represented in the photograph itself to the image or the text comments. My respondents described the affective impact of positive immediacy carried by tagging Facebook images as "closeness." For them, being tagged and tagging renews or extended feeling "close" to others. The digital exchanges of tagging enabled people to build a common pool of shared global experiences by feeling Facebook "closeness." In these tagging practices, their hometowns in the Philippines were socially and spiritually central.

Tags attached to images that didn't show the tag-ee were "vacant tags." If you went to the image to find the person tagged, his or her face was not there. There were two ways in which this kind of tagging worked: (1) to reveal the global span of networks of care and (2) to make visible a local absence, often as a kind of implicit critique or haunting. It was often not quite clear in which mode the tag had been made or what the tagger intended to convey by tagging. Instead, the tag-ee and her "friends" who viewed the photo and "liked" or commented on it attached their own meanings to the tag. Kankanaey Facebook images were also about absence and ghosts, capable of producing haunting effects as well as closeness.

Tagging thus instantiated a new ethics of revealing, commenting, making present, and highlighting absence that sustained a particular kind of belonging.

Empty face boxes were the first kind of vacant tag. These were text boxes appearing on the Facebook image marking another person on Facebook in a particular location in the image. People used this tagging strategy to absent migrants by tagging their names on to photographs they should see and, by implication, should have been in. Taggers put the migrants' name where their face ought to have been—had they had been there in person. Tagging a photo this way showed people on "friends" list and "friends of friends" list (depending on privacy settings) that a tag-ee had missed a key family or ritual event. This kind of vacant tag not only showed the image to the absent migrant but carried a charge that recipients felt as anger. For example, when Geya M.'s brother married in a registry ceremony in Katangoan, Geya was tagged into the wedding photos slightly to the left of her brother's head. But she hadn't been there. Instead, she had overstayed her tourist visa in London and was struggling financially. She had been unable to send all the money her family had requested. Buying a ticket home would have seen her unable to reenter the United Kingdom, leaving her effectively stranded in the Philippines with no savings to draw on and no means of supporting herself. She interpreted her tagging, instead of sharing the photograph to her own profile, as accusing her of failing her family.

> It was hard to see that. Seeing my name. And I know all the others looking at that picture, they would also see my name there. But no face. I am absent. And I didn't send what I should have. I couldn't be there. I didn't make my contribution. And everyone can see I'm not there, can see that it is just a simple wedding, even though . . . Here I am, the daughter working abroad (laughs) . . . You know, they could just share me the photo. They do know how to do that! But just not that time. Then, they need to let everyone see my absence. And what everyone knows is that I am earning . . . that I am ok here in London, you know. Like other people here, that I could just go home for a visit—if I wanted. They don't know about . . . that I have no papers. So, to them, as if I don't want.

The vacant tag brought Geya's anxieties about family expectations to the fore. Perhaps her relative posting the photo had only intended to be sure everyone in the family saw it, but Geya felt the tag suggested something more. For Geya, tagging triggered shame.

Tagged absences arguably set up the imagination—in the tag-ee—of a kind of corporate and public nagging. Those on the receiving end of tagging in such photographs understood these images as indexing their own and others' feelings of loss, abandonment, distance, and disappointment in relationships. The tag-ee knew that they had been asked to respond, to give something, to assuage hurt feelings. Vacant tags absented from images people who had absented themselves and had not yet repaid the foundational debts their absence incurred. This happened because images on Facebook were secondary events. These images continued to reverberate in and around places, long after the primary events they documented had ended. Thus tagging practices haunted. Because Facebook enabled additional people to comment on the image over time, tagging could carry persistent negative affect, producing ongoing feelings of exposure and abjection.

The second kind of vacant tag mapped global networks. In this tagging practice, "friends" were tagged into the text of the post, not in the image itself. This practice both drew their attention to it (via Facebook notifications) and set out the global network of care surrounding the person or event for other viewers. Respondents found this practice was less affectively charged than the empty face box, largely because nobody lost face. Instead, tagging this way claimed global influence and flows of care. For example, when Labanet (in London) posted a photograph from her daughter's birthday celebration (in Baguio City), "likes" showing care came from both Labanet's and Biag's villages of origin, but also from kin and friends in the United Kingdom, Germany, Spain, Canada, and the United States. Some of these people Labanet had tagged into her comments on the photo, even if they were not themselves in it, interpreted the tag as an invitation to view the image and comment on it. Labanet followed up by commenting on the global greetings, thanking people for their phone calls and gifts and remembrances. To one response she added a Skype-shot of her daughter wearing a gift sent by her aunt. This more expansive tagging practice was deployed to draw—agreement in number others' attention to the scope of the poster's broader "friends" network.

These vacant tags mapping global networks typically featured in reinvented Kankanaey rituals. Such rituals were life-course events marked by celebrations that would have happened regardless. Facebook enabled them to be intensified and transformed. When birthday gifts began to be presented globally and publicly on Facebook, they became more important to send and acknowledge. Even older members of Biag's family who lacked their own Facebook accounts started to celebrate global birthdays. One of their children in the Philippines would post a portrait and the extended family and friends' networks would send greetings and make comments. The comments and memes or images received in reply would be shared with the birthday celebrant on a laptop or read aloud. Facebook thus gave some previously more family-focused and private rituals new life.

Vehicle blessings—once small and fairly informal events during which the priest was invited to say a short prayer over a new vehicle—exemplified this change. Now these blessings involve large gatherings of families and neighbors on Gameng's main street, are followed by a special meal, and are posted in their own Facebook album. On Facebook, family and friends overseas are tagged in the text of the post and invited to comment. Every spring, as the dry season rolls around and cars and trucks are acquired, the global network contributing to the purchase is invited to witness the success of the family who purchased the vehicle. This ritual is recorded, shared, "liked," and commented on through Facebook tags.

## Digital Haunting

Pictures of graves made the dead present on Facebook. These photographs were taken on death anniversaries and at All Souls' Day rituals. Abandoning the graves of the dead is *inayan*, but the ritual responsibility of maintaining gravesites falls to those who remain at home. Kankanaey people believe that, without propitiating the past properly—at home, in the *ili*, on the gravesite—the ghost of the dead can bother the living. While ritual propitiation of the dead is local, the scope of potential haunting is global. So Facebook posts documented graveside rituals to show these had been conducted properly. Sometimes people posted rephotographed pictures of the deceased. People used tags and comments on these images to bring to bear the supposed will of the dead on the actions of the faraway living. Such posts indexed anxieties about current relationships. They acted on the absent viewer by bringing him or her back to thoughts of the dead person and to their relationship with them and also to the broader context in which this person had been mourned and buried.

The effect of haunting came from the response of the person encountering the image of the dead person on Facebook. The tagged photographs did not, in themselves, function as ghosts, but seeing these images could precipitate experiences of paranormal activity for migrants. Labanet confided:

> Usually, someone would see a photo on Facebook . . . Like that, the grave or one of the dead, on their death anniversary. Then something would happen to them. For Domia, she told it was a bump. She felt going down the stairs, as if she had been passed by someone. Sometimes a cold feeling and you shake. Or something falls and becomes broken—just for no reason. So that's the dead. And you must go to your relatives in Katangoan and they will make the ritual. They do it there, near the grave. You can't do it here, in the UK. It won't work. Only then will you be relieved—no more ghost.

Labanet's friends recognized, in these bumps and chills, their affective ties to home.[9] Affect flowing through the circulation of photographs made these ties manifest, supernaturally, in London. Thus Facebook mediated haunting. Posting such photos motivated migrants to contact their nearest relatives, discover something was amiss, and organize a ritual propitiating the ghost. These rituals redistributed hospitality and food through the extended kin network, renewing migrants' ties to their sending villages. Facebook hosted ghostly activities that drew people back into the past to heal old conflicts, reexamine what had been done to see if it was lacking, and renew promises of mutual aid or assistance.

This posting practice could work as a kind of "emotional blackmail," as in the following example, in which Yakabow A. responded to the death of her niece in London: "Did you see on my Facebook? They said the worst thing. Just there, under the photograph of her coffin, you can see it. They wrote: 'if anything happens, it will be your fault'! Can you imagine that? It's emotional blackmail. Something is always going to happen, somewhere. But it only won't be our fault if we spend the money to send her body home and they are the ones to bury her there. Not her family here. They can't accept, at home, that [her family] are staying here, permanently, that this is their home now." Yakabow's niece had died and was buried in the United Kingdom and her immediate family did not travel home with the body for a ritual burial. Instead, an accommodation was reached to prevent ghostly interference with the living. Rituals at home were held without the body present and were modified to prevent haunting. But relatives reported to Yakabow that they had anxious dreams about what this accommodation meant and whether it would succeed, thinking they would have to return to local ritual specialists if (unspecified) problems should arise in the future.

Oedma reported a similar example had appeared in comments on an All Souls' Day photograph of the grave of her young cousin. Oedma's aunt took the photograph to show that his grave had been ritually "warmed" with a pine-pitch fire and to remember him to his kin beyond Gameng. Somehow, through lapses in privacy settings, the comments alongside the image included speculation by non-relatives on whether his death had been accidental or self-inflicted. Finally, *inayan* was invoked: "Peace. No bad words . . ." Oedma did not ask her aunt to delete these comments; she found them useful: "Well . . . they really said that gossip and they can't deny. . . . That's recorded now. So if anything bad happens, it's right there on Facebook. We know who it was." In other words, if the comments had disturbed the ghost, the person who posted them would be responsible for any ill effects.

Facebook images reminded people they were bearers of Kankanaey culture. As such, they were still obliged to care for the dead, and the shadow side of *inayan*—ghostly retribution—would be enacted if they failed. Through *inayan*, the digital ghosts of ancestors and expectations of family underpinned migrants' daily routine of providing comfort, recognition, tenderness, support, and engagement for employers and wards. Not surprisingly, migrants' images of employers and wards, too, turn up on Facebook feeds.

## Making Care Global

Photographs of employers and places of work form the final genre of images posted by my respondents. These photographs never had vacant tags attached. Instead, all the text appeared in the comments as "friends" saw the images. Moreover, unlike other image genres, employer's images were not shared from profile to profile, but stayed with the poster. Comments on employer photos were largely directed to congratulating, consoling, or otherwise recognizing and supporting the "friend" posting the photo.

Kod-as A., for instance, posted a series of pictures of her employers' cats. Care for the cats formed much of her job while she was waiting for a decision on her application to remain in the United Kingdom as a spouse after overstaying a tourist visa. She received many comments complementing her on the way the cats' appearance was evidence of her care for them and the lovely West London flat in which the cats lived. She was working without papers, so images of her adult human employers did not feature.

Daguon and Basig, both nannies, posted regular photos of their wards, outdoing even Labanet. Both with grown children of their own and waiting to become grandmothers, they were in the life stage when their evident affection for the toddlers in their charge was no threat to their equally prominent commitment to their families at home. Their cute charges' images gathered lots of comments, typically along the lines of "KUUUIT!" [cute], expressing how lucky they were to have such cuddly work.

Nathan, before he went back to the Philippines, posted images of himself sitting at his employer's desk in a penthouse office in East London. Wearing a suit and tie, he joked about his executive cleaning role: "In another life, this could have been me." The joke garnered over thirty "likes" and comments suggesting images his "friends" could post in response, illustrating how they might look in their employers' roles. Not many of his "friends" posted these imagined images, of course. They were likely afraid of being discovered and potentially humiliated or of losing their jobs.

When Adamey R. was struggling with her caregiver role, she posted a series of photographs of her employer's wife, for whom she cared. Her ward had problems with alcohol and what Adamey suspected was early-onset dementia. At breaking point one evening, Adamey posted a picture of this woman, holding a glass and apparently tipsy, with an account of being offered money to take her out of the house to a pub for another drink. Adamey had been verbally abused when she refused. Within an hour, Adamey had over thirty-five consoling responses, the last advising her to take the image down from her profile, now that she had assuaged her feelings. Adamey followed this advice. She acknowledged to me, later, that her post had been ill-considered. Her job would likely have been endangered if her employer had found out she had vented her frustration under his wife's photo on Facebook.

Other postings were much more considerate and dignified. Oedma P., who had been without steady work for six months after the death of the older woman she had cared for, posted news of a new job. After nine years of overstaying in London, and with three of her four children in university, she had been desperate for work. She found a role as caregiver for an older man. With her phone, she photographed him sitting, bent over his desk, from behind. The text accompanying the image read, "a [nationality of origin] writer, tall and sturdy . . . Just last week, his doctor's said he's got less than 6mos to live, cos of Leukemia. And he does not even know about it . . ." Within four days her post had ninety-two likes and twenty-five comments. The comments that garnered the most "likes" were ones predicting that Oedma's care would help him live longer. For example, "Your TLC can prolong his life. Can even cure him. Our prayers." Many comments offered advice about diet and asked about his treatment, offering advice based on their knowledge of cancer patients either in their own family or for whom they had been caregivers. Comments came from people in the United Kingdom, Canada, the United States, Germany, Norway, and Spain, as well as the Philippines. Some of the final comments referred back to the principles of *inayan* as they applied to Oedma's work: "*wen ading*, [yes, younger sister] do the best service you can." The last poster reiterated that the employer was lucky to have Oedma on hand: "*Swerte na dyta lakay anti ta ada ka dta mang pamper kenyana* [That man is very lucky to have you there to pamper him.] Tender love and care is very important in times like this." Oedma responded by thanking those who had commented: "Thanks everyone for the advice and sympathy. I am happy that you show your care."

Facebook was also a key tool in linking migrants to potential employers. Labanet used her iPhone and Facebook to connect would-be workers to job opportunities in the wealthy neighborhoods of West London.

One Sunday, after church and not long before Christmas, Labanet and I left her Essex Street house to get food for lunch. We were the only ones with valid travel cards, so we took the bus to the supermarket to buy roast chicken. In the mall, Labanet's phone rang. Whoever it was wouldn't go to voicemail—they just kept calling back. Labanet checked the number. It was the husband of one of the two couples who employed her. She called him back. Did she have a recommendation for a babysitter, immediately? They were supposed to be attending a school social event the following evening and their neighbors' babysitter had cancelled. They needed someone who could come to the house in West London at 4:00 p.m. Labanet rang off. Standing to the side of the crowds of shoppers streaming from the mall to the exit for the Tube, she posted a query on Facebook. She began to text and check Facebook status updates. Between her seven-minute investment in this task and our purchase of chicken, biscuits, and ice cream for Sunday tea, she had several responses. She settled on one of her cousins, a student, who would cut classes at her college on Monday due to "illness." Working between Facebook profiles and e-mail on her phone, she sent a photograph and short biography of her cousin to her employer to pass on to his neighbors and also forwarded the neighbors' photo address and number to her cousin, all before we left the mall. She explained, "This happens all the time. I should maybe charge a fee!"

Labanet's Facebook networking ability also came into play when one of her former employers moved from the United States to Dubai. She'd stayed in touch with the family via e-mail after they'd left London. Now they were looking for a domestic helper. Again turning to Facebook, Labanet posted a general enquiry, in Kankanaey on her own profile, illustrated with an old photo of her with the employer's children. She explained they were looking for someone already in Dubai and with papers because visa sponsorship was not possible. She garnered several expressions of interest from her networks in the Philippines, but the only person in Dubai who was interested was her sister. Labanet considered her sister unreliable, even though she was close kin. So she told her sister that she would find no improvement on her current salary. She looked through her sister's "friends" list to find more contacts in Dubai who might be interested. Eventually a cousin of one of her sister's former classmates e-mailed her. Labanet was able to broker an interview for her with her former employer. "Even if they leave the UK, and I can't, you never know when they're going to contact you. You don't know where they'll go. And it's always good to help out. They're good employers. I know. Lenient. The kids are nice, polite. So my helping out will help my family. The woman in Dubai already, her family will be happy with us that I could give the recommendation."

Migrants' Facebook employer and ward images were limited and partial in what they revealed. My respondents kept many aspects of their work lives beyond the purview of Facebook friends. Some of these networks and events were, like Adamey R.'s photograph of her drunken, abusive charge, only made visible and shared for a fleeting moment. Other aspects of work were kept away from the platform because they contravened the norms for good persons or citizens performed there.

## What's Not There?

Much happening in migrants' social networks was not made visible on Facebook. Instances of withdrawal and absence in images and off-profile chat on private messaging represented choices to conceal particular affects, topics, and interactions from public view. Facebook marked and made visible social withdrawal and cuts in the network. People who didn't respond, didn't log in, didn't comment, and could not give became notable through their inaction and lack of visibility. Meanwhile, the visual politics of digital image display and tagging expanded the impact and affective import of gaps opening up between migrants and with those back home. Some people, confronted with this gap on Facebook, became and remained T&T, because of the difficulty in repairing a rupture made painfully public on line.

In Fely S.'s case, she had signed up to a Facebook group for graduates of her village elementary school. This group had been set up by a classmate still resident in her Philippine sending village. The group attracted members from around the world. After marking a death anniversary and making a few posts on local community activities, the founder tried to involve the group in fund-raising for local causes. Fely S. had been T&T in London for several years and had recently been caught by the UKBA in a raid, so she had financial problems. She posted to explain that she could not contribute at the moment. The founder publicly queried her post. Fely S. felt shamed for not donating and being forced to explain her situation to the group, posting, "It's difficult for me now. I'm having some problems fixing my papers here in the UK." She did not receive the kind responses she had anticipated from the group. She received no response at all from the founder and only lukewarm acknowledgements that perhaps things would change from two other members of the group. So she had left the group. She attempted to find routes to remain in the United Kingdom, because of her difficulty in returning home: "As if I cannot go back there. That everyone will know I am not the successful person I left to become here. It's just better I find a way to stay now. Because they expected more from me . . . And I can't be the one to give it." In Fely S.'s online interaction, she had no private communication with her old classmate around the posts. Publicness was part of the problem. The entire interaction had been visible to the group and to the "friends" following Fely S.'s posts. She felt hurt and exposed because her classmate had chosen a public forum instead of sending a private message. This kind of exchange was why my respondents felt reluctant to post more personal things and restricted them to Facebook's chat and e-mail.

For Labanet, one of these hidden topics was her "closeness" to and pride in the achievements of her wards in the United Kingdom. Posting this publicly would have overshadowed her posts on her own children's accomplishments in the Philippines. Thus her pride in her work remained off her timeline, in private messaging to a limited number of friends. In one example she shared her feeling of exhilaration over her success in tutoring:

Labanet, 10:04 a.m.—Subject: What a feeling!
Feeling very, very nervous waiting for the result of the "School Annual Public Speaking" [competition] with [name] who is an actress, author and judge for said event. Per class, two were selected. My two kids (Year 1 and Year 2) were qualified for the finals. Everybody was brilliant with their own piece. I think I'm more nervous than their parents, especially as I did most of the job. Wheeeewwww

Labanet, 10:41 a.m.—Subject: What a feeling!
Yes! The younger one is the winner for the Junior section, which is composed of Year 1 and 2. She is still in Year 1. Unfortunately, the other one who is in Year 3 who competed with Year 4 is not very lucky. He was very good and to be qualified for the Finals is already amazing! Per section, there are 8 entries . . .

Deirdre. 16:03 p.m. Subject: Re: What a feeling!
WHEEEE!! You are an amazing teacher and clearly helped them get there! Says something for [Kankanaey] standards of English grammar and enunciation, does not it? A finalist in the upper group is super, but a Year 1 topping the group with Year 2s is amazing!! They must both be thrilled. And their parents, too! (I hope you get a bonus?!) Congratulations! Let's try to meet up soon!

Labanet, 18:33 p.m.—Subject: Re: Re: What a feeling!
The bonus is that I'm over the moon and my employers are more than proud and delighted to have me as their nanny.
See you soon and have a lovely weekend.
Lots of love,
Labanetxx

The affective charge of Labanet's messages was unmistakable. She was looking for someone to recognize and share in her elation and success. But she could not post this to Facebook. Facebook thus did not offer a full picture of Labanet's social and emotional life, it refracted only particular examples. But Facebook had nonetheless become a vital node within global networks where affective charges circulate to particular ends.

Part of the affective work on Facebook is in imagining a Facebook self, standing back, and viewing one's presentation through the imagined eyes of others. But Facebook was also a much more practical technology for channeling affect for my respondents. Through Facebook, care, in the sense of information, support, recognition, and advice sustaining caring work, wasn't coming necessarily from migrants' families at home. Instead care came from friends, fellow migrants, extended kin, church congregants, and former neighbors in the form of affirming words, job offers, recommendations, and practical tips. Facebook enabled migrants to tie *inayan* to particular employers and kinds of caregiving through this global recognition, sharing, and long-distance bonding.

Facebook also shows us that, while people might describe these networks as open and expansive, they are not. Care stops, fails, and is turned away, too. Affective flows were negative and connections ruptured or refused on Facebook, with the cuts made visible in images. Facebook revealed digital exclusions (the cropping of photographs and not-tagging of their subjects) and lacunae (who is not present and which conversations are not made public) to be a powerful tool for shaping relationships and selves, as well as a public disciplinary strategy, amenable to surveillance.

## Notes

1. Madianou and Miller, 2013, p. 170.
2. Miller and Slater, 2001.

3. Miller, 2011.
4. Madianou and Miller, 2013; Miller, 2016; Costa et al., 2016.
5. Voida and Mynatt, 2005.
6. McKay, 2010.
7. See Madianou and Miller, 2012.
8. McKay, 2010 and 2012.
9. See Gordon 1997, p. 8.

# 4   In the Community Center

"THE MORE WE get together, together, together, the more we get together, the happier we'll be. Cause your friends are my friends, and my friends are your friends. The more we get together, the happier we'll be." The emcee on the community center stage was leading us in this traditional British folk song. She had the audience singing it as a round in two parts while we waited for the seats to fill. The space was already packed and hot. We were sitting near the front, Labanet and I, and we were both perspiring. The voices behind us felt joyful, but Labanet's normally smooth alto sounded forced. I tried to focus on the swell of shared feeling, the harmonious blend of voices, but Labanet's mood was heavy. She didn't want to join the performers, or even be there at all. The song was becoming wearing . . . "Your friends are my friends." Well, clearly they weren't all already, or at least not close friends! If they had been, going to such events wouldn't be of much value for Labanet.

Earlier, on the bus, Labanet had explained why she felt compelled to attend. She'd recently lost her Tuesday, part-time cleaning job when her employers moved back to Sweden. She needed another part-time post to make up her £1,400 ($2,274) monthly remittance to the Philippines. To find work, she needed to activate networks, both with employers and with the broadest reach of *kailians* (fellow villagers) and fellow Filipinos in London: "Yes, sure . . . I can just text my sister-in-law, or my cousins, but . . . Really, they are not always the ones who will know about part-time work. I need a wide coverage of people who will recommend me. You never know who can help! My family? I love to help them. It's my obligation. But if they were going to make me rich . . . I'd be rich already." She felt pressured by the shortfall in her budget, but had other reasons for her anxious, irritable energy. At the tenth chorus, Labanet turned to me. "I see her," she said. "Sabet—I need to collect from her . . . she will not be seeing me, isn't it?!" This missed connection had a convoluted story of debt behind it.

Labanet had loaned £300 ($462) to her sister-in-law, Basig. But Basig had only been able to repay £50 ($77). For the remaining £250 ($385), plus interest, Labanet would have to ask Sabet. Sabet had borrowed the money from Basig, her housemate, three months previously. Sabet had subsequently moved out without repaying. Basig didn't exert the kind of interpersonal suasion to make repayment Sabet's first priority. Labanet, with her extensive networks, did. Labanet needed this money to pay her kids' school fees, due the next week. Sabet wasn't someone

Labanet knew well, thus she felt caught between two conflicting imperatives. She needed to build smooth interpersonal relations, to make people feel good about themselves, so she could secure recommendations for work. She also needed to retrieve the loan.

The sound of the voices, the movements of the dancers, the melodies of the gongs, the smell of the food, the colors of the indigenous dress—none of it distracted Labanet from her purpose. "She'll say, 'Labanet, let's just enjoy and talk later,'" explained Labanet. "I'll have to be hardheaded." And she was. She got the money two days later, but Sabet disappeared from her Facebook "friends" list. Labanet, jaded, sighed, "At socials like that, she just wants to enjoy. That's what you do! But there's no other time to see her. And our purpose here in the UK is not our cultural performances, our bonding. Our purpose: it's our work. We're working to help those at home. If you will forget that, your first purpose, any reputation you have here will be . . . empty. But it is hard to find work without also doing the bonding you need with the rest!" I offered, "Well, you got your money from Basig, even if it was work. No *pa-utang* [an extra amount returned to indicate the exchange should continue] or *anak* [interest] then [from Sabet]?"

Labanet replied, "*Manang* [older sister] Basig is too softhearted to really lend out money. It was just on five to six [a loan with monthly interest], not a gift she should return, so no, no *pa-utang*, small *anak*. She [Sabet] was dismayed that I asked at a social, but what can I do? She was avoiding Basig. Sure, she may not be close to me, but if she does not like to pay, she's not really our friend."

Like church, community center events offered migrants experiences of a connected, entitled, cared-about form of personhood and a chance to make friends and meet UK nationals. Migrants could gain recognition for their performing skills, speaking, dancing, singing or volunteering here. Yet there was also a shadow side to this space, as Labanet suggested. The feeling of belonging, the bonding, the sharing, came at a price. By refusing the norm of positive affective exchange in the space, Labanet got her money but cut her networks. The flow of affect around the community center also carried feelings of watching, evaluating, exchanging, and betraying.

This chapter explores experiences of citizenship and surveillance in the community center space. The community center is another node where networks were cut and conjugated. Its activities and relationships folded into, and out of, church and Facebook, houses in London and homes back in the Philippines. However, community center dynamics combined surveillance and citizenship in a way unique to London's shatter zone. A variety of third-sector groups—charities, advocacy, and activist organizations—came here to meet Filipino migrants. These groups offered services and sought migrants' support, often in lobbying to change migration policy. The NGO activities subjected migrants to new forms of surveillance, enabling people to assess others' migration status by watching their engagement with the programs on offer. Some aspects of this surveillance had a harsh edge, with care from within the community negotiated around refusals to disclose migration status. Migrants strategized to gain what they needed without making themselves vulnerable to exploitation—or even deportation—through relationships brokered here.

## A Space for Bonding

The community center hosted face-to-face encounters where migrants exchanged food and cultural performances of song, dance, and music, as well as cash, and sometimes even clothing and household goods. Here, they held wakes for the dead and took up collections to send to bereaved families in the Philippines and organized special thanksgiving celebrations to mark festivals back home. Virtually all visitors to the community center shared in the swell of positive feeling, brought about by the laughter and music-filled celebratory atmosphere as networks drew together and fell apart, only to reconfigure again. Yet of all things exchanged in the community center, information was the most vital. Migrants learned who had work, who had a new friendship, who had fallen out, and how to interpret indirect comments on Facebook posts while they swapped phone numbers, Facebook "friend" invites, and Skype addresses.

The norm for community center events included expressions of unity and a focus on the here and now. Migrants were expected to put aside worries about UK work and migration status and the situation of family back home to celebrate community. Despite this norm, the community center was a site of intense interpersonal and intracommunal politics. Some people were distressed because the singing and dancing had a competitive edge; it wasn't only for pleasure. Groups of performers practiced for hours for line dancing competitions, or to offer new and distinctive songs and dances from their village of origin. Public recognition was their reward. Responses to video grabs and photographs from these events, attested to by the tags and comments posted to Facebook, raised their global profiles. Competition in dress, performance, and appearance engaged both women and men. Some resented the fact just being in the audience meant negotiating demands to invest in or renew social ties. Labanet grumbled:

> As if you cannot absent yourself. If they don't see you, they will complain. Me, I've got my babysitting on Saturdays and—the bonding or socials—it's usually Saturday nights. Or Sunday, after church. And that's my off day and I want to Skype the kids. I'm tired then. I need to do my laundry, my groceries. Last time I went to [NGO community center], they stole my phone. I don't mean they stole it, just that they kept it, so I wouldn't leave earlier. Not early, but just ten o'clock. I don't want to stay with those women, being awake late and drinking. Bonding, yes, but not so I wreck my chance of earning! I have work on Monday morning! That's really my purpose here in London, earning!!

They always call me to join the dancing, to come to practice two, three times a week, evenings at someone's house. Well . . . it's not for me. It's not my interest. I'm working. That's my purpose here in London, isn't it?! If I'd wanted to do cultural performances, I could have stayed back home! Maybe not quite every weekend, but at least one weekend a month!! And then special occasions . . . on top. So two, three events a month.

That's really a lot of money . . . Especially, say, for a student. Probably £30–£40 ($46–$61), even £50 ($77) pounds per [event]. You have your transport—and it's often quite far, so not just your regular Zone 1–3 travel card will cover it. There's the £5 ($8) or £10 ($15) you pay at the door. Yes, it's for charity and it covers the cost of the hall, but it costs you. That charity, it's not for you or your family, just your earnings from work supports them. Then you have the food you must prepare and bring to donate. Because I am one already established here, for me it should usually be meat. Chicken or beef. For 10–12 people. That's expensive, again. It is shameful to just come and eat, not bringing any food to share, isn't it? Also, there will be some special attire you need to buy for your presentation. And you gotta get to practice sessions before . . . get home from work early to prepare your food to donate. It adds up! Some, they're spending £250 plus ($385) per month just on socials! Bonding is good and, yes, they are our community leaders here, the organizers, everyone knows them . . . But those who cannot become permanent here, what are they doing? Scattering money! What's the effect on their projects back home? Unless they can be sure it will make them a permanent or get them more work, it's nothing.

But I have to go sometimes. Otherwise, they think I am snubbing them! That I don't care! You know, that I am more . . . [focused] on my employers and housemates, and not always wanting to bond with my far cousins and my old batchmates from school, my younger sister's batchmates, even . . . or whoever's just arrived here, like that. What can I do for them? It's hard. And what will they do for me? Mostly, none . . . Do I want them to share their problems to me? So difficult. There's always someone asking to borrow, for a recommendation to a new employer, do I know a house with space . . .

For me, I'd rather just go to church. The expenses are less. The time is not so much. You can also do bonding, afterwards at the coffee time, isn't it? And I don't have to attend practice to sing!

Labanet nonetheless found consolation and built friendships at the community center, though she resented the surveillance and expectations it entailed. Having to make herself available to community organizers, campaigners, and activists here presented problems. The community center was at the interface between London's third sector groups—NGOs and community organizations—and their intended clients. Attendees at such events tacitly accepted being approached as potential recruits or beneficiaries of these groups. NGOs sometimes sent representatives who were also in Kankanaey networks, like Calangbay, but more often they were represented by mainstream Tagalog-speaking Catholics or non-Filipinos. So there was often an edge of ethnic and religious tension in these events. NGO representatives used the space to consult community members and collect details on possible clients. They organized pre- or after the event information sessions intended to help community members understand immigration regulations and changes in government policy, explained how to access health care, and invited them to join various campaigns for migrants' rights. Yet, in NGO meetings, the affective fullness of singing, traditional dancing, music, and line dancing competitions suddenly evaporated into a thin atmosphere of paranoia. Labanet wanted to avoid those spaces.

## Surveillance and Belonging

For irregular migrants, like Labanet and Biag, their claim to belonging in London was always in question. Different to belonging were made visible in NGO sessions at the community center.

One such event was a roundtable discussion on immigration issues and activist agendas for migrants' rights. UK-Filipino NGO-1 brokered this session through Father Alabag's church congregation. UK-Filipino NGO-1 had helped some congregants with their immigration questions and campaigned for recognition for the United Kingdom's Filipino community, so congregants felt indebted to them. But this particular session was offered by an organizer from an allied group—London NGO. London NGO wanted to affiliate with the church congregation. The affiliation relationship required the church to commit a revolving rota of congregants to London NGO's activities. London NGO wanted people—specifically migrants—to join in public meetings, attend street demonstrations, and plan public protest actions, advancing a migrants' rights agenda. Nine of the twelve congregants who attended the meeting were Filipino, and four were irregular migrants. I was unsure about the other five. London NGO's community organizer, chairing the meeting, was an earnest and pleasant young woman, herself from a migrant family and raised in London. She cared passionately about migrants' rights and led a discussion of the opportunities, potentials, and reciprocal expectations affiliating entailed.

Migrants' casual working practices (and irregularity) meant that they worried about making commitments they could not keep. Meetings with inflexible timings could be addressed with rotas and alternates. The next concern was, how much of a public profile would migrants' individual participation require? London NGO saw it as desirable to have articulate, deserving, well-integrated migrants at the forefront of their campaigns, no matter their visa status. Irregular migrants considered this a personal risk. Their fundamental question was "Does one have to be a (full, real) citizen to participate?" The discussion ground to a halt. To restart it, the London NGO organizer asked everyone to introduce himself or herself and to outline the issues they wanted to address.

The first eight Filipinos talked about being migrants, new to the place and not knowing much about London, and then stared at the table. Dave, a non-Filipino who had just moved to London from the north of England, said he wanted to know the problems of his local community a bit better. Biag asked him, "The north—can we see your papers, then?" Biag's query was followed by a shared spurt of laughter. Finally, Adamey broke the impasse: "I'm Adamey. And my issue—and I'm not the only one—is that I don't have papers anymore. I'm supposed to go home. But I can't, now. I came as a student and my course finished. But I was also working. And then there was a family problem and we needed the money. And I didn't leave. So, for me, it's most important that I'm not caught. I can't leave . . . not until I am prepared to go home." After Adamey had spoken, there was palpable loosening of tension. People stopped gazing down, sat back, and relaxed.

Slowly, their issues emerged. People were confused over Home Office decisions they had heard about for Indefinite Leave to Remain applicants and asylum seekers. They didn't understand the rules for claiming asylum and the various categories of protection and restrictions on work attached to them. Some of the irregular migrants and a few with work visas had problems with employers. Irregular migrants were particularly concerned about the Transport Police stopping and searching people at the local Tube station, asking them to prove their identity and status, and handing suspected irregular migrants over to the UKBA. Migrants wanted London NGO to help them make sense, individually, of what seemed to be a random system of regulation, recognition, and enforcement of immigration rules. Was it possible that UKBA was able to track movements by looking at the activity on your Oyster card? Bugan—a student friend of Biag's—had been caught at the Tube station the previous month and deported. He'd heard she'd been caught, but now knew it was true: she had updated her Facebook status from the Philippines. Could the authorities identify an irregular migrant worker by the pattern of their movements on public transport?

No specific answers were forthcoming from London NGO. There was a mismatch between migrants' needs and NGO expectations. The community organizer encouraged people to join together with like-minded Londoners to campaign for regularization of irregular migrants. She reassured reluctant and anxious people that they would be supported and would feel safe going public as irregular, but couldn't offer concrete, personal advice. Silence descended again. This silence now held long-simmering community tensions brought from the Philippines.

Kankanaey people come from a region of the Philippines that has hosted communist revolutionaries' longstanding attempts to overthrow the Philippine government for several decades.[1] The forty-year-old communist insurgency has used Kankanaey ancestral lands as a base and has recruited there, too. The leftist rhetoric and community organizing strategy of London NGO was familiar to Filipino migrants; several of the migrants had previously been community organizers themselves, back home. Not only was the lack of security and implicit threat of exposure activating repressed personal histories, but London NGO's familiar leftist approach made people uneasy.

## The Exported Shatter Zone

Sitting across the table from Biag and me was Domia, a former teacher in her late fifties. Domia had come to the United Kingdom on a family visit visa three years earlier. Ostensibly visiting her eldest child, a former student married to a UK national, Domia had taken a cash-in-hand housekeeper job and overstayed. Two more of her children had since arrived on student visas and married UK nationals. Domia's earnings helped to support her remaining four children, university students and early career professionals in the Philippines, as well as building her dream home on the outskirts of Baguio City. Domia's wider family had been active in the Philippine left in the 1970s and 1980s. Her first cousin had been a serving cadre with the New People's Army (NPA)—the armed wing of the Communist Party of the Philippines. One of Domia's sisters had been an organizer with an NPA-allied community health NGO. I already knew Domia came from the leftist elite. If not herself an ex-rebel, she had certainly heard most of the rhetoric of London NGO before: organize, build coalitions, agitate, demonstrate, follow the advice of the leaders, and have faith that changes will happen. But nobody else at the meeting necessarily knew that Domia's visa had expired. Watching her face, I admired her cool demeanor and thought about what might lie underneath. From whom had she borrowed how much money? Who relied on her to hold the tenancy for the flat she shared with two students and another overstayer? Revealing her status and her history could endanger her leadership position in the community.

Biag was in a similar bind. He had spent much of the meeting tilting his chair back, gaze averted to the table or floor. Biag had come to the United Kingdom to avoid threats from the New People's Army. After graduating from university, Biag had managed infrastructure projects for a provincial government department north of Baguio City. Travelling for work in a remote area, he had come across an NPA training camp. He said nothing about this to anyone, but the camp was raided by the Armed Forces of the Philippines two days later. Several people had died in the ensuing gunfight.[2] The NPA then threatened Biag with retribution. These threats had been verbal, passed on through neighbors. He and Labanet had moved to Baguio City to find other ways to earn a living. They had borrowed money—with interest—to come to the United Kingdom, intending to overstay and work. They wanted to save enough money to set themselves up with a new life away from their old home. In 2008, Biag was caught in a stop and search at a local Tube station. The police had told him that he met the general description of someone sought for questioning over a recent burglary. When Biag could not produce valid documents, he was turned over to the UKBA. He spent several weeks in immigration detention before filing an asylum claim. Biag, too, was reluctant to speak about his status.

Biag was not worried about his church congregation or Dave—or the London NGO community organizer. He was worried about migrants like Domia, those with NPA connections. The UK-Filipino NGO-1 organizer who had brokered the meeting with London NGO had NPA connections, too. In fact, UK-Filipino NGO-1 was affiliated with a whole global network of NPA-associated activist groups and NGOs in the Philippines and beyond. Sharing his story here could put Biag at risk. Though Kankanaey, these people might not support him. Revealing he had been progovernment might cause NPA supporters to cut ties with him. And there were other considerations. Some of the people at the table owed Labanet money. If they knew Labanet and Biag might be deported at moment's notice, would they repay? Or would they have motivation to report them? He and Labanet had borrowed from distant kin and a rural bank and were still repaying loans back home. If word of their status got back to their creditors, their loans might be called in. Their first priority was thus to conceal their problems in regularizing their stay in the United Kingdom. They needed to keep their asylum claim secret and act as if they belonged in London already.

Sitting at this table, surveillance and belonging went hand in hand. Surveillance is a way of policing or acknowledging another's belonging and confirming one's own, and it must be met with a strategic response. Transport Police and Border Agency surveillance at the Tube station is not even the worst aspect of it. Labanet explained to me later that she had opted not to attend this meeting because sitting in such a circle with people from her village or kin networks scared her. Housemates, fellow members of a church congregation, coworkers—all were unlikely to know a migrant's true immigration status, but everybody speculated. Labanet was convinced, "It's your *kababayan*—your fellow Filipino—who may be your Judas." Anxiety about publicness and betrayal was why London NGO's offer was largely ignored.

London NGO found one irregular migrant there to join their campaign activities long term. Yunnia had nothing much left to lose, already having been exposed both to the community and to UKBA. She had been caught in a raid on a house occupied by three Filipinos working in a restaurant. Yunnia's EU-citizen boyfriend would eventually marry her, enabling her to avoid being deported, so she had no fear of being further exposed. Domia, too, became involved with London NGO, though briefly. In a meeting brokered by the London NGO organizer, she did an interview with a national newspaper. She spoke as an irregular migrant but was frustrated by the results. Domia found that her comments had been selectively edited to produce the familiar story about long-distance mothering attached to Filipino women:

> What I really said, they didn't use. Yes, of course she asked. I told her. I do miss my children and wish all my family was together! I'm human! But the kids are all now having families of their own. My oldest is 36!! And the youngest will complete college this year. It's not about what I am sacrificing abroad, to raise my children. I've already raised them! All seven. Back then, I left my work as a teacher so we could transfer to the city and then we depended to my husband's earnings. Now, he will retire next year. Our house is still under construction!! But his pension will be less than we have now. And I'm here, working. Working for me! It's about how there's no available work for me there. I can't go back to working in my profession any more in the Philippines. So I have to come here to secure my retirement; I won't be depending to my kids when I'm old!

Yunnia remained active in London NGO events, posting regular Facebook status updates and photo albums, but Domia dropped out. Biag and others expressed polite interest in future activities but made no commitments.

## Proliferating Citizenships

At this meeting, participants heard the organizer reassuring them that everyone belonged in London, regardless of their formal migration status. This claim echoed the comments of the priest at their church. However, the participants were uneasy—and unfamiliar—with arguments advocating citizenship through residence. Substantive citizenship—belonging to the city simply by dint of dwelling in and contributing to it—was not something they recognized.[3] Instead, formal citizenship—having the right to reside and work in the United Kingdom, or "full papers"—was, for them, the dividing line between belonging and faking it. The distinctions between formal citizens and temporary migrants occupied much of their focus, structuring their strategies for coping with surveillance.

My respondents encountered multiple forms of surveillance. Students were concerned about meeting attendance requirements at their schools. If migrants were overstayers or were breaking their visa conditions and working extra hours or irregularly, they worried about their movements being recorded not only by their Oyster cards on public transportation, but also by CCTV cameras in public areas. Some migrants worked for employers who had CCTV at home or in the workplace to monitor their activities. Formal, state, and private digital surveillance came together with the surveillance the community conducted on itself via social media, church, and community center events. It was easy for migrants to feel paranoid and overwhelmed here. Much of the affective charge behind the awkward silences of the community center meeting came from the conjugation of social media with imagined and face-to-face encounters.

Close and distant kin, flatmates, and village-mates from home monitored others' attendance and behavior at social events and spread gossip, trying to find advantage in knowing others' statuses. Their monitoring activity was made semipublic by recording detailed images and video clips of community events to upload on Facebook. People used Facebook's "check in" place-based alerting service to tell their friends of their whereabouts in the city. They posted pictures and updates mapping their movements—attending church, working, going to the *karbut* [car boot sales], visiting the countryside with friends. Thus attending church or a community center event or meeting in person meant interacting with Facebook "friends" who knew what a migrant had been doing. This facility also offered migrants a way to manipulate perceptions. Even migrants who were limiting their movements around the city—going from home to work to the shops and back along the route least likely to attract the attention of the Transport Police or UKBA—could be active on Facebook. They "friended" other London-based Filipinos and church congregants, had extensive "friend" networks in the Philippines, joined groups, and "liked" pages. Their Facebook profiles showed family and relations through comment strings and "friends" lists and they felt impelled to leave these open to "friends of friends." Instead of documenting their life in London as precarious and marginal, they performed networked success. They used social media to hide evidence of their irregularity. There were thus few differences between the Facebook posts of irregular migrants and those of temporary workers, permanent residents, or citizens. What suggested migration status was a migrant's reluctance or enthusiasm to post material on irregularity and how to cope with it: irregular migrants rarely commented on irregularity directly.

Their strategy of acting as if they had valid visas meant that irregular migrants opened themselves up to social media surveillance, despite their vulnerability to UKBA. This apparent contradiction arose because migrants' conceptions of personhood relied on the possibility of expanding their networks through undiscovered connections whose potential couldn't be dismissed. Migrants believed there were no strangers on Facebook, only friends they had yet to meet. The potential of these "friend" networks to support the further expansion of migrants' reputations and influence was reason enough to hold them open. Beyond future bonding, there was another purpose for migrants coming out, seeing and being seen in the community center and thus on Facebook. That purpose was to manipulate surveillance to legitimate their own actions and strengthen their putative connections to place and to others. As London's shatter zone brought together congregations, NGOs, and migrants' own networks from home, conjugating them through Facebook, forms of belonging and citizenship proliferated.

*Facebook Belonging*

Facebook belonging emerged through migrants making public reciprocity, consociality, and the space of bonding in a global frame. On social media, the community center was a vital site in which to document this expansion of personal ties. Like Labanet, approximately 85 percent of the sixty-one Kankanaey migrants I interviewed for this project were active on Facebook, posting at least three status updates per week. To follow these activities, I "friended" a smaller group of twenty people I met through community center events, and also followed the groups pages of several NGOs with which they interacted. One of the churches ran a Facebook group, posting announcements and photographs of events held in their hall and elsewhere, which I also joined and followed.

Photographs from community center socials received enthusiastic responses on Facebook profiles. Photographs and video grabs of these gatherings were regularly shared from profile to profile, with people in the United Kingdom tagging themselves and other Filipinos who appeared in them, eliciting comments from "friends" around the world. Such images showed people being taken care of, with the community center as the venue for photographs documenting community, church, and life-course events: birthdays, baptisms, funerals, wakes, and weddings. Facebook enabled these images themselves to become actors, shaping new norms for relationships from kinship to romance to friendship to regional Cordillera belonging.[4] The London-based community center "bonding" group photos became a new visual trope for migrant success and security.

Photographs from the community center often documented either parallel events or replacement events held in lieu of activities in migrants' sending villages. These images were usually captioned with the name of a Kankanaey ritual. For example, Biag posted photos of a *begnas* thanksgiving ritual held by his family in the Philippines alongside his participation in the equivalent social event, captioned "Begnas, London." This kind of digital "being with" image carried a positive affective charge. More images and video grabs from the community center showed friends and relatives hanging out, eating Filipino delicacies, having fun, making faces, jamming with a guitar in the community center after midnight mass on Christmas Eve—being, laughing, together. One photograph I took of Biag, elated, playing gongs in the community center, garnered over a hundred "likes" and five "shares" on Facebook. When I visited his family in the Philippines, I saw that they had downloaded and printed the image.

These images also mapped exclusions, showing who had been cut out of community center events. However, who, among the friends of friends, lurked and "facestalked" profiles would not be made evident. Thus this category of stalkers and lurkers was equivalent to the omnipresent and rarely specified "they" of village talk—the "they" who often engaged in gossip, censure, and exclusion, reported, second-hand, as a form of community discipline. Filipino migrants in London felt exposed to a much larger, more global "they" than ever before. In an example of this global Facebook belonging, Labanet updated her Facebook status on Christmas Eve, inviting all her "friends" to join her at midnight mass. Father Alabag, Adamey (her housemate), and her sister Oedma in the Philippines all responded to her post by "liking" it. Later in the night, her aunt in Germany and her niece in the Philippines posted responses. Through Labanet's profile page and friends list, her relatives were able to access each other's pages, the current priest's personal page, and the church's Facebook site. They saw photographs of London Christmas activities—caroling, parties—in which Labanet had participated, identifying the people who had also attended the event and leaving comments. Using these digital networks, one of Labanet's fifth cousins in Jordan emailed through Facebook, asking Labanet to meet his daughter who would be visiting London the following month, then added her to his own list as a "friend."

> Labanet commented on her own Facebook photo post: "Attending midnight mass. Join us!"
>
> Father Alabag [vicar] and Oedma like this.
>
> Father Philip: "Merry Christmas sister . . ."
>
> Oedma: "Likewise sis. Miss yah!"
>
> Mona: "We joined the midnight mass, through television. [Germany]"
>
> Labanet: "That's gud auntie. Happy a blessed Xmas"
>
> Mona: "Yes! We have. Very holy WHITE CHRISTMAS."
>
> Delia: "merry x mass ant."
>
> Labanet: "Likewise sis. Miss yah!"

Labanet's photos traveling with these comments depicted not the midnight mass itself but the after-party at the community center.

Facebook's privacy settings enabled users to choose between potentially disclosing themselves to strangers and restricting their networks and activities by holding images back from exchange. My respondents were uncertain about who, in their transnational social circles, would have access to Facebook and when. A few had tried selecting "friends only," but found offline friends were unable to locate them, restricting the pleasure they could draw from participating. Having an accessible profile meant they felt obliged to accept almost all friend requests, particularly when these came from senior kin and older family friends. In addition to changing their profile shots regularly, they tagged friends in images and in non-image photos (text memes, usually) to draw attention to particular posts.

Images, whether photos or memes, iterated and thus sustained relationships and created this feeling of belonging.

Producing these images intensified my respondents' practices of performing culture. So while their posts looked like "just more Kankanaey socials," they hid political agency. Facebook, together with the church and the community center, offered migrants a way of "friending" host nationals and inscribing Kankanaey culture onto them. Some of the most globally "liked" photos displayed migrants' integration through their inscription of Kankanaey culture onto non-Filipino bodies. Images of white, English people trying Kankanaey dance moves or eating Filipino food were popular, "liked" by both Filipinos and non-Filipinos in the networks of both the photographers/posters and the people depicted. Rather than isolating migrants, Facebook contributed to migrants' orientation toward their host society. This occurred in terms of an explicit expression of care and cultural contribution, where Facebook was used primarily for social, personal purposes. Facebook images of integration and cultural sharing were another kind of bonding, one done with the United Kingdom.

## Cutting People Out

Facebook also offered a subtle but forceful way of making cuts in networks visible. Scrolling through Labanet's photographs, I noticed that Conyap, one of the senior Filipino congregants and Labanet's former landlady, had not been tagged. Conyap had been cropped out of other photos of the same community center event, photos Labanet had posted directly to her own profile. I asked Labanet about this and she explained that she could no longer trust Auntie Conyap. Conyap had been one of the first members of the Kanakaey-speaking Filipino community to settle in East London. She had arrived in the 1970s as a nurse and married a UK national. She owned a house in East London and rented rooms to recent migrant arrivals. When one of her children graduated from university and moved back home, problems arose. The house was overcrowded and Conyap's tenants rapidly departed. Conyap had cut back her nursing home hours and switched to part-time private caregiving work, relying on her tenants' rents to pay part of her mortgage. Their sudden departure caused her financial stress. She felt betrayed. In turn, she was cut out of Facebook photos.

Basig, Labanet's sister-in-law, was one of the tenants who left Conyap's house. Basig became worried about Conyap's anger and began avoiding church services and community center events. The departed tenants stayed in touch through Facebook, text messages, and phone calls instead, hoping Conyap's feelings would fade. But Basig was close in age to Conyap and they had been coworkers at her private caregiving job—peers, of sorts. Conyap had full papers; Basig had overstayed on a tourist visa and was irregular, so of lower status. When Conyap had heart palpitations because of her financial situation, she sent Basig an accusatory letter, implying that Basig had used witchcraft to make problems in the house. Conyap repeated the accusation to other members of the congregation.

Labanet thought Conyap was silly to claim witchcraft. A Kankanaey witch was someone who held himself or herself outside society and lived on the margins of the community. Witches didn't share with others and contribute to church and community events like Basig had been doing. But the accusation was still insulting. Even worse, Conyap had threatened to inform the new priest—replacing Father Alabag—and the UKBA that Basig was irregular. This was *inayan*. Basig found a room to rent farther from the church and stayed on the periphery of church activities, rarely returning to the community center. She remained scared of Conyap. Basig's extended kin responded by creating a Facebook gap around Conyap. They refused to tag her and framed their photographs to exclude her or cropped her out. Since Conyap was not on Facebook herself, the activities of Basig's kin were directed toward the watching "they"—to show that Basig's family supported her. The anger and the witchcraft accusation were one thing, but Conyap had broken a fundamental rule by threatening to denounce an irregular migrant to the authorities and the church. Conyap's threat rebounded on her, seeing her "unbelonged" from the Facebook community.

In this instance, Labanet and her networks deployed Facebook belonging as form of substantive citizenship to counter Conyap's formal UK citizenship. Though Conyap was a citizen, she now lacked the support of some of her church congregation and her wider ethnic community. *Inayan*—she had used her own secure belonging in the United Kingdom to threaten others' less secure status and thus, indirectly, their families back home.

Kankanaey Facebook was not only about personal networks or grudges. Yes, being on Facebook was fun and compelling, broke isolation, and performed migrants' success—thus possibly making it real—but it could also be more overtly civic-minded.

## Netizenship

Layered on Facebook belonging was another form of citizenship, an older kind of Filipino digital citizenship called netizenship. If belonging worked through its performance—and migrants' willingness to reveal seemingly all activities and connections to the scrutiny of others—netizenship was more individuated. Netizens were much like the activists London NGO was trying to recruit. Thus the apathy my respondents apparently expressed in response was not reluctance to engage with activism or government, merely a judicious choice of arenas for political action. They were already familiar with what active citizenship looked like, online and from the Philippines.

For Domia and Biag, their distance from campaigns to recognize their contribution to the United Kingdom and improve their living conditions was strategic.

They recognized how these campaigns created a space of legitimacy for their irregular work. But as irregular migrants, they were not seeking permanent residency
in the United Kingdom. Instead, they retained their formal political engage-
ments with their substantive and formal citizenship and investments back home.
Because their UK sojourns funded those commitments and projects, they tracked
local politics in the Philippines online as netizens. Netizenship first emerged in
the Filipino diaspora through e-mail discussion lists in the 1990s. Some netizen
groups began as traditional, village political fora, like Domia's clan association.
Other groups emerged in the 1990s as new electronic iterations of local pressure
groups, like Biag's group opposing the extension of a Gameng road into a forest
reserve. Most of these netizen groups had transferred to Facebook by 2010.

For example, BIBKANETS was an original Listserv netizen forum for the
Philippine Cordillera.[5] The forum incorporated local elders, local government
officials, and migrants. Its members compared it to the Kankanaey village institu-
tion of the *dap-ay*—a council of neighborhood male heads of household in which
the right to participate came from descent, residence, or initiation, but status
came from care, contributions of work, and the wisdom members displayed. Most
of my respondents over forty-five years of age were members of BIBAKNETS.
The group had always been open to women, and its founders had been part of
the professional diaspora of the 1960s and 1970s. The group was dominated by
a regional elite who exercised civic responsibility through long-distance advice
to local politicians and community leaders. On BIBAKNETS's Facebook page,
Philippine citizenship was expressed through debates about indigenous cultural
dignity and control over natural resources. The group discussed contemporary
provincial and municipal projects. The individual-posting model of the Listserv
had assumed people were largely individual entrepreneurs, while Facebook made
their group identities more apparent. So Facebook was almost a welcome switch.
Since Kankanaey society is built on a redistributional regime operating beneath
state level through corporate groups, people valued a chance to see members'
"friends" lists and locations. Such clan networks had often captured the state's
local iterations, and this was still evident in political campaigns and lobbying on
BIBAKNETS. BIBAKNETS also expressed one of the shared dissatisfactions of
my UK respondents. They were convinced that fraud was the norm of settlement,
both in their urban land purchases and in rural property disputes in the Philippines as well as, increasingly, in immigration matters in the United Kingdom.
BIBAKNETS members were regularly engaged in party political campaigning
in their hometowns, trying to recruit community members at home to exert
influence over elected officials. BIBAKNETS tended to emphasize the requirement for "proper" legal citizenship in the United Kingdom as part of being a
virtuous migrant. Exercises of netizenship thus became a locus to police formal
citizenship instead of the more substantive kind that arose through Facebook

belonging. BIBAKNETS assumed netizens would be legitimate migrants over-seas—good citizens both at home and abroad.

BIBAKNETS competed with several other networks to organize Kankanaey migrant netizens for local development. One, the Cordillera Global Network, offered the following mission statement: "CORDILLERA GLOBAL NETWORK (CGN) aims to develop within its members the knowledge, skills and cultural understanding to help Cordillera achieve its goals and be proud and responsible citizens in a global society. To this end, CGN encourages all members to become active, life-long learners and good citizens who, by creative and critical thinking, can make positive contributions to their community." These good citizens are global, but Philippine-focused in their values and futures. Migrants must negotiate multiple citizenships and belongings so the "good citizen" can emerge. But the "good" attributes of this citizen were tied to the idea of luck.

Kankanaey people considered routes to formal citizenship to be governed by *inayan*, so that someone's "luck" or "chance" depended on their virtuous actions. A representative of UK-Filipino NGO-2 circulated the following Facebook message to organize a community center event: "Free immigration workshop *id . . .* [at—location, time, date]. A team of immigration lawyers will be accommodating a 1-1 discussion re your immigration status, so bring all your documents and prepare your questions to ask. Again *LIBRE daytoy kakabsat* [FREE here siblings], and they are upfront *haan da nga agpabayad* [no payment required] so grab the chance and know your chances. PM [personal message] me if you want more clarification." Migration success—becoming regularized or legitimately working and living in the United Kingdom—was considered a matter of chance in migrants' encounters with the immigration bureaucracy. Even though someone might appear to be a "good" Filipino citizen, it seemed to observers to be luck that would let him or her stay in the United Kingdom. Bad luck suggested that people had committed some as yet hidden infraction—*inayan* was at work. For migrants who thought as Conyap did, examining who joined in the netizenship networks offered a measure of how good these people were as citizens and, indirectly, suggested their UK migration status.

## Subversive Citizenship

Good people on the way to becoming good UK citizens needed supporters and advocates who already had this status. London NGO's efforts were part of a larger campaign to extend formal citizenship to all migrants who were long-term UK residents. In the community center, migrants thus met with sympathetic, activist formal citizens who practiced their own, subversive version of UK citizenship. These subversive citizens argued that long residence should be the basis for people's belonging. They didn't support current migration regulations. Like the priest who preached "migrants welcome" in chapter 2, they refused to police the border themselves. Instead, they believed residents should eventually gain rights—rights to make claims on the state—by arguing for them on the basis of their substantive contributions to the country.[6] Migrants, they argued, should gain formal citizenship by first attaining public recognition for their substantive citizenship. To help migrants do so, the task of subversive citizens was to compel the rest of the United Kingdom's formal citizens to recognize migrants' vital contributions to British society.[7] This was why London NGO wanted to recruit charismatic irregular migrants for its campaign and had encouraged Domia to speak to journalists: to make the UK public appreciate the contributions of irregular migrants.

Subversive citizens are formal citizens who are critical of citizenship's contemporary boundaries. Their advocacy comes from concern for migrants' rights and well-being but also from their sense that it is their public duty to correct inequalities produced by state regulation of migration. In their framing of citizenship, citizenship exists anywhere there is a large corporation to formalize the belonging of its members. This kind of citizenship is not dependent on the state for its creation, only for formal recognition. Their approach to belonging and citizenship comes from within a particular Western intellectual history.

Kankanaey Filipinos, in contrast, come from a society in which membership in corporate groups—clans and villages—is determined largely by birth and marriage, not necessarily by contribution and residence. Birth order and marriage control status, land ownership, and residence. Layer on top of these norms decades of insurgency and a remote and predatory state and the combination explains why Kankanaey people might think that individual citizens would need to betray their noncitizen fellows to attain formal citizenship. Such a betrayal would not be treason, in the eyes of the state, but its opposite: loyalty, placing state above family, and friendship. If, as migrants, they had developed loyalty to their state of sojourn, they were not sympathetic to subversive citizens' arguments. In comments on netizen forums, Kankanaey British citizens claimed they had a moral duty to the United Kingdom and to their church to discourage and possibly report people who were breaking immigration rules, even if those people were in their social networks. Some Kankanaey British citizens were concerned about the reputation of the Filipino community and the impact of migration on families at home. Conyap explained, "First, in my time, we were all coming to the UK as professionals with papers. Now they are just coming on any visa—tourist, student—but still working. They are giving us Filipinos a bad reputation, as if we are all T&Ts [overstayers]. But some of us are citizens here now and we follow the laws." Conyap's "we," however, was not cohesive.

Some Kankanaey migrants were subversive UK citizens, too. Respondents who were born UK citizens or naturalized many years ago and enjoyed formal citizenship rights could see how citizens' rights and benefits now depended on the work of noncitizens. They realized that formal citizenship increasingly worked as a mechanism to distribute inequality, instead of creating equality. They noted gradations of citizenship often mapped onto geographical zones. Irregular migrants were stuck in the poverty-stricken, heavily policed inner city, while formal citizens lived in much more salubrious areas beyond. Having come from the Philippine shatter zone, Kankanaey speakers had grown up knowing that their own claims to substantive citizenship in the Philippines were considered weak, even if they had Philippine passports. For them, active netizenship was necessary because state projects and interests regularly attempted to dispossess or exclude Kankanaey people. They felt national government and the national mainstream had often treated Kankanaey communities as if their formal citizenship didn't exist. Circumstances for migrants in East London seemed similar, with the Transport Police and UKBA setting up sweeps at the Tube stations there, where migrants lived, as opposed to in the more affluent West London areas where their employers did. Subversive citizens were sympathetic to irregular workers' concerns over racial profiling.

Indeed, the type of police action that apprehended Biag potentially contravened the United Kingdom's stop and search laws. Stop and search actions often seemed to be directed at visible minorities—that is, largely recent migrants from outside the European Union—through racial profiling. This approach to policing produced ethical dilemmas for the United Kingdom's full citizens. Citizens perceived that the fullness of their own citizenship gave them unimpeded access to recourse against discrimination and inequitable treatment. Treating migrants this way showed that them that nonbelonging was the underlying norm, revealing that the fullness of their own citizenship could also be stripped away. They knew that migrants' cheap caring labor shored up the government services—health care and home care—making life tolerable for the formal-citizen majority. It was the exceptional position of migrant workers that enabled the United Kingdom to continue to recognize citizens' rights to access these government services largely free of charge.

On top of intensified policing, government information campaigns encouraged irregular migrants to exit the United Kingdom. Some of these campaigns were bullying, including a series of advertisements that appeared on the side panels of vans. Driven through the streets of East London in the summer of 2013, these mobile messages exhorted irregular migrants to leave the country voluntarily, before they were caught. Subversive citizens quickly organized to support migrants in resisting this campaign. The following statement appeared on Facebook, originating from the NGO Migrant Voice. It was shared widely through Father Alabag's congregation and UK-Filipino NGO-2's networks:

> We are appalled at the current campaign of threats and intimidation by the Home Office.
>
> These tactics which include racial profiling are attempting to bring division, suspicion, fear and anger to our communities, sentiments only the

extreme and racist fringe can benefit from. They are also a cowardly attempt to attack the most vulnerable in order to gain populist votes.

Many of the so-called "Illegals" are people who have fled violence, persecution, oppression, torture and violent conflict in their countries of origin.

Only a fraction of those needing protection are granted asylum in the UK. But they cannot return home for fear of their lives.

Targeting these vulnerable and traumatized people, just in order to appear "tough on immigration" is cruel and inhuman.

Last year London has been celebrated internationally as a city that proved that multiculturalism works. London has benefitted for centuries from migration, and today as before Refugees and Migrants are contributing hugely to the success and the vibrancy of this city and its communities.

We demand a stop to the current campaign of intimidation by billboards, stop and search and other methods. We propose to sponsor a van advertising a different message:

Refugees are welcome here! Stop the scapegoating!

Many so-called "illegals" have fled violence, oppression, persecution, torture and violent conflict.

They cannot return home.

But they make great contributions to the UK whenever they are allowed to.

Refugees and Migrants are welcome![8]

A broader NGO campaign on this same theme was created by Citizens UK: "Strangers into Citizens." This campaign advocated formal citizenship for long-term irregular migrants, calling on the government to offer the following:

- A pathway to citizenship for migrants who have put down roots in the UK
- A recognition that migrants remain vital to the UK economy and society, even in the downturn
- An end to limbo for people fleeing persecution who have waited on a decision for many years[9]

Through these campaigns, subversive citizen groups sought regularization or conditional amnesty to enable refused asylum seekers and overstayers to acquire legal status. Migrants' social contributions, in the past and, potentially, in the future provided the basis for the campaigns' claims. In 2008, London's mayor, Boris Johnson, addressed the Mayoral Assembly to make this very point: "Where people have been here a long time and have no prospect of being able to be sent back then an amnesty could be considered so that they can pay taxes and legally contribute to the British economy."[10] In this amnesty proposal, their substantive citizenship contributions would entitle migrants to formal citizenship. Similarly, one strand of the Strangers into Citizens campaign (reason 4 for regularization) argued, "By not regularizing, the UK is permitting a substantial subclass of citizen to exist outside the law."[11] By citizens, Strangers into Citizens evidently means substantive citizens, rather than formal citizens. The campaign suggested that, after five years of residence, migrants should be given a pathway to formal citizenship, bringing them into the space of legal protection and regulation. Yet, despite the benefits of becoming British citizens, the "strangers'" social space remained attractive to my respondents.

As "strangers," migrants inhabit the global shatter zone. This is a global space in Britain but outside government regulation. People dwelling here are intimately tied to global networks, but largely invisible to the British state. Having "done the math" on citizenship, some of my respondents calculated that they were significantly better off with cash-in-hand and casual work than if they did the same job as a visa holder in the formal economy. From the shatter zone, they could access informal work, housing, and even banking, operating in the shadows of the formal economy. They minimized costs for housing by subletting informally or renting outside local council rules, tolerating substandard buildings and overcrowded conditions as a result. Remitting cash over the counter from high-street banks and wire transfer services or using shipping firms to send goods home, they moved any surplus wages they earned out of the United Kingdom as soon as they could, with few questions asked. They relied on activist groups to direct them to charity-funded health services that treated without requiring patients to present a passport. Sometimes they consulted medically qualified community members for informal diagnosis and treatment, then asked friends and family to carry medicine from the Philippines for them. They could sustain themselves in this way for many years, building relations of trust, exchange, and sometimes mutual care with employers, landlords, bankers, and medical workers. By ignoring or refusing to implement government regulations on proof of the right to work, identity, visa validity, or provenance of funds, these people—subversive citizens, other residents and businesses seeking profits—cocreated the shatter zone space, enabling migrants to survive and even prosper. Some migrants I met were in this global space only temporarily; others found the shatter zone key to their longer-term migration strategy.

Migrants dwelling in the shatter zone were very aware of public opinion and grateful for the support of subversive-citizen UK nationals. To persist here, they had to negotiate claims to substantive citizenship. Collaborating with activists helped them gain public recognition for deeds, merit, and caring. Even if migrants never intended to regularize, they understood claims to substantive citizenship performed an implicit exchange at a symbolic level. If migrants indicated formal citizenship was their eventual goal and long-term dream, they were more likely to enjoy support from or simply tolerance within wider British society. So irregular migrants put much energy into performing "as if" they were future citizens, if only as a way of shoring up their claims to the substantive citizenship that helped them remain in the global shatter zone.

Reflecting on the politics here, Labanet explained, "[Mayor] Boris agreed that long-term overstayers should be regularized," but that "is not going to happen soon, is it?" Labanet and Biag tried to demonstrate their good character and contribution to the wider British community in order to appear as if they were among those who would be regularized. Labanet's strategy was to cultivate her own networks of good employers. These were people sympathetic to her presence and projects in the United Kingdom who would hire her—and people she recommended—without undertaking thorough visa checks. Or they would accept, for their records, a copy of someone else's passport (borrowed) with a valid work visa in it.

Subversive citizens thus played a vital role in supporting and recognizing migrants' substantive citizenship. Subversive citizen employers flouted the rules, possibly more for their own ends. Advocates, like London NGO and the church, refused to recognize or take seriously the gradations of citizenship migration produced. Subversive citizens all refused to accept state-assigned responsibility for evaluating others' citizenship statuses. They pushed the delegated problem of checking workers' papers and verifying visa statuses back to the state. Subversive citizens expressed a superior, critical form of loyalty to the higher ideals of nationhood, refusing to see those ideals debased in everyday surveillance and its uneven implementation. For them, subverting state regulations of migrants was a duty, but it also expressed privilege. Their ability to act as if citizenship, formally, didn't matter was characteristic of elites who considered themselves "citizens of the world" and were uneasy with nationalisms. In subversive citizens' conception of their own relationship with the global, they were obliged to oppose the distribution of inequalities through citizenship and indebted to migrants.

Subversive citizens networks organized through UK-Filipino NGO-2 supported migrants seeking work. They posted messages such as this on Facebook: "An employer in Fulham road, Chelsea is looking for a living-in housekeeper/nanny. Even if your docu's are not yet ok but have lodged an application and have received a letter of acknowledgement from the HO, you can apply." This offer of work didn't follow migration and employment regulations to the letter—the employee's documents are supposed to be verified as "OK"—it offered a workaround. Such minor subversions of the rules were a lifeline for migrants with outstanding applications or without papers. This would-be employer seemed willing to take the small risk of a fine if they were discovered not to have checked the worker's documents in full in order to support migrants by offering work.

Subversive citizens, like Dave, above, also used their community center–brokered networks to helping migrants navigate the affective charge of UKBA enforcement activities targeting irregular migrants. Dave posted practical advice to Facebook:

UK Border Agency (UKBA) officers go to . . . to the bustling hearts of London's multicultural experiment, and they check your papers. Burly, aggressive men stop passers-by as they walk into the tube station, in a bid to find out their immigration status. Ordinary Londoners trying to get to work are subject to a humiliating and threatening ordeal.

Officers know their legal right to do so is highly questionable but they also know one of the great truths of human interaction: that when an official questions a minority, the law means nothing. They act with the confidence of the uniform, the unwavering assumption from the minority that the law is not on their side. But one of the great things about this country is that the law is on your side. You have substantial rights and immigration officials have very few.

Immigration officers' right to stop and question people away from ports of entry are governed by paragraph 2, schedule 2 of the *Immigration Act* 1971, as supported by the long standing judgment of Singh v Hammond. There are strong restrictions on what they can do.

Here is the relevant passage from chapter 31 of UKBA's *Operational Enforcement Activity* manual:

"Before seeking to question someone, an IO [immigration officer] will need to have information in his possession which suggests that the person may be of immigration interest (that is there are doubts about that person's leave status). The information in the IO's possession should be sufficient to constitute a reasonable suspicion that that particular person may be an immigration offender. Any IO stopping and questioning an individual will need to be in a position to justify the reasons why they considered that threshold to be satisfied in that particular case. Any questioning must be consensual."

The paragraph 2 power to examine does not include a power to compel someone to stop or to require someone to comply with that examination. Should a person seek to exercise their right not to answer questions and leave, there is no power to arrest that person purely on suspicion committing an immigration offence.

This is a very high standard. It is illegal for an officer to conduct a speculative check on your immigration status. If you are a commuter simply going to the Tube station, you do not satisfy this standard. Demand to know why you are being questioned. If you do not receive a decent answer, inform the officer of your rights and walk away. You can walk away, because this is a free country.

This will be a threatening situation, with an unfriendly and often physically imposing officer. The reason they are being threatening is because they are hoping to scare people out of recognizing their rights. It is a coup of charisma, of confidence. Don't let them do it. Hold your nerve.

When you first see the UKBA presence do not do anything which raises suspicion. This is referred to as "having an adverse reaction to an immigration presence." Doing so gives the officers reasonable suspicion.

Do not change the speed of your walking or suddenly change direction. Maintain a steady pace. Do not hang back from the barriers. Do not behave confrontationally or aggressively. Enter into the conversation willingly, and then state that you are aware of your rights and can walk away unless the officer can give a reason for having reasonable suspicion of your status.[12]

Subversive citizenship was thus expressed by making interventions in everyday affective politics. At the same time, irregular migrants mobilized affect to cope with such encounters in other ways, shaping themselves to better conceal their status.

## Prosthetic Citizenship

Facebook belonging, netizenship, and subversive citizenship intersected, opening up a new space for migrant belonging in the shatter zone: prosthetic citizenship. Migrants could now manipulate their online and public self-presentation through their presence, their actions, and the circulation of particular digital images, appending to themselves the qualities and attributes of a good citizen of both the Philippines and the United Kingdom.[13] By acting at all times as if they were, if not citizens already, on a legitimate pathway to UK citizenship, they could even convince themselves of their entitlement to be in the United Kingdom. They used Facebook to publicly archive evidence that they had become good UK citizens in the substantive sense, implying that they were on track to formal citizenship.[14]

Prosthetic citizenship extended the internalized self-surveillance needed to navigate Kankanaey village life into global, digital, and substantive citizenship spaces. Labanet explained:

> Sure, I check in on Facebook when I'm working—like last week when I took the kids to Gambardos, or to see the lions in Trafalgar Square. I post pictures from my employers' house—just of me, of course. I post pictures when I attend our socials in the [community center]. You see, I know they are looking at my status and pictures to see what I'm doing. If they are really my friends, my family, it's ok and I can trust them not to report me. But if they are not, I am showing what I do like I have nothing to hide, so maybe they will think I've got papers. Only those who are absent are hiding something, that's what they will think.

Labanet used Facebook to append to herself a kind of belonging she had yet to secure. Because only "the absent" had something to hide, she hid in plain sight. On her Christmas posting, above, she said, "Of course I want everyone to know I will be attending church. I need them to know that I'm doing good things while I'm here. It's good that they see I am 'friends' with our new vicar, that I'm encouraging our kababayans here in London to attend mass, stuff like that. They don't need to see that I am one of those who . . . Well, I am not one to just enjoy-enjoy [party] when I don't have work." When I asked who "them" might refer to, Labanet was not concerned about delimiting "them" as a group. She explained, "I am not hiding anything." Labanet thus took the affective openness required to accept surveillance and transmuted that orientation into prosthetic citizenship. She "checked in" where she imagined she would be if she held the appropriate work visa. Portraying herself as if she were on a pathway to settlement and to being a full participant in mainstream UK society explained her mosque photos and the pictures with her employers' children in Trafalgar Square.

With prosthetic citizenship, migrants took Facebook belonging and re-created an alternative citizenship in which gradations of visa status could be equalized through performance. Facebook, combined with church and the community center, offered a public forum in which to demonstrate kindness, reliability, industry, and good relations with others—being a good citizen. If formal citizenship was individuating—perhaps actively requiring a betrayal of one's fellows, as Conyap contemplated, above—the well-documented activities of the community center worked, publicly, against such betrayals, bringing together subversive citizens with those performing prosthetic citizenship. Hence we find Dave, who led the congregation's contributions to London NGO, on Labanet's "friends" list and tagged beside her in her photographs of after church community center gatherings. Online and in the wider community, any evidence that prosthetic citizenship translates into the real thing was highly prized.

When people secured residency, they added evidence to their Facebook archives. For instance, Gonay A. and Malecdan posted a photograph of their letter from the UK Home Office granting them Indefinite Leave to Remain and their pink-and-blue Residence Permit cards. Labanet "liked" the post and commented, "Happy for you both, you are blessed . . . may you become a blessing for others too." These others—for whom they would become a blessing by sharing their good fortune—were members of their wider social and community networks in the United Kingdom. Other migrants responded to this with congratulatory comments and "likes." Doing so, they appended to themselves a kind of vicarious virtue, proclaiming their own worth by documenting their associations with recognized "good citizens." Labanet curated her own Facebook profile and presence to show herself as if she had a work visa, separating her profile images from the realities of her life with judicious selection and editing.

What Labanet didn't share, post, or discuss was her own letter from the Home Office acknowledging her as a beneficiary of Biag's claim for asylum. As the claim was being processed and appealed, carrying this letter allowed her to move freely across London. Appending possible citizenship in the "to come" to her presence in the United Kingdom, these papers documenting a submitted claim for asylum enabled her to pass through two spot checks at her local Tube station. But she didn't discuss those experiences in the community center, post about them on Facebook, or even "like" the advice on UKBA spot checks circulated by Dave. She left the posting and circulation of testimonies of spot checks and details on migrants' rights to the subversive citizens. Online, she pretended she was not affected, even as she took the advice to heart. We discussed Dave's posting on UKBA enforcement, above, in an interview. She envisioned a day when she would no longer have the letter. The advice about holding your nerve against a coup of charisma and avoiding showing an adverse reaction was good, but not news to her. "Last time, when I was stopped at the Tube station, I just smiled and got in the queue where they motioned me and got my papers ready. Of course, the officer accepted the papers but asked me if I was working, even before they started reading them! I said, 'You see, sir, I am required to be reporting to my case officer regularly, so I have told them there.' Because I always carry my papers, I was able to be confident."

## Navigating the Shatter Zone

In the community center, migrants appropriated the affect of subversive citizenship—the warm solidarity expressed by UK nationals—to themselves in order to navigate the global shatter zone. The discourses of chance and blessing that surrounded formal citizenship also supported those acting "as if" with prosthetic citizenship, too. Facebook provided a record and an audience to recognize the ways in which migrants became deserving and successful—good citizens. Facebook also mediated their mutual exposure in ways that dissuaded migrants from taking the risk of arguing, publicly, for changes in migration policy to resolve their own problems. Meanwhile, the UK government had decided that subversive citizenship and chain migration were responsible for sustaining the large number of overstayers in the United Kingdom. In late 2013, they introduced regulations attached to a new immigration bill intended to prevent irregular migrants from accessing private, rented housing and health care. At this point, there were at least 618,000 irregular migrants living in the United Kingdom.[15] When I learned that the regulations on renting would be changed to fine private landlords who did not establish their tenants' right to be in the country, I contacted Labanet. She didn't respond to text messages or phone calls, but I found her on Facebook. I sent her a chat message, and she replied saying she would get back to me in a few days. She was, she explained, incredibly busy with her netizenship, campaigning for the elections in Katangoan, her thoughts on the other side of the shatter zone.

Labanet was delivering the overseas workers vote from the United Kingdom to the allies of an uncle running for office. She and Biag had made a substantial donation—£2,000 ($3,082 or PHP 143,320)—to his campaign. Indebted to them, they anticipated that he would foster their projects and business interests after his election. She wasn't immediately worried about new fines for landlords! When we did chat, Labanet explained that she did not think the regulation would be easily implemented, particularly for sublets. And new requirements certainly would not affect informal rentals where no contract was signed, rent was paid in cash, and no records were kept. Labanet envisioned that borrowing passports—which migrants did to access work—would also circumvent the new rental policy. She thought the renting of rooms in private homes, as opposed to entire flats, would continue to be difficult for the authorities to regulate. My sense that she might have felt abject in the face of UK government policy was wrong. She displaced her anxiety by shifting focus toward securing her investments at home. Her entanglements in personal and formal electoral politics in her exercise of Filipino citizenship, netizenship, and Facebook belonging came together here. Though she appreciated the care extended to her by subversive citizens like Dave, her prosthetic citizenship in the United Kingdom was a means to prepare for her return home. For her, the shatter zone was a desirable space from which to operate. Even though her status made it precarious, her techniques of affective self-management sustained her.

## Notes

1. Rutten, 2008.
2. I was able to verify the story of the raid on the training camp and the subsequent deaths through reports in the *Philippine Daily Inquirer* and in an NPA-affiliated online newsletter.
3. Holston, 2008.
4. Miller, 2007.
5. Longboan, 2011.
6. Holston, 2008.
7. Holston, 2008.
8. www.migrantvoice.org, last accessed September 15, 2014.
9. (http://www.strangersintocitizens.org.uk/?page_id=9), last accessed May 28, 2012.
10. Boris Johnson, Mayor of London, speaking to the London Mayoral Assembly, 2008. The Mayor's comments were widely reported including by BBC News (see http://news.bbc.co.uk/1/hi/uk_politics/7338950.stm, last accessed June 28, 2016) and campaign groups, including Citizens UK (see http://www.strangersintocitizens.org.uk/, last accessed May 28, 2012.)
11. http://www.strangersintocitizens.org.uk/?page_id=9, last accessed May 28, 2012.
12. This text was shared across Facebook unsourced and circulated as a meme, with a cartoon UKBA policeman beside it. The text is Ian Dunt's (2013) UKBA spot checks are an abuse of power—but you can stop them, posted to politics.co.uk August 2. See http://www.politics.co.uk/comment-analysis/2013/08/02/comment-ukba-spot-checks-are-an-abuse-of-power-but-you-can-s. Last accessed June 28, 2016.
13. I am indebted here to Celia Lury's (1998, p. 3) discussion of the operation of prosthetic biography through portrait photographs and Mattia Fumanti's (2010) description of migrants' "virtuous citizenship."
14. Lazar, 2013.
15. Dorling, 2013.

# 5   At Our House

East London: bricks and mortar, stucco and pebbledash, all in gray and beige, made up the terraced streets. The lots were long and narrow and the houses pressed onto the footpath. What were once small front gardens were given over to waste and recycling bins. Because numerous houses were being renovated, skips and piles of waste materials dominated the streetscape. Mattresses, bits of furniture, the odd bit of porcelain bath set poked up above the skips' edges. There was some greenery—the occasional tree or flower—but not much. Cheaper housing built for postwar workers, in the main, these were modest family homes for the working class. Now only a few of the older generation remained, with their families living out in the leafy suburbs or beyond, in London's vast commuter belt. The new occupants were a mix of young professionals at the anxious front edge of gentrification and migrants. Landlords snapped up these properties, rented them as boarding houses for migrants, and saved up the money to renovate and resell to the young professionals. From the back gardens, it was an even more ramshackle view. Landlords, tenants, and homeowners all built extensions, usually to increase the number of bedrooms, and often without planning permission. Some of these extensions were unheated, unsafe, and slapdash. They had exposed wiring, a few leaky windows (if any), and roofing made of corrugated iron and, sometimes, plastic sheet—the infamous beds in sheds. These sheds were not only bedrooms: people cooked on hotplates and used their beds as living areas, too, though they usually had access to a toilet and shower in the main house.

Biag and Labanet rented on these streets after moving out of Conyap's house. They were lucky. They found their three-bedroom unextended property for £500 ($771) per month through church. It was a nondescript gray pebbledashed house located in the middle of Essex Street. A deceased estate, they took it on when the fabric of the house badly needed renovation and redecoration, before it could be sold or rented for a premium. The owner who inherited it was happy to have it occupied by reliable tenants until she could save up to renovate and sell. Biag did some of the most immediately necessary repairs. The heating was always dodgy—the radiators leaked—and the bathroom was moldy and cold. Over the five years they rented the house, they lived in one room and sublet the rest to an ebb and flow of fellow migrants. Their housemates were friends and sometimes kin—usually distant—from their Philippine villages of Gameng and Katangoan, and also fellow Kankanaey speakers they met at church and the community center, and even sometimes through Facebook. Usually they had six other people formally subletting bed space in the bedrooms. But transient visitors would sleep on the couches in the shared living room or on the bedroom floors for weeks at a time. Essex Street was so close—via public transportation—to work in West London and so cheap that the crowding was tolerable.

Labanet and Biag's house was another affective node where friendship and kin networks came together and reconfigured, cutting and conjugating each other in intimate ways. Known as "Essex Street," it was recognized as a way station and safe haven, welcoming new arrivals from the Philippines and migrants who had fallen on hard times in the United Kingdom. The house was where migrants spoke most freely about sensitive issues: money and power. They discussed the going wages for particular jobs and shared their strategies for finding, managing, and communicating with UK employers and immigration authorities. They spoke about money loaned, owed, and sent home as well as the yield from their various investments. They expressed their frustrations with their families and their intimate relationships.

Essex Street held the everyday rituals of caring for selves and friends through daily chores, sharing of food and drink, chatting, gossiping, and hanging out. Affect flowed through these daily interactions as housemates shared the space and their stories. Care in the house came to each resident or visitor through food, shared cooking, conversation, greetings, cleaning, accommodating their friends, and loans of clothing, funds, and goods. Labanet and Biag allocated no rotas of chores and virtually all of the food in the fridge was shared. When someone had some special ingredients or limited snacks, it was either reserved in the fridge in a plastic bag or box with a note or kept in people's rooms. Everyone pitched in, hosting friends for an evening sing-along or a movie night or having after church gatherings on Sundays. Somebody would gather together the money to get ingredients for a special meal of Filipino delicacies and cook. With the crowding, people socialized while flopped across beds or couches-cum-beds. Labanet described it: "This is how we spend our days off, you know? We just sit around, on our phones, texting, e-mailing, Skyping, and Facebook. Actually, we lie around. See, it's all beds! And we just eat. And eat some more. It relieves us of our heavy feelings, to taste the tastes of home. It's the day we're in the Philippines together." Within her friendship networks, this Sunday afternoon gathering moved from house to house each week. At these events, people garnered information from new arrivals and old friends, and arranged to move between houses.

The materiality of the house was vital to the global shatter zone. While the church and the community center were spaces, places, and institutions, they hosted public rituals and performances. Often empty, they waited to again be filled with ritual and affective flow. Migrants' houses, in contrast, channeled the affects of everyday livedness, expressing the intensity of migrants' connections to the Philippines through their material fullness. At Essex Street, networks were cut and conjugated through material objects—by the selection, storage, and sending of gifts. By accumulating gifts to be sent home in the house, migrants made it a sacred space of care.

## Mapping London

The house on Essex Street sat centrally in migrants' social maps of London. I learned about these maps from back-of-envelope directions I was given to after church socials drawn for me by respondents. I also put such maps together from Facebook check-ins, sites of Facebook photo albums, and conversations about what people had done on their days off. Migrants mapped others from their region into place in ways that merged London and the Philippines. People talked about Biag and Labanet's rented house on Essex Street as being "Essex" from the street name, but also as a "Katangoan house" or a place for *iGameng* (people from Gameng). Residents in these shared houses typically came from across several Philippine municipalities. People within the diasporic Kankanaey community recognized these houses as nodes within similar kinds of networks, roughly equivalent to extensions of municipalities. At a 2011 event for Bacayan, returning home to the Philippines, the community staged a series of performances. Performers were grouped by the names of both their municipalities and their London streets. So Oedma performed twice. She danced and sang as a member of *iKatangoan* (from Katangoan) and sang, again, as a resident of Essex Street. Like municipal identities, the house-share street name identities were based on friendship, distant kinship, or kinship via marriage, with propinquity *kailian* (fellow villager) ties added in to the mix. The titles of photograph albums participants posted on Facebook showed how people in the Philippines used the photographs of house groups to navigate London networks. House-share or flatmate groups defined by street names were easily grasped as corporate groups.

At Essex Street, Labanet and Adamey told me how they were fielding constant requests from the Philippines. Adamey, sounding indignant: "My niece Facebooked me, telling me about what we would give for the donation to our cousin's wedding. It's PHP 10,000 [$216] she says. But then she tells me, 'Don't worry, auntie! I have a job now; I'll be the one to pay it!' As if she is expecting me to pay. She is so gracious, offering to put her own money after so many months of asking me, asking me. I am laughing! It's incredible."

Labanet sighed. "Did you tell her you're pregnant? That you need to save for your confinement here and the baby?" Adamey shot back, "Not yet. I was just . . . it's incredible. That she thinks it would just be my obligation anyway and she's the one doing me a favor!"

Labanet spoke to me, "Always the same for me, too. Our relatives . . . You remember, I have my sister in Australia, one in Dubai, and a brother in Hong Kong. So they have other relatives abroad to ask . . . But they always ask us— London, Essex Street. As if they know that we are good for it—that we will help. The others might decline, but we will make ways and means." Adamey interjected, "I think we now have a reputation [laughs] with ALL our relatives—even the ones I don't already know! 'Essex Street'—they'll give. They're the solution to your problem! Everybody is asking money." I queried, "Is it that you get text messages, always asking, from people who are not really even that close kin now?" Labanet stated, "Not text messages any more. It's always Facebook. You can't say you had no load or the message got lost . . . Or anything . . . It's there, sitting in your inbox or your conversation, asking . . ." Adamey interrupted her: "Or they just wait online until you log on and then, 'bink,' there they are on chat! And if you don't pick up their chat, they e-mail you right then. It cannot be avoided. You cannot say that your computer isn't working because . . . there you are! Just like when they are coming to the door of your house in the Philippines, evenings, after work and before dinner, or after church on Sunday—instead, now it's Facebook. They see your pictures, taken at Essex Street. You're tagged. Then it's in the comments, the Essex Street group, here or wherever we have visited. And they are watching you! They comment to your new handbag or haircut, that it suits you. And you feel guilty to say 'no' when they ask." When Adamey said "There you are," she expressed an experience of being folded back in to the space of the Philippines through the house, not only by digital technology, but also by norms and practices for care.[1]

The Essex Street house drew together people who would have been in each other's middle-distance networks in the Philippines. Their proximity made the house a powerful affective node. Because housemates were not strangers, but rarely close (first degree) kin, there was scope to draw closer, or to come into conflict. Housemates formed what Filipinos call *barkada*—an emotionally supportive and close group of largely unrelated peers.[2] At Essex Street, Adamey addressed Labanet as aunt to indicate generation, but in English kinship she would be Adamey's second cousin once removed by marriage. Oedma was one of Biag's family's neighbors from Katangoan but not a relative. Kod-as was likewise a Katangoan neighbor. Domia L. was a former classmate of Labanet's younger sister from Gameng. Her husband, Eric, was a UK citizen. Biag and Labanet's first-degree kin in London included Labanet's sister-in-law, Basig, and Biag's cousin Daguon S. Both socialized with them regularly, but lived at other houses nearby.

Labanet, having worked in London for the longest time and knowing the landlord, managed the rent and distributed work through Essex Street. Oedma and Kod-as had arrived on student visas, then overstayed. Domia had a spousal visa. Labanet was their contact for part-time, cash-paid caregiving, cleaning, and housekeeping jobs. Essex Street was also the locus for Labanet's own plans and ambitions. In a mid-2011 conversation with Oedma, who was bemoaning the difficulties of her new job, Labanet offered some advice:

> Oedma: Will it always be like this? My employer, she is so . . . speaking so harsh . . . As if I am so small to her, the way she speaks to me. If I do some . . . thing she does not like, she is shouting. Shouting in front of the kids, her husband. She does not consider my feeling . . . Ok, she shouts a lot, with her husband and her kids, too. It's a house with shouting all the time. I am fed up . . .

> Labanet: Most British [people] just say how they feel, right away. They show you all their feeling. And it's for you to cope. You know? That's your work. They are not trying to shame you, just calling your attention to . . . whatever they see that they don't like. Just hold your patience and be gentle. Show them by your own . . . how to behave, how to care. Show you listen to them, that you care about the corrections she gives and they'll stop speaking so harsh . . . Like this: for me, she wanted me to put the glasses in the cabinet upside down, so no dust. I am busy with the kids when I take the things from the dishwasher, so I forgot. I get shouting. Ok, her house, I do it. And she's happy to see I listened. She shouts because her husband and kids don't listen. They don't listen because she shouts. If you're the one listening, you can easily adjust to each other . . . Show you care to listen. Isn't it? And give it time. Most times, that's what works.

> [To me] If you like, you can always resign. You find another employer, then you give your notice. And you can always just go home, too. There's no contract, now that you're private and also T&T. If you've got your travel document, you just fix your ticket and go to the airport.

Labanet then confided that she felt frustrated by one of her long-term part-time arrangements and wanted to change employers. She was considering going to Australia. Her sister, Ros-al N., was working there, also as a housekeeper/nanny. Ros-al, she thought, might be able to find her a good employer. I naively asked how Ros-al had acquired the right to work in Australia, and Labanet laughed. Ros-al has gone to Australia as a tourist and overstayed, just as Labanet had in London. There was no work visa or possibility of permanent residency on this new horizon either. Labanet was considering moving again, but would remain in the shatter zone, an irregular migrant doing cash-in-hand work. I asked why she wanted to switch countries for no apparent gain in security or income. She explained that immigration enforcement was comparatively lax in Australia. There, she would be less worried about the authorities detaining and deporting her. The United Kingdom was growing more precarious for irregular migrants.

Precarity was evident in the material conditions of Essex Street. The house was more than a boarding house but less than what Biag and Labanet would consider a home. Instead, it was a stopping point in their sojourn and a node in their networks, never quite a place of dwelling. The fabric of the house itself showed how everyone—and everything—inside it was either coming or going through the affective press of its clutter.

## Stuff to Ship Home

Essex Street was always cluttered. Large cardboard boxes dominated the living room, hallways and bedrooms. These were *balikbayan* boxes—3 × 2 × 2 cardboard boxes, three for £100 ($154) for door-to-door delivery in the Philippines.[3] The boxes were being packed or waiting for collection. They were picked up from the house by a London-based Kankanaey freight-forwarding company every three months. Most of the time the boxes seemed to be some way toward full, surrounded by toys and canned goods. The furniture was usually pushed back to the walls, draped with drying clothes purchased at the *karbut* (car boot sale). People followed narrow paths across floors crowded with piles of stuff to be packed to get from room to room. Care for distant others, made material, thus impinged on their everyday activities.

The clutter became a frequent point of tension among the housemates. One person's boxes packed and waiting for pickup would be obstructing someone else's packing or taking up the sleeping-and-suitcase space they'd promised to an out-of-town visitor. Someone would have taken up more than their fair share of packing space or used the space for too long. Migrants accused each other of caring less for their housemates than they did for their reputations and projects back in the Philippines and their employers in London. These inevitable ructions led to departures and arrivals. People moved through Essex Street so frequently, it was difficult to keep track. Labanet even had to decline offers of work in order to move boxes: "You know, I have a new housemate? After Domia left, we needed someone for the rent. And my three boxes are ready; they are somewhat blocking her door for the room, though . . . on the landing. She is only here one week, but she's annoyed. I can tell. She's the one climbing over, every time she's leaving the room. And she wants to use that space to pack her own. We are still looking for one more person to share that room. It's all beds inside. But she won't recommend it to another if I'm still not moving the boxes."

Sending goods was such a fundamental obligation for Kankanaey migrants that locating, selecting, and acquiring these goods formed a big part of their leisure activity in London. Acquiring stuff for their boxes, housemates scoured weekend car boot sales—*karbut*—together. Sometimes they included friends from other houses. They cleaned, packed, admired, and discussed their bargains after work. Making up these boxes diverted value, time, and space from their United Kingdom–based activities and relationships, crowding non-Filipino partners and visitors out. Eric, Domia's husband, told me he found the clutter oppressive; it was all laid out for an anticipated height of about five foot two, instead of his own five foot ten. Meanwhile, filling the boxes sustained the United Kingdom's sizeable informal economy.[4]

Putting together a box was a kind of competition. While migrants also sought out conventional retail sales and frequented charity shops, car boot items were recognized as being the best value purchases. Even better were donations of employers' discards: free, except for transport. The traffic in boxes thus sustained car boot sales, but also enabled migrants to be rewarded in kind by their employers. Having been given good things to send marked a good employee. Choosing goods and sending the boxes expressed migrants' continued care for those they'd left behind. Sending more things or spending more money indicated greater care. So migrants evaluated each other's abilities to source bargains, elicit gifts, and practice self-denial.[5] Migrants would deny themselves skills training, health care, haircuts, new clothes, and vacations to send boxes. The boxes reinforced migrants' inclinations to seek more work, longer hours, and more and better stuff to pay off their social debts and gain acknowledgment of their sacrifices from those at home, instead of thinking of the long term.

Father Alabag, considering Essex Street's box-strewn front room, noted that this applied even when migrants finally had their papers:

> What I observe here in the community is that people do not stay in education. They look for their Indefinite Leave [to Remain] but then they work sixty hours per week, because they need the money. But it is only short-term thinking. If they go to college, if they take a course, they could earn another £10,000 [$15,393] per year if they reclassify their position or apply for a higher position. They could invest in themselves to improve their chances. That won't happen like this . . . not by just working extra hours, extra hours at the same low rate and spending their money on these . . . gifts.
>
> Most of the caregivers here are nurses in the Philippines, or occupational therapists, or midwives. They have some training like that. But they need to recuperate their professions—to requalify here. So many are deskilled—their skills are not practiced and then lost. But they really have so much more they could contribute. If only they could find the time and the support to attend a course. For some, they can see. My *kailian* [village-mate], Malecdan, he went to Manchester, worked in a care home on a temporary work permit. Then he did two years of night school to get his Mental Health Nursing. Because he saw that would be the qualification that would be recognized to get him a better position. Now he has his residency [permit] and he has his family here in the UK. But he wasn't able to send like this [gestures to boxes] so much.

Father Alabag's observations seemed accurate. When Oedma's student visa elapsed at the end of the school year, she overstayed to continue working, part time, as a nanny/housekeeper. Looking for another part-time job to make up her hours, she went into debt to Labanet for her rent. Still, she continued to use what money she had to ship gifts home, even though she was accruing interest. She was only half-joking when she said, in July of that year, "I can't go home now, the *karbut* isn't finished!"

## Unpacking Boxes

In the Philippines, the stuff migrants send was not always wanted or valued. The contents of the boxes produced unintended outcomes, including economic stagnation. In Gameng and Katangoan, the goods sent by migrants undermined their own investments of remitted cash in local enterprises, like the *sari-sari* stores (corner shops) intended to support their left-behind families. Not many households wanted to buy a regular selection of dry goods at a local store when boxes of cheap but prestigious stuff arrived every three months from relatives abroad.

Households here benefitted from global bargain hunting. Migrants in different countries supporting the same household used Skype to compare prices and vary box contents from multiple recipient nations. Often migrants were able to purchase and ship goods from bulk barns or supermarket specials. Meanwhile local transportation costs and a minimum mark up of 15 percent to break even placed the owners of *sari-sari* stores at a disadvantage. Migrants also remitted money to purchase family vehicles. These cars meant more frequent trips to Baguio City or Manila to provision households with cheaper goods. In Gameng and Katongoan corner shops, stock with a long shelf life now often sat idle. The fresh food market appeared a bit more resilient. However, when their *sari-sari* stores failed, families were no longer partners in managing investments and became more dependent on remitted cash allowances. Thus migrants' strategy of sending gifts to keep families independent had the perverse effect of undermining local development.

People at home recognized how boxes expressed migrants' urge to share the material, sensual experiences of everyday life abroad, but they also saw this stuff as an attempt to exert financial control. Sending boxes made a gift or remembrance of what, if given as cash value, could have become an entitlement or allowance. Stuff sent in the boxes preempted more distant relatives' requests for cash and limited the ability of closer relatives to request allowances. Other than the really significant gifts of new purchases, much of the stuff in the boxes consisted of generic grocery items or used goods. Used goods tended to arrive as extras, clutter, or seconds, and more or less remain so. Inside a typical box, recipients typically found dry goods and household items for everyday family use: towels, soap, shampoo, toothpaste, coffee, tea, biscuits, and the like. Special gift and personal items were mixed in. The special items in boxes could be varied, though. From Essex Street, I saw migrants ship food for Domia's wedding reception, Biag's flat-screen TV (a cast-off from an employer), and an entire carpentry workshop he'd picked up at sequential *karbut* and then shipped back home. But the bulk of the goods in the boxes was not souvenirs of the global city of London or prestige goods, instead they were generic items.

The things sent in the boxes replaced what migrants would have bought for daily domestic life and their own chores back home. Carefully collected by migrants' frugal shopping over several months, these items might be a different brand, or better quality, or a slightly different taste, but they were fundamentally recognizable as staples and thus formed part of the general consumption in the receiving household. Some of the special items in the box, through their brand names or new tastes, did tell stories about global identities. However, much of the typical box was taken up with bulk items; towels and soap and tinned meat, used often and replaced regularly, sustain households every day. Sending the boxes was a kind of global grocery shopping through which migrants continued their roles in the households they'd left behind. By giving things to be used daily, migrants constituted, in a material way, their participation in making their Philippine houses into homes, while making their London houses storage depots. Other than these general household goods, there were two broad classes of gift items in the boxes.

### Gifts Seeking Recipients

The first kind of gift was given for generalized reciprocity: something to be distributed along other networks by the box's initial recipients. Such gifts were special items—*karbut* finds—that were still seeking a recipient when they were sent. Sometimes what was in a box was simply the best set of bargains to be found, an expression of *ayew*—the globalized general care preventing of waste.[6] Frugal migrants simply couldn't bear to pass these things up, even if they had no obvious recipient or purpose. They considered them potentially useful for extending networks back home. Biag, for instance, bought a distinctive, brightly colored leather motorcycle jacket at the *karbut*. It was too big for him. When he sent it home for his family to distribute, he didn't know who would be given it. He laughed, "The leather jacket is so nice. So I want to impress the person, but I don't know him . . . yet. I just don't know who he is . . . But he is going to be very happy with me that I care so much for him!"

Biag became a bit of a *karbut* legend. He sent six leather jackets, fittings for a galley kitchen in the house they were renovating for rental, and two small motorbikes, as well as his carpentry and handy-man tools. He developed a reputation for being astute at spotting bargains and making deals, including bargaining down, at the *karbut*. I asked him if it was worth his money and effort to send these things, if they would not be cheaper back home. Biag was offended:

> No, it's a gift. You just don't think about it that way. So what if it would be cheaper for someone to go to SM [a mall] in Baguio and buy it for himself? That's not a gift. It's shopping already. And, you know, he'll just put the money to something else and . . . no leather jacket. He'll deny himself. So I like to give, to share what I have here. So the feeling is there for him, when he is wearing

it, that someone abroad cares about him. And that other people can see that, you know?

Other items, like Biag's shop tools, were intended to provide for future life in the Philippines, just like cash remitted to savings and investments. Biag, again: "My family, they receive my boxes. They put it all in a room, at the back of our house. But it's overflowing. And everyone who visits can see what I'm sending. My belt sander. My circular saw. All these tools. Those are so expensive at home! So it's good that I have also got something nice to give others. That I'm sharing my leather jackets, you know? They won't be so jealous."

East London being part of the UK shatter zone meant that some *karbut* bargains were too good to be true. Migrants could not necessarily spot stolen goods! After the London riots in 2011, Labanet told me about Gely S., who had purchased two iPads at the *karbut* the following weekend. The vendors warned her that she should not turn them on, but ship them out of the country immediately in one of her boxes. However, she couldn't resist temptation. And she wasn't even buying them for anyone specific, only for her family to enjoy. She was tracked, through the activated iPad, and arrested for receiving stolen goods. The police discovered she had overstayed her tourist visa and handed her over to UKBA. They deported her. This story was circulated widely to warn bargain hunters about traceable electronic gadgets at the *karbut*. Biag was more sanguine about the shop tools he had acquired, noting that few circular saws would be as easy to find as an iPad.

## (Not So) Personal Gifts?

The second kind of gift consisted of specific items for particular individuals, materializing key relationships. Migrants most often bought conservative and personal gifts with recipients in mind. Packing her box at Essex Street, Oedma explained, "This T-shirt is for my nephew, and one for my brother-in-law. And these bed sheets are still very good—someone can use these. Only £2.50 [$3.84]." The specific gifts in Oedma's box were carefully laundered, good-quality used clothing items, but mixed in with the general household consumption items. Her family would separate out these items on advice she'd provide by email or Skype. I asked her if it would not be cheaper and more efficient to send cash. She, too, pointed out her intention of making a gift. Oedma explained that gifts fell outside the usual norms of economic calculation for household provisioning. She laughed at my question: "I like to do this. It's as if I am there, in my thinking when I'm packing my box. You know, I'll see these things being used on Facebook and when I go home. The rest, I'm sharing." The nature of the gift, instead of its market value, was the point of the exercise. Both Oedma and Biag also sent money. They knew they were going to go home soon, so they were preparing for their return.

When it came to sending cash, temporary migrant overstayers were the most regular remitters. They could not open UK bank accounts and were paid cash in hand. Depending on their work, they would send £200–£1500 ($307–$2,309) per month as allowances for family members, loan repayments to cover costs of migration, savings, and investments, usually in real property. But this flow of cash meant that the stuff they sent could go unappreciated, with recipients having the sense that the real riches of migration were being invested elsewhere. Back home, families were stuck with used goods!

During my fieldwork, Filipino-Canadian singer Mikey Bustos's video "Balikbayan Box" went viral across Facebook.[7] The video was shared and liked by Biag, Alabag, Labanet, and many more of my respondents because it satirized unappreciated gifts. The song—a spoof of Miley Cyrus's "Wrecking Ball"—has the narrator singing to his mother who works abroad:

> You called and told me "*Anak ko* [my child] we sent you *balikbayan* box."
> I jumped and screamed imagining having all those foreign products!
>
> I'll have Coffeemate, lotion, chocolate, shampoo even if I'm *kalbo* [bald],
> Second hand *damit* [clothing], I don't care I still want it,
> As long as there's brand name to show!
>
> I got my *balikbayan* box; I waited for it for two months. I bet it's full of awesome stuff. Some Colgate and new briefs, imported corn beef . . .
>
> I got my balikbayan box, so full of imported products, I know I will feel so *sosyal* [elite] *parang* foreigner *lang* [just like a foreigner] . . . Thanks to my Mommy, I'll have Nikes on my feet!
>
> I just want to say, to my dear Mommy, I will always love you.
> But I got my *balikbayan* box and everything inside it sucks . . .
> Some medicine for chicken pox, holy water in case of what? Conjuring?! You sent oil of oregano (*ano 'to?*) [what's that?], a winter coat in case it snows (it's so hot!), a pair of sexy panty hose, *ay naku* [oh, dear]. What is this? Melted ice cream! And this? Always with wings! Ay naku! [oh, dear] *Medyas* [socks] that stink![8]

Bustos's lyrics parody the expectations of those at home. He captures the moment of negative affect for the recipient when the gifts, despite the love, turn out to be awful. The box unpacked in the video contains used, smelly clothing; strange health cures; unwanted spiritual resources; and spoiled food. All are inappropriate to the way the narrator now sees himself. People hoped for gifts and goods of great value to give them social mobility and make them like a foreigner in easily recognized—brand name—ways in the Philippines. They wanted their relatives abroad to help them transcend their current social positions. But what was inside was not what they wanted, but merely stuff. The way the stuff "sucks" materializes, for recipients, their sense of affective disconnect with the sender. This stuff jars with their desires and with the local environment, and overshadows and even trivializes migrants' gifts of cash. The gift's recipients have not received is the social mobility they felt they were owed by migrants. Boxes of material goods are not enough to repay social debts.

If Mikey Bustos had received a box from a settled migrant, he might have been happier. Permanent residents and those migrants on longer-term work visas with the possibility of converting to residency did not remit cash as often. They typically no longer had to service debts at home and they usually had invested locally to provide a regular income for their Filipino family. They sent boxes of personal gifts, not domestic things, for birthdays, graduations, or the start of the school year. A box described by a baffled British husband had more "sharing the good life" special items, instead of grocery shopping and used clothing: "Spam, corned beef, Cadburys chocolate, Swiss chocolates, Gillette razors, Swiss watches, Triumph bra and panties, Armani Jeans, Gucci shoes, Prada eyewear, Dolce and Gabanna fragrance, Louis Vuitton bag, Gap baby clothes, boot fair clap trap, baseball caps, England football shirts, makeup sets, grooming tools, razors, more Cadbury's chocolate bars—lots of them—more colognes from Boots the Chemist. . . . All of it, packed in a huge cardboard box called a *balikbayan* box, sent twice yearly at a sending fee that's higher than the value of the contents, and then the *kapamilya* [family] still complain!"[9] The family still complains because these gifts of remembrance only give them a taste of the good life from the United Kingdom, not secure social mobility. They were seeking a donation of fungible value that would let them transform their lives in the same way they imagined the settled migrant had transformed his or hers. The prestige gifts suggested to them that migrants were not really sharing their luck, or their blessings, as they ought.

The stuff in the boxes carried an affective charge. The kinds and states of objects sent delimited specific parameters within relationships, cutting and conjugating them. For example, take Oedma's used T-shirts: her nephew and brother-in-law were remembered, but were not given regular allowances or prestige items, only nice, simple things to use. Biag's leather jackets, on the other hand, were gorgeous items bought for some as yet unidentified recipient, and said things about his potency and possible future closeness. These gifts appended their ontologies to the donor in a generalized exchange, making Biag look knowledgeable and potent in his selection of leather and motocross styles. Oedma's T-shirts gave the opposite message: "We're still poor, so don't expect more; this is the best I can do for you." Because images of both these classes of objects circulated on Facebook, the migrants who sent them followed the objects' eventual fates.

Meanwhile, back at Essex Street, the constantly cluttered rooms were also collecting transient people.

## Hosting Visitors

Visitors occupied living spaces in the Essex Street house from week to week and month to month. Sometimes they would visit for a few days, sleeping on the floor or on Adamey's bed when she had an overnight shift. When two people arrived at once, one might sleep on the couch in the living room, separated from the kitchen by a heavy curtain to provide some quiet and privacy. Visits were often draining and fraught for the residents, with visitors' sleeping arrangements and personal effects competing for space with the stuff in the house.

### An Overstaying Student

The first person to visit and vanish was an overstayer who had entered the United Kingdom on a student visa. Yakabow B. was Labanet's distant cousin from Gameng, and in her early twenties. She had come to London to study for a National Vocational Qualification Level 3 in social care. (Someone with an NVQ 3 qualification has the basic skills required for entry-level work in the formal economy as a care assistant in a nursing home or as a visiting careworker for an elderly or disabled client.) Yakabow's parents had sent her to stay with Labanet and Biag. Their plan was for Labanet to help her find an employer and keep an eye on her until she settled into earning in the United Kingdom. Labanet had only met her once or twice, when she was a child. Yakabow's family had expected her to work part time as an informal, cash-paid caregiver while meeting the requirements for her studies. They had heard this was possible from other families who had daughters working in London.

At first, Yakabow had her own room and attended church with Labanet, though her family belonged to an evangelical congregation at home. But Yakabow did not like her course. She insisted on being independent, not wanting Labanet's recommendations for work. She sought out her own employment instead and had several bad experiences with employers she found on Gumtree.com. These experiences included sexual harassment, unpaid overtime, and unpaid wages. Yakabow resented her situation. Her working hours contravened her student visa conditions and she was angry with her family for putting her in this position. After Yakabow quit her second caregiving job, she couldn't contribute to the rent or pay for her food. She was no longer able to send funds to her family. Instead, she became dependent on Labanet and Biag, which she also resented. She began to avoid them, failing to greet them when they returned to the house and not joining in communal meals. She ate leftovers on her own, after the rest of the housemates had finished. The housemates suspected Yakabow was no longer regularly attending some of the classes for her course. Adamey and Oedma were fed up and finally spoke to Labanet and Biag, noting that Yakabow wasn't contributing her share of the work or bills but was depending on Biag and

Labanet like a child, while shunning contact with them. She was taking advantage not only of them, but also of the other housemates, to whom she was not related. Yakabow's presence destabilized relations among all the housemates.

Labanet decided to move Yakabow to a shared room with Adamey and Oedma and to rent out her old room to Gayagay. Gayagay was another Gameng village-mate who had recently separated from his wife. He had part-time caring responsibilities for their seven-year-old son. Gayagay was out of work and living on his savings while looking for a new job. When Gayagay moved to Essex Street, he and Yakabow started an affair. Yakabow stopped attending church and the classes for her course altogether, and stopped seeking work. She began avoiding Labanet and Biag entirely, coming in and out of the house when they were at work and otherwise shutting herself away in her room or Gayagay's. Adamey and Oedma spoke to Labanet again, requesting that she put an end to the situation. At the same time, Yakabow's father in the Philippines phoned Labanet to discover why his daughter had stopped sending money. He had yet to pay off the debt he'd incurred to pay her plane ticket and visa fees. Labanet fielded calls from him and from Yakabow's aunt in Australia, trying to sort out what to do. Eventually the father called Gayagay directly and had a frank discussion in which Gayagay explained that he had no plans to marry Yakabow. Labanet and Biag, at their uncle's request, approached Gayagay to give voice to the family's disgust at the situation, highlighting the impact on them, as senior kin. Yakabow and Gayagay soon split up, moving out of the house at the same time, but to different destinations. Gayagay found paying work. Yakabow lived with another set of distant cousins as an unpaid household helper and babysitter—an arrangement brokered by her aunt in Australia—and refused to take Labanet's calls.

Labanet took responsibility for this rupture. Yakabow's father stood to lose his mortgaged land and had become ill. Labanet diverted money from her investment projects with Biag to cover her uncle's medical expenses as a way of apologizing for their failure to guide Yakabow appropriately. "As if we couldn't care for her, but we tried," said Labanet. Labanet had been humiliated in front of her family, her housemates, and her church because she couldn't influence Yakabow's behavior. Yakabow's father felt his extended family had let him down, but was most disappointed in his eldest daughter. She had failed in her filial obligation to put the needs of her family and siblings before her own pleasure and to make the most of the opportunities given her. His dependence on Labanet's financial help for his medical expenses meant that he had publicly forgiven Labanet and Biag for not being able to manage his daughter. All of this took about four months to transpire, though Yakabow lived in London for another two and a half years. She eventually posted pictures of her return celebration in Baguio City on Facebook. Labanet viewed them with incredulity. After the payment to Yakabow's father, his relationship with Labanet cooled. Labanet heard nothing further from him or from Yakabow.

*A Frustrated Careworker*

Shortly after Yakabow left, a former college classmate of Labanet's, Pul-ot, arrived to spend a series of long weekends in London, looking for employment. Pul-ot had migrated to the United Kingdom as a senior care assistant and had worked in two nursing homes. She had recently been granted Indefinite Leave to Remain and had a citizenship application in progress. She had no prospect of bringing her husband and two daughters to the United Kingdom; her salary was still too low to meet the new requirements for family reunification. Pul-ot wanted to move to London to be closer to her friends and other relatives in the United Kingdom. The northern city she lived in had few Filipinos and even fewer Kankanaey speakers. Pul-ot missed the easy camaraderie of eating familiar food and speaking dialect in her leisure time. She had grown despondent about the grind of long shifts, low wages, and the squeeze on her time to deal with patients. Pul-ot had even tried buying a car and picking up domiciliary care shifts to earn extra money, but found she earned little extra after she had covered her running expenses for the car. She found Labanet through Facebook and arranged to come to London to look for work as a live-out nanny. Weekends she slept on the couch, and she occupied Adamey's room during the week.

Pul-ot visited several times, attending two interviews with prospective employers. Oedma had located one potential employer. The other was someone Labanet had found through her own employers' networks. Both interviews were ultimately unsuccessful. Pul-ot, on the citizenship track, was looking for a salary she could live on after taxes and National Insurance were deducted. She wanted benefits, too: insurance cover while at work and one month of paid home leave each year, including the cost of her ticket back to the Philippines. Pul-ot's expectations didn't match what was on offer from possible employers. Labanet found herself embarrassed:

> My employer, she says the feedback from her friend is not good. As if Pul-ot is too hardheaded already. She expects a lot. It's a recession now and she wants to negotiate a really good package: a big salary and many benefits. They say she did not seem caring or interested in the children, really. Just wanted to know about the salary, the vacation. It's as if, maybe, her work in the care home and the hospital, well . . . it's made her too demanding. Employers now . . . there are many workers out there. And not everyone needs someone like Pul-ot who has papers, who can travel abroad, take the kids around easily. Lots of people just need someone in the house, long days, like that. I don't know what to say to her, though.

I asked, "So you believe your employer is giving you the real story about the interview?" Labanet pondered my question:

> Hmmm . . . I can't be sure, but, yes, I think there's some gap, some problem in communication. And, for me, I won't question my employer and what she

is saying is the comment of her friend. You cannot mend a gap of caring like that with making stories and explaining. It just is. Me, I need to go with my employer. That's my work. That's my skill here: caring. So if they say she is not good at caring, then they are not having the right feeling with her and they are right—about their feeling, anyway. Even if she is my classmate, before... Here, I can't be the one to question how she is with them. If they say she's like that, then that's the end. Maybe... I think the care home... the work is hard here. And it is that it teaches you not to care, to lose the orientation. So when she's thinking now about taking care of kids, it's all like a business.

I followed up: "So it's her? Or is it the case then that employers prefer workers without papers?" Labanet first paused to consider, and then continued:

Yes, I think employers want first that caring feeling coming from the work, then they will be concerned about your papers. So it's not really they "prefer." You know, first they just want a good person. It's just that they are really looking for someone who won't oblige them to follow a contract, demand their conditions all the time. You know, like your employer is coming home at the agreed time each night after work. Some employers just can't do that. Their employers don't let them!

For me, in my case, my part time now decided to hire me, even without papers. She said "I'll take a chance" because her old nanny, she came from Croatia. So she had her EU passport and could do any work here. One day, my employer was late coming back from her bank—and then some problem with the Tube—and the nanny met her at the bus stop. She—my employer—was supposed to be back at six o'clock and it was seven-thirty. But it could not be helped. Anyway, the nanny just handed her the baby and walked away. So there's my employer, standing there at the bus with the baby crying and the pushchair, in her business dress, and no nanny for the next day. And she's crying, too. She is really thinking she needs someone reliable, flexible, who can be patient when she has overtime or there's a problem with transport. Someone who has a good feeling for her. It's like that.

For Pul-ot, well, she's too much insisting on her own benefits already to cope up with that kind of job. You know, what if the employer's vacation isn't approved for one month, and Pul-ot can't adjust her plans? Can she find her own relief when she goes on her time off? Or is that going to be also for her employer?

Pul-ot eventually found a care assistant position with an NHS hospital in the north. This role was at a more senior level than her job in the nursing home and came with a bigger salary. She and Labanet remained close.

## A Nurse Who Failed Her English

Biag heard from a former high school classmate of his, Gon-ay L, after Pul-ot found her next job. In the usual way of such things, this classmate first got in touch with their flatmate, Oedma, through a cousin of hers who also attended their church. Oedma passed Gon-ay's query about possible work on to Biag to forward to Labanet. Gon-ay had trained as a nurse in the Philippines and had migrated to Saudi Arabia, where she'd worked in a large hospital. She'd been recruited from there by a staffing agency for a care assistant job with the NHS in Scotland. She'd worked in Scotland for five years, living in a dormitory and supporting her two children through high school and university in the Philippines. Finally she'd taken the examinations to have her nursing qualifications recognized. These exams were required for her NHS contract to be renewed and thus her temporary work visa to be converted to Indefinite Leave to Remain. Even though she met the income requirements at the time, she'd failed the English-language requirements. "As if my head was not so clear on that day," she explained. So Gon-ay had decided to leave nursing and overstay, traveling down to London to find other work. She, too, stayed in Adamey's bed while Adamey was working her weekday shifts, and slept on the couch, among the boxes and drying clothes, on weekends.

Gon-ay had been unable to meet the language requirement for overseas nurses to practice in the United Kingdom. The Nursing and Midwifery Council requires these nurses to be tested on reading, writing, listening, and speaking through the International English Language Testing System (IELTS). When Gon-ay took the test, all candidates needed a score of at least 7 in each subject.[10] She was one of a whole cohort of overseas-qualified nurses working in the United Kingdom as care assistants who were unable to attain this standard. There were many vacant positions for qualified nurses in the United Kingdom, but care nurses were not on the Shortage Occupation List at the time.[11] Because of the large number of potential candidates who had struggled with the examinations, the government had asked the Nursing and Midwifery Council to change the requirement to an average of 7 over all four exams. Gon-ay, who received a 6.5 in her listening and 7s in the other three exams, would have benefited had this change been in effect when she sat the test.

Unlike Pul-ot, Gon-ay knew she would be working without papers and asked Oedma and Labanet about the going rates for nannying. She eventually took a live-in job at £250 ($385) per week, food and lodging included. Since it was unlikely she could have found a nursing job in the Philippines on her return, she was making the best of a bad situation. Labanet reflected, "For me, it was much easier to find the employer for Gon-ay. She is not looking for so much, not so demanding. Just wanting to help her kids get stable in their lives, and save a bit to retire on. You know, to do some business when she goes home. So the employer, her impression is of a very caring, humble person. Very diligent. I had a good report back."

These visitors obliged all the housemates to express care, providing accommodation, food, utilities, space, loans of cash and clothes, recommendations to employers, and suggestions for interview strategies. Their presence not only brought everyone else's experience to bear on the visitors' problems, it also required rearranging the stuff in the house to make additional space for them.

The Essex Street house holds the things—space, utilities, possessions, gifts—through which migrants extend care, but failure of care is always a threat. As Labanet said of Yakabow, "If only we had known how immature she was, that she was lazy to work and that it was really her father's plan. Then we would not have found the bed space. It was too much for us to take on here. With our work, and family back home, there's no time to really give that kind of advice, that care.... To migrate, like this, you need someone who is independent already, who can manage their own things." In the main, though, having such a space of warmth and safety to offer sustained good feeling through Labanet and Biag's networks.

## Where Care is Made Material

The house on Essex Street often hosted the weekend after-party from the church and community center events. Its four walls gave migrants a space for more intimate bonding and exchange. These were long Sunday gatherings filled with clutter, food, texting, jokes, and gossip. Father Alabag observed:

> Here, at *our* house, we complain all the time. We are always talking with each other, about everything. Opening all our problems—work, family, immigration, money. We can talk. We never stop. But we do not always complain to our boss when the English people would. Because maybe something will change . . . or it is a bad day for them . . . Or . . . we just put up with it. So this attitude can make it very easy for us to be exploited by them. Even though they should know better. Because a Filipino will not always complain where an English would. But we are looking to them and thinking: you are not following the correct procedures, you are not complying to the regulations, you are not competent. They should know better. But we are not the ones to correct their mistakes. They will not accept advice from us. We express our feeling in the community. We support each other. Because we won't lose our jobs speaking to our *kailians* . . . And we gain some advice—what to do, where to find a new work, like that.

Newer arrivals sought advice from longer-term workers while housemates swapped gossip about other friends' struggles to find work, strategies to manage employers, and even how to best avoid Border Agency stop and search activities. Amidst all the stuff they had selected to ship home, migrants spoke about money and the benefits of different visa strategies most frankly.

Displays of things and discussions of money were connected to each other here. High-earning migrants usually had the best stuff for their boxes and gave the most valuable advice. Everyone tracked everyone else's purchases and earnings as best they could. Among the housemates, Adamey was most secure. Having arrived on a student visa to study social care, she was earning £500 ($770) per week, cash, for her caregiver role, with two nights and one and a half days off each week. Each month, she tried to send at least £800–£1,000 ($1,231–$1,539) back to the Philippines. This was reduced once she was on a post-study work permit, because she then had to pay taxes. Working a weekend relief shift on behalf of Adamey was a good way of topping up earnings for the other housemates, but the woman she cared for was difficult. Everyone had discussed the details and shared their strategies to manage Adamey's "patient." Labanet herself was earning £250 ($385) per week for her three-day part-time nanny/housekeeper role and £270 ($415) for her other part-time position. She topped this up with babysitting, cleaning, and weekly visits to help older employers with housework. Together the extra work gave her about £800 each month—some months more, others less. She was usually able to remit between £1,100 ($1,693) and £1,400 ($2,155) per month, attempting to limit her expenses—rent, food, utilities, phone, and travel to £600–£800 ($924–$1,231). For both of them, paying £100 ($154) per month for rent and utilities at Essex Street made this level of remittance possible. It also enabled Labanet to save for charity work and special projects, including gifts and loans to friends and family. Though Adamey was earning a higher wage, her benefits and tax ate into it, so it was Labanet who was able to remit more. Adamey considered her advantages: "Yes, it's true. I have papers. I can travel—leave the country, with my employer. I get to see Europe, to experience lots. But I just can't send as much as others. Maybe I'll stay here for ten years, if I can. But this isn't where I will be with my family. I still don't earn what I'd need to petition for them to come here. And look at where I'm living. I couldn't afford to rent a whole house like this for them. It's so expensive. It's only bearable to earn pounds but spend pesos." Labanet expanded on this:

> Really, the wages here are not so good, unless you are like me and not paying the NI and the tax. I get, now, about £35,000 [$53,876] per year, maybe. If I were paying taxes, with the proper papers, I would need to be earning nearly, what, £40,000-plus-plus [over $62,000] to have that afterwards? The employers, they can't afford to be paying £40,000 [$62,000] for their nanny. Not with the prices for everything else here . . . This is why it's us, they say, the migrants, who are making a problem here. We are not paying taxes, not getting benefits. The British workers here, they are stuck with benefits. If they earn low wages, the government gives them some more. But what I know, it's a mess. If they take just extra days of work, then no benefits. . . . So it's not worth it, for them, to work any extra. Me, I can be flexible. I've no family, no obligations. But this city is too hard if you would like to raise your family. It's only good to earn, send, and plan to go home someday.

By the end of 2012, both London's real estate boom and the authorities had caught up with Labanet and Biag. Their landlady decided to end the lease and start her renovations. She could now be charging £1,300–£1,500 ($2,076–$2,395) per month with a few small improvements to the house. The house broke up. Biag had to leave the shed in the back garden he'd eventually built to store their boxes and his *karbut* acquisitions. He and Labanet moved to a sublet room in a flat closer to Labanet's work in West London. The rent alone cost them £440 ($702) per month, more than four times what they'd paid for rent and utilities on Essex Street. But they did not tell their departing housemates that their asylum appeal had failed.

Biag and Labanet, now in the migration refusal pool, were hiding from Capita, the Home Office subcontractor. Capita was attempting to serve them notice to leave the United Kingdom. Changing addresses at this point was a convenient way for them to disappear from government records. The specifics of their case, their first rejection and appeal, were topics they didn't discuss in the house. They wanted to keep their exposure to gossip to a minimum, particularly to protect Labanet's loans in the United Kingdom and their investments in the Philippines. Leaving Essex Street, Labanet and Biag cut or attenuated some of their ties with the church congregation and Filipino NGO contacts. They stayed in touch with their housemates, of course, but no longer returned to East London to attend church or social events. They still continued to remit money and to ship stuff home from the *karbut*, though!

This chapter has revealed how the things migrants move from one place to another shape global affects and the shatter zone. Whether the things are objects migrants acquire, dispose of, or distribute, boxes or houses, these material objects extend relationships.[12] The affective charge of things gathered and sent from Essex Street translated migrants' feelings into gifts. But the practice of translating feelings inevitably created something new, whether this was new nuances of meaning, new kinds of exchange that reshaped family relationships, or different kinds of economic problems back in the Philippines.[13] Though the problems were new, they often arose from the age and status of the things sent, like Bustos' used socks. Many things were not shiny and new and evocative of global social mobility, which offended their recipients. Could something as banal a pair of second-hand socks create a rupture in relations that sees a migrant overstay her visa, a child refuse an online chat, or a tranche of money from London diverted to a heretofore unapproved use? An iPad that had been stolen in the riots would be likely have the opposite effect, however, shoring up relations through its materialization of technical potency and social mobility. Thus the stuff in Essex Street also showed how the demand for and flow of things shaped the global shatter zone in London. London's car boot sales staved off expulsion and supported the informal economy by sending objects with dodgy pasts out into global spaces beyond the governance of the state.

In the house, we saw how affect flowed through the materiality of shared lives and shared spaces: the housemates' daily routines of eating, talking, doing the housework, finding provisions, and exchanging gifts and goods. The affective charge expressed in this reciprocal care faltered with Yakabow. Pul-ot discovered that she was unable to effectively translate the care she received from Labanet, the housemates, and her extended family into an affective connection with her putative employers. Gon-ay, feeling she had failed herself, her profession, and her family, used the care in the house to seek a caring work environment. Care in the house also worked to sustain Labanet, Adamey, and Oedma, who continued to successfully hold down their own challenging work as caregivers or nanny/housekeepers in difficult circumstances. Their ability to assist friends while facing their own challenges attested to the potency of the flows of good feeling established among the housemates. When the house broke up, it was with a palpable sense of distress and loss, with the final Essex Street party becoming an album on Facebook, filled with shots of drunken jamming with a guitar, housemates sitting on the couch, some smiling, but many facing the camera with a lost look, eyes brimming with tears.

## Notes

1. Pertierra, 2002; McKay, 2012.
2. Kelly, 2000.
3. McKay, 2004 and 2007b. See also Szanton-Blanc, 1996.
4. Gregson, Crewe, and Longstaff, 1997.
5. Gregson and Crewe, 1997.
6. See also Gregson et al., 2013.
7. See http://vulcanpost.com/3490/rise-of-a-filipino-youtube-star-mikey-bustos-wrecking-ball-parody-a-hit-among-locals/, last accessed May 10, 2015.
8. Bustos, 2013. *Balikbayan Box* (*Pinoy Wrecking Ball Parody*). YouTube video with text lyrics, available on Mikey Bustos's channel, at: https://www.youtube.com/watch?v=WSMw7trHUcU, last accessed October 28, 2015.
9. Posted by ginapeterb to http://www.filipinouk.co.uk/forum/showthread.php/8894-Ungrateful-so-called-family-in-Philippines!!/page2, last accessed June 17, 2012.
10. Migration Advisory Committee, 2015.
11. Nurses were added to the Shortage Occupation List in October 2015.
12. Basu and Coleman, 2008.
13. Johnson and McKay, 2011.

# 6  Back Home

Looking out over Baguio City, as I stood beside Biag, I saw a landscape of aspiration. As the city both grew upward and spread out, most of the new residential construction was being built one floor at a time. Instead of roofs, the buildings had flat concrete top floors with concrete pillars and steel reinforcing rods jutting out of them. It was summer and the unfinished homes' roof/floors were decorated with laundry strung up on makeshift lines. I saw items shipped home from the *karbut* in London or similar gifts from receiving cities around the world. This landscape, too, was in the global shatter zone. The care being expressed through flows of affect from migrants abroad had changed culture, relationships, and landscapes back home.

Baguio is the gateway to the Philippine Cordillera. People from the surrounding agricultural and mining communities come to the city for education, medical treatment, shopping, and work. Baguio's population is made up of people from Cordillera indigenous groups—local Ibaloy and Kankanaey, Ifugao, Isneg, Gaddang, Kalanguya, and Kalinga—as well as Ilokano and Tagalog speakers from the lowlands. Mixed in are descendants of Chinese traders, Japanese carpenters, and American missionaries and administrators, plus transient Korean students studying English and a sprinkling of missionary groups. The city's residents are a global mix. On top of this mix, the local and regional governments exert weak state control and practice a great deal of flexibility in the ways they apply planning regulations. Biag spoke about the ways land tenure was constantly being challenged, unpacked, disputed, and, reportedly, changed in the records by under-the-table payments to workers in the city's registry office. Much of the city was subject to claims under ancestral domain provisions recognizing indigenous title, but this process, too, was amenable to "fixing." The city's landscape reflected this uncertainty, being rapidly denuded of trees and filled with concrete as people tried to produce material evidence that established their possessions and the boundaries of their lots.

Buying a lot and building a family home was the epitome of success for migrants who came from the remote municipalities such as Gameng and Katangoan. Like the foreign products and clothes in the *balikbayan* box that would make recipients *soysal*, (elite) moving to Baguio made statements about personal potency. Once, after a social event intended to strengthen *iGameng* (from Gameng) bonding in London, Labanet complained about one of her *kailians*,

"Manang Marlyn was making problems with our friends, the ones not from our barrio. She was drunk. And shouting, 'Don't you be the one to correct me! All the people from our barrio [name—a subdivision of Gameng] now here in London have their family homes transferred to Baguio!' That's not true . . . yet. But that's what everyone here is working for . . . It's our purpose—what they want, at home." Moving one's family and life to the city had become the currency of middle-class mobility. What made "back home" a distinct affective node was the way fundamental aspects of Kankanaey culture—debt, *inayan*, and kinship—had been reshaped by the inflation of expectations alongside land values in this process.

## Unstable Landscapes

Baguio was precarious in a physical sense. The influx of people who wanted to live in the city created traffic congestion and constant construction, like London—but when the rains came, its now-treeless hillsides were unstable. Every year the city struggled with landslides and flooding, being situated on a mountainside already subject to potent natural hazards. It is regularly in the track of powerful typhoons and two major, active seismic fault lines run through the city. All the love and care being poured into families as cash and plans from those abroad was choking Baguio. Their investment had transformed the old American hill station town into a more typical, concrete-bound Philippine conurbation. It was if the urban sprawl itself resisted governance, diverting the tools of regulation to produce additional rent for local officials. People like Biag, spending funds from abroad could—and were now expected to—pay a premium to flout the planning and building regulations in order to build. Aspiration and care thus combined to put people in harm's way.

On this landscape, returning home was different for settled as opposed to temporary UK migrants. Settled migrants found it difficult to accumulate the assets needed to fund a comfortable retirement in Britain. They imagined futures in the Philippines in which their kin would care for them and their savings and pension would go farther. They were nostalgic for the place they'd left, but also sought a more comfortable life. So instead of retiring to their village of origin, they envisioned a future in Baguio. They would be close enough to visit the village regularly, but also proximate to medical care, communications, banking, and other amenities. In contrast, irregular migrants, like Labanet and Biag, had organized their finances to set up future lives at home virtually from the moment they arrived in the United Kingdom. Remitting allowances, making gifts, and investing in property and businesses at home had been the only strategies available to them. The two groups were differentiated by the time they'd been away, the currency of their knowledge, expectations, and contacts, and their focus on investing through kin as opposed to broader, place-based networks. Both groups found managing finances, long-distance relationships, and investments a challenge. Irregular migrants developed a new set of strategies to build the security and relationships that enabled them to return, while UK citizens found instability.

This chapter contrasts Conyap's family based retirement plans with Biag and Labanet's largely friendship-based investment and business strategies to illustrate the irony of the global shatter zone. Law-abiding, settled-migrant Conyap had the more impractical plans. Labanet and Biag, though irregular, seemed to have been, from a Philippine vantage point, the cannier investors.

## Retirement Planning

Conyap's plans to return home revealed how care work constrains. Conyap had come to the United Kingdom as a nurse and now had citizenship, living in East London. She dreamed of retiring "back home." Like many older migrants in the United Kingdom, her plans necessitated that her junior relatives forgo their own opportunities to migrate—either abroad or even to Manila, the Tagalog-speaking national capital—in order to care for her investments. She had sent cash allowances and gifts to her relatives, but those relatives had largely directed the money toward increasing their social status through education or housing and, sometimes, through productive investments. They'd used this stream of value to become a different kind of person. Having done so, they were surprised that Conyap expected them to care for her in her old age. Why would she want to come back when life was clearly so much better abroad?

Her left-behind kin who became caretakers had frequently faced situations not suited to their skills or experience. Renovations, managing teams of workmen, renting equipment, complex planning approvals, and legal procedures—transfers of deed, court cases, and so forth—were all required when trying to safeguard her investments in real estate. Conyap's family had found her plans and investments a burden. Her projects had seemed underfunded or overly ambitious and their success, limited as it was, had relied on unrecompensed donations of time and labor. In Conyap's kinship networks, new ideas about migrant debt had transformed Filipino kinship and its norms of age hierarchy and deference. The younger generation of caretakers was, at best, ambivalent about at the return plans of elders abroad.

Rachel, Conyap's younger sister, explained her view of Conyap's retirement plans:

> It's good for her, there. Manang Conyap, she has her work, her house, her family in London. She was always the clever one, the valedictorian of her class. I'm proud, of course. Don't be mistaken in me. . . . She is very generous. She supported my kids in their studies. But she does not know how hard it is now for us here. I don't open it to her [discuss it] because she will think I'm asking again

more money. She should be the one to think about it, anyway . . . how it is, the way prices go up, like that, if she really cares for us . . .

This time, she is asking me to sell her house. It was our parents' house. It's good, wide grounds. She inherited it. And, since I had my house already with my husband, she put tenants. Ok, but I'm the one to manage it. She lets me keep some of the money from the rent, of course, but it's always as if there is some problem in the house I must fix. And I always need to explain how her money became smaller. So sometimes I just pay it from my own share. It's like that . . .

She's abroad. She's not here. She can't know that our brother-in-law is sick and needs a cleansing ritual. I text, but she has no load. So it's five days we wait. Then she forgets to send something for our aunt's death anniversary one year. It's ok, she's got her own concerns there. I asked her but then she has lost her phone. Then she needs to fix the tuition of her daughter. It's our sister who is in hospital and needs a scan, but Manang does not like to borrow there in London. It's too expensive to send Western Union, so she has to wait for the bank. We understand. We're the ones who will borrow here. She is helping out, yes, but we are the ones delivering it all.

Now she wants to sell and to subdivide the lot first. Ok. For her, it's a good idea. But I will be the one [to implement the plan]. I need a lawyer, I need to pay fees in the Municipal Office! There are many papers to fix. It's complicated! But she is not the one here. I will do it. Even if I am busy with my own business.

Then she wants to buy a condo. One of those new ones by Mansions!? It will be for her retirement. She wants me to put family in first, as tenants, so they will keep it for her until she comes back. So many fees!! For this one, for that one. And my two kids, they don't want to live in a condo by Mansions. They are living in [the outskirts of Baguio City], near work for my sons-in-law. And the condo will not be big enough for all a family. There's no garden, only small parking. So, who will I find?

And she is my *manang* [older sister], eight years older. She has shared her success to her *ading* [younger sibling, i.e., Rachel]. She's a good sister. But now, I'm working here in the University Office, my husband is working in the BIR [Bureau of Internal Revenue]. We like to retire, too. He has a heart disease already. He takes these tablets, they are expensive medicine. So if she will come here, back from the United Kingdom . . . Can we be the ones to help her? We'll be old ourselves. Is she preparing a fund for a caregiver? I don't like to ask. Yes, she gave money for my daughters' school, for their college, for their wedding. But they have their children now, and their work is somewhere far from Mansions, same for their school. Not far, maybe, when Conyap was here. But now, really, there's so much traffic. . . . You would be hard up to go there in two hours sometimes. So, who will stay with her? Is she thinking of that? Does she know how much things have changed here? It's not like before, when family could do everything. These days, it's not just possible anymore.

As migrants moved farther along the life course, such tensions escalated. Conyap held on to expectations of kin relations and reciprocity that dated to the time of her departure. She was often stubbornly unable to hear what her kin at home were saying. Rachel did not feel she was being ungrateful. For her, in her middle-class life in Baguio City, it was perfectly normal and expected to have help educating and marrying children from kin overseas. Remittances were how most middle-class people she knew made ends meet.[1] But the idea of an older sister, widowed and perhaps frail, coming home and expecting support loomed large on the horizon.

Conyap, in London, explained:

> When I retire, I'll go home. I've seen how older people are treated here in the UK. I have friends who've worked in care homes. It's terrible. They don't treat older people with respect. The children don't visit. The staff can be cruel. I don't want that . . . In the Philippines, we respect our elders. *Inayan*, if you do not. That's our culture. And I've helped out my sister and her family. I paid my nieces' school; I gave money for their weddings. I've fixed up my parents' house, put tenants, and my sister gets some money. When I sell, I can buy my retirement home. So then it will be my retirement and they will help me. That's how our culture cares for the old. And, after I die, if my children here in the UK don't want the condo for when they will visit—I don't think they'll like to move home permanently . . . The condo, it can go to my sister Rachel and her family. It will be a good investment for us. But when I call her, as if she's not interested. I used to call her up all the time, send boxes. But now, she says they don't need so much. And she's busy with many things . . . I worry the house isn't being fixed anymore, too . . . Sometimes . . . As if she is losing interest.

Conyap didn't have any particular family member in mind as a caregiver or companion for her retirement. In her imagined future some grateful relative would live with her in exchange for room and board in the new condo. Rachel saw instead a future in which Conyap would pay this person for their caregiving work. What Conyap envisioned as the repayment of a historic debt, from Rachel's family to her, Rachel envisioned the obverse. She thought Conyap had just about paid off the debt incurred to the family through her own migration. Rachel didn't calculate the debt her family owed to Conyap on the same basis Conyap did.

Debt remained a key theme in this affective node. Failures, distancing, shortages of money, delayed responses to messages—all this opened up the tentative agreements on the value of migrants' gifts and donations again, diminishing the importance of their contributions back home. This effect was retroactive and difficult to undo, except by donating even more value from abroad. So demands and expectations back home kept ratcheting upward, in a kind of inflationary spiral, often exceeding migrants' abilities to earn. Conyap had attempted to invest in things that would produce a dividend for their caretaker. But Conyap's gifts and house rental had not generated the "fruit" (*anak* or *bunga*, meaning interest) left-behind kin considered adequate to make up for their own sacrifices in caring for them. So the family felt Conyap still owed them something, and Conyap's retirement planning seemed destined to create further stress.

More broadly, the successful migrant retirees I met were of two kinds. One kind of retiree was a retirement migrant. Already a middle-class professional migrant who had invested in his or her children's education, they had children who had become successful, professional migrants overseas themselves. Settling abroad permanently, the children had been able to sponsor their still-young-enough parents to join them. The whole family had liquidated their assets in the Philippines to facilitate emigration. These migrant parents retired abroad and only returned to the Philippines to visit extended family. While Conyap and Rachel's family may have been middle-class, they were not in the upper fraction of this group and were unable to aspire to this kind of family reunification. In fact, they seemed to be somewhat downwardly mobile, in terms of children's education, marriage, and job outcomes.

The other successful kind of retiree was a female migrant from a working-class background who had invested in educating a daughter in a migration profession, usually nursing. When the mother retired from caring or domestic work abroad, she took over child care and household management duties for her daughter, who had replaced her, overseas, as the household's major breadwinner. Often the migrant daughter was initially a domestic worker, caregiver, maid, or nanny abroad. The family care chain saw the original migrant comparatively comfortably off, managing an extended family household in the Philippines. While this kind of household migration strategy might eventually have been transmuted into the emigration strategy, above, it would take another generation or so. In the interim, these retired migrants were well respected in their communities and often leaders in local churches or village associations.

"Back at home," care, *inayan*, and debt intersected in a different configuration from their pattern in the United Kingdom. Conyap described how the care she anticipated on her return was protected by *inayan*. For Conyap, *inayan* meant that those who did not sacrifice their own interests to repay their migrant sponsors should be punished by fate. The point at which the obligation to care ends and the notional social debt is paid off was the site of the cutting and conjugation of networks. Instead of incurring future obligations, those back home tended to understand migrants' gifts, repayments, remittances, redistributions, development assistance, charitable donations, and emergency aid as directed to discharging the social debt created by migrants' departures. Thus affective flow from home to London faltered when migrants tried to intensify these relationships. The timing of interactions and accessibility became crucial. Conyap's apparent affective withdrawal enabled Rachel to feel that Conyap owed her not only consideration in the future—the possibility of using or inheriting the condo—but also something more tangible now. She felt slighted when this did not arrive at her request. Rachel thought that Conyap's status—being permanent—should mean she had security in the United Kingdom.

On the home landscape, material things allowed family networks to play out these struggles over debt and its limits. Families neglected property to show their frustration with the quality of care they received in terms of returns on their time and earnings forgone. In the United Kingdom, however, a migrant who talked about her plans to retire at home was making a statement about status and potency, but the things sent home were largely abstract and invisible to her peers. Making such statements demonstrated how migrants had managed debts to their advantage. Retirement plans announced their networks at home were still intact and functioning: people still cared for them. In the Philippines, this care was found in things. And things on the ground in the Philippines were quite different to a migrant's imaginings. When families received boxes of second-hand junk, this stuff became a potent metaphor for migrants' care for them.

Successful investment back home required a delicate balancing act of migrants: they needed to nurture relations with key kin and limit donations to others. Yet the currency of affective flow or care underpinning these exchanges had no fixed value. Instead, the value of what a migrant sent and what time they offered was renegotiated. Migrants and their kin had to cut some networked ties while intensifying others. They understandably didn't always agree on which ties were which. Rachel, if not pushing for a rupture in the sisterly care under-pinning her relationship with Conyap, was moving toward an attenuation of previously close sibling ties. Cutting these networks was the way people opera-tionalized the apparently limitless concepts of family to produce social effects such as familial/household exchange and intimacy. In Baguio, we see the cutting of family ties from extended families in a system based on reciprocal exchange, trimming this down to nuclear families in a system based on intergenerational flows of resources.

Migration thus reshaped kinship, redefining familiar forms of Filipino fami-lies. Some strategies of investment back home pushed families toward a nuclear form. Others encouraged an extended form. While Conyap had directed her energies to first- and second-degree relatives already in Baguio City, she now may have to focus on second and third cousins or beyond from her Gameng networks to secure care for her old age. This struggle over the meanings of family hap-pened because Filipino distinctions between kinship and commerce have never had attached to them the modern, Euro-American ideals of fixity and contain-ment that neoliberal economics would expect. Recall how Filipino kin beyond the first or second degree will charge each other interest—albeit at lower rates? But can one now charge a sister-in-law interest? Migrating to London, a migrant may well have to, even if she would not in Baguio. In the Philippines, a choice like this feels like stopping the positive affective flow that sustains kinship.

For migrants who wished to retire back home, the extended-kin reciprocities of the Philippines must be extended and retained, not purified into the nuclear-family relations typical in the United Kingdom. But close kin in the Philippines likely did not want to share. How migrants planned for the goodwill, reciprocal care, and capital necessary for retirement required an awareness of how to play these two network strategies off each other to conserve scarce resources. The tensions within these relationships produced both centripetal and centrifugal effects, pushing some migrants to settle abroad at great personal cost. Other migrants chose, on the basis of incomplete information, to negotiate risky investments at home. Permanent settlement abroad, ironically, seemed to increase the risk to a migrant's plans at home, as well as the stress on their relationships.

## Building a Return Project

Biag and Labanet had never intended to become permanent residents in the United Kingdom. They had migrated so they could set themselves up in business back home. They managed their finances to anticipate returning home at a moment's notice, remitting cash to support their children and money to their Philippine bank accounts. As opposed to Conyap's hazy idea of her eventual retirement, they measured the time to their return(s) in months and years and calculated the amount of Philippine pesos they'd need to have in savings to execute their plans. From London, as soon as Labanet had steady work, they had borrowed money from a relative to buy a property on one of the public transportation routes into Baguio's colleges. This investment property was let out to students as a boarding house. Labanet asked her sister, Fely, and brother-in-law, Herbert, who were also caring for their two children, to manage the property. The rent from the students should have covered the food and travel allowances of Biag and Labanet's children. This arrangement, made in their first year in London, worked well for the next three years of their sojourn. They repaid this first loan within eighteen months but, three years on, the family plan faltered.

Biag and Labanet's investment strategy then became more complex. Their rental property needed expensive renovations that Herbert and Fely couldn't manage, having neither the time nor the necessary knowledge. Meanwhile Biag—engineer, carpenter, and handy man—never found steady work in London. He had only worked occasional cash-in-hand jobs. A few days' work in a good week had topped up Labanet's earnings, but he was her dependent. Thus, even before his application for asylum failed, Biag had been thinking about going home. He eventually withdrew his application. Instead of making a second appeal, he returned to Baguio, leaving Labanet earning in London, on her own. Once the first loan was paid in full and with this first property as collateral, Biag arranged a PHP 2 million ($44,984) low-interest loan from a rural bank in Katangoan. Biag combined this with money from their savings—about PHP

4 million ($90,765)—and what was left from Labanet's monthly remittance of £1,400 ($2,297) after household expenses. He used these funds to set himself up in business as a construction contractor, while renovating the boarding house to become their family home. In executing this plan, Biag and Labanet consciously limited their reliance on close family for support and investment.

Biag decided to rely on friendship networks, instead of close kin, to develop his contracting business. He put a lot of thought into his strategy, and approached two of his older cousins from Katangoan for advice, but choose not to go into partnership with them. Both offered to rent him equipment at a small discount, in return for a share (larger) of the proceeds from contracts won by his firm. He declined. Instead he found a former college classmate to be his business partner and a former college lecturer, now retired, who became his ongoing employee. He hired another classmate's brother as a driver. He decided not to bid on contracts in the Katangoan area because of his history with the NPA guerillas. Instead, he bid on government road projects near Labanet's home village of Gameng. Thus he chose Gameng-area people as his partners and employees, but ensured that none of them were his own relatives, and no closer than third or fourth cousins to Labanet.

To set up his business, Biag paid PHP 115,000 ($2,588) for a contractor's permit, P5000 ($112) for tax clearance, and P1500 ($34) and P7,000 ($158) for business permits covering his intended area of operation. He bought equipment: a converted dump truck, PHP 250,000 ($5,630); a cement mixer, PHP 1,000,000 ($22,505); a hollow-block maker for PHP 60,000 ($1,350); and a truck, PHP 100,000 ($2,250). So before he even submitted his first bid, Biag had expended over PHP 1,600,000 ($36,010) on permits and equipment, as well as another PHP 100,000 ($2,250) on travel and communications. At the same time, he had spent PHP 400,000 ($9,000) on excavating the area underneath the house. He was running the household using money remitted each month by Labanet. At this point the additional challenges of negotiating the shatter zone came into play.

For Biag—or any contractor—to bid for a contract worth more than PHP 20 million ($450,000), there was a formal requirement to show he had PHP 5 million ($112,483) in the bank. An even more important informal requirement was for bidders to pay a 10 percent kickback. Out of this, 7 percent went to the politician controlling the budget for the roadworks projects and 3 percent went to the bidding committee. This was when the Facebook belonging and netizenship work Labanet had done from London yielded results.

Labanet had donated to the campaign funds of her uncle and campaigned for him on Facebook, over a year earlier, before they left Essex Street. Using her name and Biag's, she had given him £2,000 ($3,281) for election expenses, making them major campaign donors. Now he was incumbent in the position and Biag had connections they could use. The uncle called in a few debts of his own to bring suasion on a more senior politician involved in the approval of bids. At the same time, Labanet scrambled to remit enough funds to fill in the hole in their bank account. She explained the situation to her employer and got a £1,000 ($1,620) advance on her wages. The bid process required that a bank statement be submitted before the proposed contract had funds approved. While Biag's bank statement was a bit short of the full five million amount at submission, it was approved anyway, thanks to the suasion exerted by their politician patron. One installment of the kickback had to be paid in advance, to ensure that the contract, if approved, would go to Biag's bid. The kickback system meant that people from outside the Kankanaey-speaking area with competing bids would be unable to outbid local contractors. Biag paid an initial PHP 1,350,000 ($30,065) to a fixer working for the politician and they waited. And waited. Biag was finally awarded a PHP 21,500,000 ($483,588) contract for road construction. His balance of PHP 800,000 ($17,994) for the kickback came due immediately on release of the funds. He had established himself as a local contractor.

Now all Biag had to do was build the road, to specifications, with a substantial cut to his budget, and support the household in the interim! Without Labanet in London, laying the political and financial groundwork of sharing, caring relationships, this apparent overnight success would not have been possible. Nor would the road.

Biag's travels back and forth from Baguio City to the Gameng area to organize his team and his bid demonstrated how affective flows had shaped his success. Firstly, the small gifts that Biag and Labanet had sent to sustain their friendship networks, the charitable fund-raising, and efforts to build ties with former classmates on Facebook had produced results. Almost by chance, Biag's classmate had dropped in to visit Biag's family in Katangoan on a day trip the previous year. Biag's family had given him one of the largest leather jackets as a remembrance from Biag, a kind of ongoing *barkada* hug. So this classmate was well disposed to a shared business venture. Secondly, Biag, by keeping his plans out of Katangoan networks and thus under the radar, was able to circumvent his senior kin in their attempts to extract rent from his potential bid. His trusted friends, not his family, formed the safety net for his return and investment program and would benefit most from it.

## Coping with Inflation

Inflation was the other challenge Biag—and Labanet, at a distance—had to confront: inflation of both prices and expectations. Biag had been away in the United Kingdom for almost six years. He found it difficult to accept how much prices for basic goods, materials, and vehicles had increased. "As if Baguio is now the same as London," he explained, as we traveled through the city in his truck. "Nobody can afford to live in the center except the *buayas* [corrupt politicians]. It's as if it's still the UK. Almost everyone is struggling with broken-down houses, leaking roofs, and not knowing about where they will next find their food." Over the phone and via Skype, he and Labanet kept revising their budget. Back in London, Labanet was concerned and felt pressured: "I know he is a responsible man, a good father. A caring husband. But the expenses! It's such a big project. And the expenses grow and grow. But I've observed him; he does not scatter money. That must really be how it is, now. I trust him. But, for me, I'm in debt with my employer and looking for a part-time again for my day off. I need to send at least £1,400 [$2,155] or more. As if I can't sustain it. I want to be sure it's all there, complete. That I see where our money has gone."

One of the things Labanet asked me for during my visit to the Philippines was a series of emailed portraits of Biag's heavy equipment. Biag himself had arranged for the vehicles to be blessed. It was *inayan* for the trucks to be put into service without this ritual, but he didn't want it documented. When I took these shots, he asked me to send instructions—from him—for Labanet to refrain from posting these photos to Facebook. Biag didn't want people in her wider networks to know—yet—that he was going into contracting. "Then we'll have more *gastos* [expenses] and less money coming in, just because they'll be asking us for something . . . Asking her! To them, it looks like we have a lot saved, a lot stored. And Labanet is still in London. They don't know her situation. They don't need to know." Labanet's ongoing employment was bankrolling the business. Her remittances covered the renovation of their house, loan repayments, the kids' school fees, Biag's truck and travel, and the costs of food.

Though Biag was investing with friends, he did not neglect his family. He and their two children traveled to Gameng and Katangoan regularly to set up the contracting enterprise and to visit. Biag maintained an ongoing involvement in his family's ritual obligations within their *ili* (village), provided labor for weddings and house construction, offered sacrifices for thanksgiving rituals, and attended wakes for the dead. *Inayan* applied; he couldn't do otherwise.

Biag expressed traditional family care not only in these ways but also by organizing long-distance provisioning. Biag's parents' cupboards were stocked with a combination of dry goods from the United Kingdom and Canada. Pride of place on top of the refrigerator was given to a display of everyday comestibles—juice crystals, peanut butter spread, coffee whitener—labeled in French and English. Biag, Labanet in London, and his sister in Winnipeg, Canada, coordinated their shopping for their parents' box over Skype, comparing discount offers and ensuring that a box arrived in Katangoan every six to eight weeks. New products and tastes were on hand, even if people from Katangoan weren't sure they needed them or wanted the global brands, with their chemical preservatives and garish colors. Gesturing to a packet of Jell-O pudding, Biag's father told me, "That? We reserve it for the kids." They had a sense that the real value Biag and Labanet had created was elsewhere, and their gifts only exotic consumer goods, part of the village's closer integration into global consumer culture, but not the real investment.

Biag's home of Katangoan had changed a great deal since Biag's childhood, in large part because of an influx of money remitted from *iKatangoan* migrants overseas. Discussing the village building boom, and the cutting of trees and paving of access roads it required, Biag's family neighbor, Lucy, remarked on a Facebook group, "It's everywhere, like a ubiquitous plague. The sound of the chainsaw resonates almost daily from every corner of this valley. Structures are being built incessantly at a pace that policies regarding that seem to lag behind or are just completely forgotten as time goes by. Sadly, people just keep mum about this and go on with their lives, stuck in a mantra of that's the way it is and it's their own property anyway. Then one day, we might just wake up in a completely different place, it's because we paved paradise and put up a concrete jungle." In what seemed to be a competition to have an improved house and parking for several new vehicles, it was evident from the size of the buildings and their cost that many families in Katangoan were ahead of Biag's own natal household. Biag was someone from the small end of town, trying to catch up. Even with his contracting business, he and Labanet still felt they had somehow fallen behind.

Looking at Katangoan for opportunities, Biag saw he had not much choice other than to invest elsewhere. Little work would be available to him other than poorly paid, casual day labor on construction projects or perhaps guiding tourists. None of this work would use his engineering degree or provide wages sufficient to support a family. Biag did not stand to inherit any of his family's farmland. Setting himself up as farmer or worker were options he had written off long ago and were not worth revisiting now, even with capital saved from Labanet's earnings in London. On Katangoan's edges, Biag could see these lessons made material in much larger projects—ones with a municipal or national scope—that had many times more than his own savings invested in them.

Katangoan elites were involved in a large land dispute. They had contested the title over a coveted development site outside the village and the matter had gone to court. As Biag's neighbors tutted about the shame of an interfamilial conflict, one party hung a banner defending their claim. They argued that they were in the right on the basis of past care for the land, because care substantiated occupancy and ownership. The last line of this banner read, "[Name] believes in tradition and the saying '*inayan* or *lawa*.' *Igad di adi kaila*. [May karmic justice prevail]." *Inayan* was being put to work to defend the interests of tradition here, too.

Ordinary people in Katangoan felt increasingly alienated by the machinations between parties in such conflicts, and shut out from access to jobs and resources. Biag had been able to migrate, but many of his neighbors and classmates had not. Their mounting frustrations had supported the New People's

Army (NPA) communist guerillas. The NPA had, in previous years, set up training camps much further outside Katangoan town proper. The NPA collected so-
called progressive taxes from local businesses and wealthy elites. Moving NPA
camps and roving cadres had not exactly been welcomed by Katangoan's wealthier
residents. Instead, the NPA had been tolerated. The guerillas had been a resource
to be mobilized to defend more local interests against national-level attempts to
grab resources or shut local contractors and laborers out of prime projects. While
Biag was planning his return from the United Kingdom to Baguio, the army had
raided another one of these camps and several people had again died in the ensuing gun battle. This time, unlike Biag's own encounter with such a camp a decade
earlier, the blame apportioned by the NPA was more generalized. The guerillas
decided to target not one individual for informing but elements within the wider
community in the Katangoan area—those who desired law and order. Several
months later, in a retaliatory strike, the NPA ambushed a police training exercise.
Four Katangoan police cadets were caught in the ambush and, while none were
killed, they saw one of their officer-instructors die. This ambush marked a rupture between the global Katangoan community and the NPA.

Katangoan Facebook pages erupted with outrage. Mothers working overseas
to fund the education and training of the police trainees who had been attacked
posted scathing comments about the intracommunal tensions. The ambush had
seen mostly Kankanaey rebels attack mostly Kankanaey police trainees. On a
widely shared news story about the ambush, comments revealed that community
members now overseas saw such retaliation as *inayan*.

Oedma M wrote:

> They were young, just starting to enjoy professional life and enjoy the fruit of
> their sweat and labor not to mention the moral and financial support from
> parents. They were unarmed and harmless. They are everybody's children. We
> salute the victims, you are the real heroes. *Ken dakayo ay nin ambush, gawis
> nan activista no ilaban yo nan prinsipyo yo* in a fair and square manner [But
> about the ambush, it's good if the activists explain their principles in a fair and
> square manner], but what you did today shows you are losers ever. Unneces-
> sary killing is not the solution.

To this, Labanet replied, "Come to think of it, most if not all are Cordillerans.
Just wondering if they are not relatives by affinity or consanguinity, neighbors
or acquaintances???" In other words, she pointed out the obvious fact that the
attackers and the cadets/police were in the same networks.

Both comments received many likes. Finally, some three months later, one
of the United Kingdom-based activist allies of the NPA, a member of Filipino
NGO-1, posting from London, replied, "One of the most difficult situations is
when we are told stories of people or families about their bad experiences as a
result of the processes of change (revolution) which were inevitable and however

we explain why how etc., the more we feel apart. What is challenging is how to create unity. . . . So that we all understand that 'change' is the only option." This comment was not dignified with a response or a like. "Change" was something Biag and Labanet wanted to define on their own terms, not take direction on from activists.

These comments showed migrants in the United Kingdom the extent to which their remittances ensured family livelihoods were protected from the fallout of such conflicts. Whether it was the NPA or government line agencies, authority could not be relied on to care for the everyday villager. Government departments were untrustworthy and their officials were, in their experience, out to extract maximum value from the little guy. Kod-as L. posted about her experiences working in the Philippines with the Philippine tax authorities:

> BIR [Philippine Bureau of Internal Revenue] harassed and intimidated small business/farmers for their *lagay* [kickbacks] and ignored the rich and *buayas* [crocodiles, a derogatory term for politicians] my experience with BIR as an accountant and doing small business is stressing and depressing. Am away now [in the United Kingdom] and see how good governments spend tax, and educate people on their responsibility to pay tax, how to see where their tax is going. It is very encouraging to pay tax. Where I am now, people pay massive tax on everything but never complain because they see where the government puts their tax.

Kod-as L. was typical in the origins of her cynicism about the Philippine state. Most of my migrant respondents in London still identified as middle-class Filipino professionals, whatever their work or status in London. Kod-as had worked as an accountant, Father Alabag was a priest, Labanet, a teacher, Biag, an engineer. Many more of my respondents were clerks, nurses, administrators, accountants, and so forth before they had left the Philippines. They were deeply suspicious of government and the transparency of its processes back home. They felt that their only chance for security was to earn enough in the United Kingdom to invest in projects so large that they could, themselves, join the governing elite. There was no other way of attaining a sustainable middle-class lifestyle but operating strategically across the global shatter zone.

Labanet, discussing Kod-as's comment, explained, "For us, I really have to stay here, working. You know, until Biag will get his business stable back home. He has to fix his tax. He has to fix his employees—their wages. We will need maybe another five to seven million plus in the bank, just to keep going from this contract to the next. There's no way . . . back home. It's got to be me, earning for it here. And for the school fees, for the kids. Otherwise, our plans will become . . . nothing." At the same time this comment was made, a meme circulated on Facebook stating, "Is going abroad the only way," showing the national flag painted across the face of a young girl. It struck me that this "way" people sought was not an escape from poverty, per se, but intended to assure middle-class security. They wanted their electricity, running water, childhood health care, decent education, cars, and careers to be sustained and passed on to their children. Their biggest fear was slipping back into the poverty that had limited the lives of their parents and grandparents, hence their migration. It is was this emergent global middle class who really paid the kickbacks for government workers and governing elites alike. Migrants, it seemed, were also obliged to settle a foundational debt to government workers. To thrive in this shatter zone space, migrants needed to play the corruption game through their long-distance and lateral connections.

Biag had returned to find that inflation had not only increased the prices of goods and services, but had also raised the stakes for precarious livelihoods. He could only press forward, making huge bets with their savings and Labanet's future earnings. They both hoped he would not be trapped between the corrupt petty officials, the guerillas, and the established rich as he tried to build a future for them. Biag had thus focused on building lateral networks to expand the number of sites in which they had invested care and money, giving them further potential to negotiate business and support.

## Affect and Global Precarity

This chapter has shown how, although the shatter zone came into being as a space on the geographical margins of the state where people took refuge from, avoided, and repressed state-making projects, this space has become a global one. On the Cordillera and in the Kankanaey ancestral domain, the presence of national government has remained remote, deferred, and largely ineffectual. Informal economies of exchange, corruption, and criminality have prevailed, exerting their own governmentality to incorporate those nominally identified as state agents into competing networks. The Philippine state has been captured or repressed by these networks through bribery and corruption.[2] What sustains people within this shatter zone is not effective governance but the migrants' networks connecting them to similar zones elsewhere.

It is care that joins the shatter zone on the Philippine Cordillera Central to the shatter zone inhabited by migrants in East London. This care is made material in the built and human landscape. We have seen how roads and policemen depend on the archipelago of care, sustained by global flows of money and positive affect. Roads were being paved not because of the wise investment of properly raised local taxes, but through the leverage of migrants like Labanet, mediated by Facebook belonging, netizenship, and her own prosthetic citizenship in the United Kingdom. These roads were not so much public works as they were the materialized care of migrants abroad. Likewise, recruiting for the police force relied on migrants' remitted investments in education, with routes to college education and advanced training largely out of reach of young people whose families did not receive remittances. At the top of the government hierarchy, elected officials were both taking a cut from these investments of care and manipulating what taxes were collected in order to reward supporters in their own networks—people who cared for them and vice versa. Knowing all this, Biag and Labanet have positioned themselves strategically in networks, while Conyap's plans are more individual and vulnerable.

The communist insurgency, meanwhile, remains at a critical but unpredictable remove. It is still fighting a conflict in which its cadres envision themselves to be mobilizing peasants. Doing so, they fail to raise the class consciousness of West London nannies like Labanet who are navigating those same corrupt relations with a hard-nosed pragmatism and foreign currency earnings. On this landscape, what looks like development brought about by an increasingly effective state in action—paving roads, improving law and order—is enabled, subsidized, and beholden to the entrepreneurial and affective nous of its absent citizens. Development here works through flows of affect in a space beneath or beyond the state and outside the law.

The Cordillera landscape enhances this precarity because it is a shatter zone in another sense. Its newly-built environment is vulnerable, too—particularly government buildings and projects. Vernacular building forms here were always constructed low to the ground, and made of local wood, bamboo, and cogon grass, the better to withstand regular typhoons, earthquakes, and landslides. New asphalt roads, large concrete office buildings and markets, even four- or five-story concrete residential houses are now the desired norm. Yet, as we saw, these buildings and grounds were neglected when relationships with kin abroad became strained. When kin left behind didn't feel cared-for or close, they didn't rent out, maintain, repair, or care for migrants' real property. But this minor risk only exacerbated the much less visible but nonetheless inevitable threat of landslides and seismic activity.

In 2009, Typhoon Parma, a slow-moving tropical storm, dumped weeks of rain on the Cordillera's already saturated soils. Many of the recently cleared slopes gave way. Previous generations had avoided building on these slopes because they recognized their vulnerability, but the combination of population pressure, increasing income and aspiration, and the ability to circumvent planning restrictions with bribes proved lethal. Most people who were killed by the typhoon-induced landslides died of suffocation after encavement. Meanwhile, Baguio has not had a major earthquake since the city was devastated by a 7.1 earthquake in 1990, but such an event is inevitable. The upthrust karst landscape of Baguio's new suburbs features sinkholes likely to liquefy in a quake, destroying newly built homes and killing their residents. Both Biag's new home and Conyap's condo lie close to one of the city's two active fault lines. Their houses and families are unlikely to be spared.

Baguio is a remittance landscape—a spatial organization largely determined by the priorities of investors elsewhere and the actions of their local agents, trying to generate profit. Real property—these houses and their subdivisions—has replaced migrants' original site of investment in fields and agricultural crops. Agriculture initially served as a make-work project for their left-behind kin and provided an income stream. Agricultural investments were intended to sustain families, relax the pressure on migrants for continual allowances, and enable returns and retirements, but were largely unsuccessful. So people turned to the cities. Twenty years later, Katangoan and Gameng migrants' families are now part of the emerging urban middle class. Having learned that agriculture does not offer either the prestige or the returns on investment they seek, migrants and their families are focused on acquiring urban real estate. Migrants still expect kin to manage these properties and maintain them so their value does not depreciate, but they know most of the value is in the land, despite the precarity.

One way of looking at migrants' newly built houses would be as investments of affect made by migrants in the long-distance field between abroad and back home.[3] Migrants' decisions to buy property at home are clearly shaped not only by their understanding of real estate markets and capitalism, but by state policies. They are even more strongly shaped by the ways they come to understand their lives. For my respondents in East London, the key concepts are care—a flow of positive feeling shown, shared, and made material—and *inayan*. Migrants' caring about, practices of showing care, and efforts to care for others were translated, on the ground, into material things, communications, and mobility carrying affective charges. In this field of affective flows, self-care and care for others intersected. So, if we read this urban landscape as part of the global shatter zone, we see what affective flows sustain and work against.

The global shatter zone extends onto this landscape, and *inayan* here means migrants are depending on fate, on luck, on debt, and on karmic justice to protect their investments, their persons, and those of their kin from future landslides and earthquakes. As elsewhere in the world, the costs of consumer goods such as televisions and cars in the Philippines has fallen relative to earnings and remittances. At the same time, higher education, health care, and real estate have been slipping out of reach for this emerging middle class. Thus in Baguio and the Cordillera region, people increasingly pay for college, health care, and improved housing with overseas, not in-country, earnings. Where the middle class is largely dependent on remittances for its livelihood as well as its social mobility, people seek other avenues to earn (illicit) money, but these depend on and expand the culture of *lagay* (kickbacks) and corruption in government. The irony of Baguio's remittance suburbs is that materializing this care on the vulnerable landscape puts the cared-for, their investments, and migrants' investment strategies at risk. When I asked Biag about this, he shrugged and said, "What can you do but this? There's nothing for us in Katangoan or Gameng. And the whole of Baguio is like this, now. I just try not to think of it and pray we will not be the ones affected. It's what our kids want. They don't like to be farmers in the barrios. Just like us. It wasn't the life we wanted, either. Why should the kids go back to the life of their grandfathers?"

With migrants' remittances being invested in urban property, the aggregated effect has been to produce a real estate bubble in the Philippines' major cities.[4] After the financial crisis in 2007 and 2008, global flows of investments were redirected from Western economies into emerging markets like the Philippines. Ultra-low interest rates enabled the government to invest in infrastructure—like the road Biag was paving—and this property bubble. The flow of capital into the country, after 2008 and 2009, saw the Philippine peso rise 25 percent against the US dollar. So Conyap's family was quite correct: she did not grasp how much less her gifts buy when the money is spent on imported goods and fuel for transportation or cooking. At the same time, the Philippine stock market tripled in value, with the Philippine economy being one of the world's fastest growing in 2013. Consumer spending shot up, personal savings dropped, and loans for cars expanded by 50 percent. All those new-car blessings in Katangoan posted to Facebook? They likely represented ongoing debts investors intended to service with remittances instead of outright purchases.

The cheap credit and asset bubble has inflated the value of the rest of the nation's economic activity. While earnings from call centers and remittances have increased, they are only 10.4 percent and 4.4 percent of the country's economy, respectively. Much money has been invested in new condominiums in the middle of the market, like the one Conyap wished to buy as her retirement home. Migrants working abroad have been able to purchase these units with a 20 percent deposit and no proof of income. Overseas Filipino buyers have been the target market for 80 percent of new residential construction. The risk has always been that migrants' short-term contracts abroad may not be renewed. Or they may become overstayers, as some of my respondents in London had become, and be vulnerable to a sudden loss of employment and repatriation. This instability aside, when the global economy next falters and remittances decrease, the asset bubble will likely burst, creating a new kind of crisis alongside, or even along with, the impacts of typhoons and earthquakes.

How did this shatter zone space feel to live in? My Kankanaey friends didn't talk about emotions much in the sense of using categorical terms. Instead, they spoke more frequently of embodied experiences of affect—of being made to feel big or small as a person, or someone feeling heavy or light inside himself or herself in response to an interpersonal encounter or experience. My attempts to get them to translate English emotion discourse into their Filipino dialects had thus met with confusion. In London, when I was doing the "our house" interviews at Essex Street, I had offered, "So you felt humiliated when your employer . . . ," and Biag and his friends had given replies along the lines of, "Ummm . . . yes . . . , I felt small inside; my feeling was heavy feeling." The "umm . . . yes" had meant nothing much more than "I hear what you are saying, but back off with your categories, because I want to see that you are sincere in learning about our experience." What they held back or stifled—they'd say *kimkim*—was the expression of their affective response. This was not translated into an emotional display at the time, but came out afterward in their talking and gossiping and, sometimes, on Facebook. There was no magical act of translation that could shift English terms entirely accurately into Kankanaey and vice versa. More importantly, people did not see that they needed one. One of the funniest moments of my research was leaving Biag's family home in Katangoan on the last evening of our visit. Beside the light switch at the front door was a wonderful chart of emoticons—little faces—with the English emotion words beneath. I looked at Biag and said, "So you need to make a study in advance to go abroad," and Biag replied, "No, it's just schoolwork. We don't need that! Not even you and I! You're always asking me how I feel? But you know already! Why is it that you need words for what is a feeling? As if that is [gesturing at the chart] for . . . someone with a . . . sort of disability." Had I been lacking emotional intelligence, ignoring his affective messages? This said, and not particularly gently, we held each other's gazes as we erupted into sidesplitting laughter with the surge of relief.

In the global shatter zone, flows of affect sustain networks of relationships. Gifts and remittances provided for the private development of what only appeared to be public spaces and services, while state activities were dislocated into intimate networks with their roots far away. Strategies of settlement and kin, such as Conyap had followed, were failing to produce secure futures. Instead, irregularity and lateral networks appeared to yield greater returns to canny migrants. Thus, to secure their own future and their family's, Biag and Labanet needed their archipelago's other spatially and socially dispersed affective nodes to care for them through economic exchange, trust, support, and advice. The new kind of security they were producing for themselves to combat precarity emerged from the global scale and scope of these networks. For them, a sister in Winnipeg, a classmate turned business partner north of Baguio, a sister in Sydney, an employer in London were all vital connections to be cultivated against precarity.

## Notes

1. Katigbak, 2013.
2. Abinales and Amorsolo, 2005.
3. See Faier, 2013.
4. Colombo, 2013.

# 7  In Transit

THE LONGER SHE stayed in the United Kingdom, the more Labanet's daily life felt restricted. Starting in 2013, the British government began to introduce new policies designed to deter irregular migrants from remaining in the country. Speaking to the press, in the summer of 2015, about would-be migrants attempting to enter the United Kingdom by rail, truck, and car from the French port of Calais, Prime Minister David Cameron explained, "We are passing legislation, we have done this very recently, to make sure you can't get a driving license, you can't rent a house, you can't take out a bank account, and we will remove more illegal migrants from our country so people know it's not a safe haven once you're there."[1] The prime minister was referring to the 2014 Immigration Act. Labanet knew she would have to circumvent these new regulations in order to remain in the United Kingdom.[2] She used both spatial and temporal tactics, living her life while in motion across London.

Movement assuaged Labanet's feelings of exposure and lack of control. She spent a great deal of her day moving herself both physically and psychically from one space to the next. She lived, phone in hand, on a circuit, from work to her shared flat and shared flat to her work, with occasional detours to socialize or remit money. In her mind, she rotated her focus through her various problems and vulnerabilities, shifting from her kids in Baguio to her employer's kids in London to Facebook friends to investments and back to her own migration status. Both Labanet's mobile strategy and the features of the United Kingdom's shatter zone space held the authority of the UK government at bay.

Negotiating public transit was one of Labanet's key tactics. Instead of using the Tube, she took the bus back and forth from work to her flat and to social events. Because she wanted to conceal her irregular status from the public and her flatmates and not remind her employer of it, she considered discretion first. As she was moving across the city, buses were one of the few places we could talk. We took advantage of Londoners' reluctance to eavesdrop on buses and then moved to text messages and Facebook's chat function to keep in touch between interviews.

Labanet's journeys through the city weren't always smooth, affectively or ethically. Shortly after she sorted out a new, shared flat closer to her work in West London, and farther away from regular immigration spot checks at the Tube stations in East London, she had been in a bus accident. She was a passenger on a bus that hit a wall. She texted me, called, and finally switched to Facebook chat, all while she was leaving the bus. On Facebook, she explained.

> Labanet: Yeah, I'm fine, just a little bit shocked. I needed to have a little rest before I can go home since my feet went wobbly. Now I'm home and just now realize my blouse was ripped. For some reason, I don't know. Above all, I'm fine. Thanks God.

> Me: Oh, dear. . . . That sounds really horrible! What happened?

> Labanet: I'm not sure if the bus driver turned a little bit early or something happened to him. There was a big bump then he managed to go to the right path then again the second time. A disabled woman was thrown and I managed to go and help her stand. Until I went out of the bus and saw the driver and the bus there I realized we had an accident.
> A big metal and the wall I think. Something might have happened to the driver beforehand. I think he's not conscious after that. Paramedics and police were around the area after a few minutes, so I need to move.

Even in this extreme of vulnerability, *inayan* had driven Labanet's actions. Over the voice call that preceded this chat exchange, Labanet's concern was finding someone else to take over helping the disabled woman. This would have enabled her to leave the scene before being asked to present any identity papers. "*Inayan* if I cannot find someone else to help her," she explained. Labanet's first priority was her global, ethical responsibility to help this person and the possible repercussions if she failed to do so. I suggested that she find a middle-aged woman and ask gently, explaining she had a doctor's appointment close by and would be charged if she were to miss it. It worked; she found a volunteer. For Labanet, this experience of the bus crash tied together the affect of sudden violence with that of global care and its obligations. It brought together the potential repercussions of her failure to care with her possible exposure as an irregular migrant. Labanet found that the combination had given her a rare moment of affective overload which she shared with me across polymedia.

On Facebook chat, and in the aftermath of her successful exit from the scene, I commiserated with her:

> Me: *Piman* [poor you]. . . . Are you still reporting or are you (explosive used in mines) [T&T—a play on TNT and meaning irregular and hiding]?

> Labanet: The HO [Home Office] cannot find my apps [applications] so I didn't go."

> Me: Are you going to chase that up with your lawyer? Did he ever file the new appeal?

> Labanet: Don't know. Got tired following up. I will just wait, as they say.

Most of the time, Labanet was discerning and self-regulating; she had to be, as so much depended on it. Thus she brought the chat conversation round to an upbeat conclusion.

Labanet: Let's just be optimistic

Me: Sometimes it seems optimism is all there is to hold on to . . .

Labanet: Hehe so true

Some weeks later, Labanet and I met up face-to-face for an interview, and she explained the weight of expectation she was carrying: "As if I can't bear living in the Philippines . . . Where can I earn the same kind of money there? It's not possible. We thought 2,000,000 ($44,878) would be enough to secure a life in the Philippines, but it isn't . . . From now, maybe I'll need to send another 3,000,000 ($67,317) or 4,000,000 ($89,756) until we're just ok. There's been an inflation." At this point, Labanet had been earning about £700–£720 ($1,078–$1,109) per week from her combined part-time work and still remitting £1,400 ($2,308 or PHP 102,857) each month. Her aim had been to give Biag PHP 100,000 monthly for regular expenses—children's school fees, utilities, transport, and subsistence— but also to have extra savings to cover the one-off special expenditures for setting up the contracting business and renovating their house in Baguio City. She had also been covering the costs of dialysis for her father, who had developed kidney problems, by sending money in rotation with her siblings every few months (PHP 30,000 or £408). Her typical pattern had been to save up her earnings for a month and remit in a single transaction from one of the High Street bank branches near her employer's residence in West London. This reduced the bank fees charged.

Because she could have no bank account of her own in the United Kingdom, Labanet carried the cash around with her or stored some of it in a locked cabinet where she lived. One of the first problems she had with her three new flatmates in her shared room was that they had become aware of how much she had on hand at any one time. Betty, who was struggling to meet her rent payment, asked to have a short-term loan from Labanet's savings almost as soon as she saw Labanet's envelope of bills. This new stage in Labanet's London sojourn was thus marked not only by the everyday burdens of irregularity, as in the bus crash, but also by desperate and self-interested actions on the part of her new housemates. The negative affects here were met with a countervailing upswell in care from her employer.

Labanet navigated precarity and affective overload with culture, using *alayan* and *inayan*. We can see these concepts at work in the ways Labanet spent her time off after work, but also in her dealings with employers and immigration authorities. After leaving Essex Street, Labanet made regular visits to the Home Office at Lunar House in Croydon, at least for the first few months. Her encounters with the Home Office had one affective charge, while a growing feeling of closeness to her main employer provided another. In between, she developed strategies to manage her increasingly chaotic living arrangements.

This chapter does not focus, in detail, on what I learned from Labanet about her particular UK employers. She wished to protect them from fines and censure and respected their confidentiality. Instead, I set the wider context by mapping how the United Kingdom's shatter zone was sustained from within the regulatory apparatus governing migration, using an example of *inayan* in action in the national public sphere. This was a front-page media story in which the United Kingdom's junior immigration minister had to resign his position after learning he had, himself, been employing an irregular migrant to do domestic work.

## *Inayan* in Action

Mark Harper, Minister of State for Immigration, resigned on February 8, 2014.[3] Harper had discovered that a person who had worked for him for seven years as a self-employed contractor did not have the right to work in the United Kingdom. UK employment regulations required employers to undertake reasonable checks on workers' rights to work and to retain copies of workers' documents. Harper's resignation letter explained that he had verified Isabella Acevedo's identity and right to work in 2007.[4] He had viewed and copied her passport and a letter from the Home Office, dated 2006, stating she had Indefinite Leave to Remain (ILR) in the United Kingdom. ILR status gave Ms. Acevedo the right to work and run her own business. In 2013, when Harper was taking the new Immigration Bill (2014) through Parliament, he found he could no longer locate the copies he had made. This bill, as outlined above, imposed heavy civil penalties on private landlords who had failed to establish that prospective tenants had a right to live in the United Kingdom. Harper wanted to ensure that he was fully compliant with the regulations governing employers, considering a similar regulatory burden would soon be imposed on landlords.

Harper asked Ms. Acevedo to provide him with her documents again and made further copies. Harper then passed these copies on to his private office to check their details with immigration officials. He learned that Ms. Acevedo did not have the right to work in the United Kingdom. Harper claimed that he had complied with the law at all times, but wanted to hold himself to a higher standard than other employers, so resigned nonetheless.

According to Isabella Acevedo, she had only met Mark Harper twice. She had been closer to his wife who, while not a friend, was "sweet" to her. Acevedo had arrived from Colombia in 2000 with her daughter, having decided to leave after her husband's father had been kidnapped for ransom. She had wanted her child to have a better life. She and her daughter shared a single bed in a room with two other migrants. Her daughter attended school. Ms. Acevedo had found cleaning work, including, in 2007, a job cleaning flats in a luxury complex in Waterloo. She started working for the Harpers on the recommendation of a member of the complex's security staff. She had received £30 ($46) in cash each week for three and one half hours of cleaning and ironing, with no sick pay or holiday pay, working as a self-employed contractor. The Harpers had given her a £30 ($46) bonus at Christmas, but she had not received a raise in pay over her seven years of work.

In 2010, Isabella Acevedo had applied for Indefinite Leave to Remain for her daughter and herself under the provisions for migrant children. Her application was turned down on the basis that her daughter had returned to Colombia for two and half years as a child and thus did not meet residency requirements. Ms. Acevedo had appealed this decision and, in February 2014, was awaiting another ruling. The 2006 letter from the Home Office she had supplied to Harper was forged. Acevedo had stopped working after Harper discovered the forgery. In July of 2014, she was arrested, only minutes before her daughter's wedding at a London registry office. She was deported back to Colombia.

As Harper's resignation played out across the media, my respondents took it up on Facebook. They were familiar with Mark Harper from his sponsorship of a campaign to encourage irregular migrants to leave the United Kingdom the previous summer: the infamous "Go home" vans that drove through East London's boroughs. My respondents saw Harper's resignation as *inayan* in action. On one of the Facebook groups I had joined, I saw the following exchange:

Flora: *grabe naman sya. Akala ko mas nakaka intindi sya.* [That's really serious. I presume he didn't know.] Oh well,,, that's life . . .

Kod-as: *Nakarma ngarud* [It's karma of course] from his being too hard from undocumented, now GOD give Him a big lesson. *Inayan.* Very good experience for him.

Simultaneously, in other fora, potential employers were saying similar things. Many pointed out that even they knew the current Home Office requirements, introduced under the 2006 Work and Families Act, better than Harper did. This act indicated that such a letter was only valid if the worker produced alongside it an official document giving the person's National Insurance Number and their name issued by either a Government agency or a previous employer.[5] So presenting the letter alongside a Colombian passport, by itself, as Ms. Acevedo apparently had, would not have enabled Harper to meet the legal requirements for employers at all.

Sameerakhan explained this in a comments thread beneath *The Telegraph* newspaper's coverage of this story:[6] "I'm very happy that this has happened to our country's supposedly-tough-on-immigration minister and that he employed an illegal immigrant for 7 long years before realizing it. If nothing else, it shows how impossibly difficult it is to keep up with the confusing bureaucratic procedures, government regulations and ever-changing laws (seriously, they've changed at least every year since the mid-2000s), especially for small businesses that can't afford legal advice every time they need to hire someone."

Pjon replied, "Employers catch it in the neck because of the abject failure of the UK Border Agency and its previous incarnations to remove illegals and failed asylum seekers in numbers significant enough to act as a deterrent to further illegal entry and working."

Following this, Manonthebus commented, "Mr Harper intended to force everybody to check fully the right to work of anybody they employed in any capacity. That is a huge burden on ordinary people. Mr Harper had the benefit of countless minions and automatic access to official documentation. And yet, he got it wrong. Why should the rest of us be expected to get it right?"

In an expression of subversive citizenship, these (potential) employers did not want to be "the border" themselves. They wanted to hire workers but expected the government to take care of all regulatory requirements surrounding migration. They considered the checks and requirements too onerous, the documents too easily faked, the process too confusing. Perhaps more importantly, the process of assessment and recognition of legitimate claims and immigration status didn't match up with public opinion on the virtues attached to migrants. Migrants themselves had picked up part of the public discourse on substantive citizenship circulated by NGOs. As we've already seen, irregular migrants made their case to stay on the basis of being deserving, making substantive citizenship claims based on their contribution to the United Kingdom. Acevedo made this same argument, saying, in an interview with *The Guardian* newspaper, "I thought because I was a hard worker, maybe someone would recognize in court that I was no problem here . . . Initially I was like 'I've ended Mr Harper's life.' Now I'm realizing his life hasn't ended, but mine has. He has a new job; I haven't got anything."

While Acevedo was reestablishing her life back in Colombia, Mark Harper became Minister of State for Disabled People. As the comments made by potential employers showed, in the end, an employer's failure to be the border and take on the work of the state was much more forgivable than a migrant falsifying documents, dissembling, and giving incomplete information to negotiate that border in everyday life. These contradictions illustrated the ironies of the global shatter zone. Subversive citizens, who refused to become an arm of the state, or who only gave a veneer of compliance, sustained the shatter zone space. But their actions arguably raised false hopes and thus frustrated migrants' long-term plans for security. Because subversive citizens were unable to effectively intervene or extend care when migrants were apprehended, migrants who considered employers' sentiments to represent a commitment ended up with nothing much to show for their years of work. However, the changes in regulatory frameworks and cultures over time made this shatter zone an unpredictable space. These frequent changes made the eventual outcome of their migration a gamble for migrants.

## Evading the Authorities

While the Harper/Acevedo story played out in the media, Labanet had given up her engagement with the appeals process for her own asylum claim. After their appeal had failed at the Immigration Tribunal, Biag had withdrawn his application and returned to the Philippines. She and Biag had already spent £2,500 ($3,850) on lawyer's fees filing the initial case and a further £2,000 ($3,080) on their appeal. At appeal, their lawyer had decided to argue that, since their application had been so long in the system, they had effectively settled in the United Kingdom—to make the substantive citizenship argument. From this, he went on to argue that refusing their application at this point would have amounted to denying them their rights under Article 8 of the European Code of Human Rights: the right to a family life. Their appeal had failed because the tribunals had tightened up on their application of the definition of family life. Having spent several years in the country with their case in an administrative backlog was no longer sufficient reason to grant them even a limited right to remain in the United Kingdom. On her lawyer's advice, Labanet had paid another £1,500 ($2,310) for the lawyer to put in a second appeal, covering her stay only, on the premise that she and Biag had separated. While this appeal was supposedly in progress, Labanet took an afternoon off every two weeks to report to the UKBA at Lunar House, Croydon, as required.

Labanet, in a later interview, explained how exhausting these reporting sessions had been and why she had eventually decided to stop. Labanet had disclosed her occasional work to the case officer who handled their initial asylum claim. Though asylum claimants were allowed to work after twelve months, Labanet should not have been self-employed. Her work situation was thus a regulatory vagary that the system had tolerated, having no effective sanction to stop her. However, Labanet felt she was constantly being tested by Home Office staff so they could intimidate her into admitting she was an economic migrant. She dreaded these confrontations.

> I went to the window to make my report. And the man is telling me, "We know you're working." Not shouting, exactly, but his voice is . . . low, loud, and so harsh. I say "Yes, sir. I have declared that already. It's just a few hours, casual babysitting. It's only just enough to support my food and transport." He is asking me where I live. I tell him, "I stay with my friends. They are helping me." He does not accept this, "Nobody's friends just let them stay like that. You are working. You should go to that window and arrange your flight home."

So he is pointing at this window. And I say, "I have still an appeal in process, sir. Have you not received the papers filed by my attorney?" And he tells me, "There's no record of any appeal." I say, "I'd better consult with my attorney then; there must be some mistake." And he tells me again to go to the window to go home. When I get out of the building . . . It takes such a long time, just to leave . . . I am shaking, again. At least he isn't seeing me react . . . I have to find a place to have coffee and just recover. As if I am in shock! My legs are shaking. I'm feeling cold.

I can't go back, I think . . . I've transferred my house. Now, the UKBA, they don't have this new address, so I am not traceable. And the lawyer? He does not return my calls. Just took the £1,500 but no output. I have followed up so much on that, I'm tired of it. The UKBA, they don't have my new paperwork. As if they lawyer just kept the money and did . . . none. But it's not certain. He is also not informing me. There's no receipt and no copy to me of what he has filed. So as if there's no appeal filed. Or they have lost it. What do I do? Pay again to the lawyer? Why? There's no proof he made the appeal! Go back to Lunar House to see if it's them who have lost the appeal? No evidence it was filed. Who do I complain to about the lawyer not filing? It's too much.

Labanet had found herself caught between what might have been a predatory service provider and an inefficient asylum system. In this node, the affective overload from the hostility of the UKBA officer, the lack of support from her lawyer and her own conscience was overwhelming. There was no care here, so she decided not to repeat the encounter.

Labanet was still part of the migration refusal pool, the regulatory black hole that meant the UKBA did not know if she had left the country or stayed on without authorization. This part of the United Kingdom's shatter zone had, in 2014, an estimated 175,000 people who had refused to comply with migration regulations and were likely still living in the country.[7] To sustain herself here, and to ensure that she could continue to sustain her family and work, Labanet turned toward places and spaces where she could allay or recover from the negative affect of Lunar House. In spaces of recognition and safety, she found the affective flows that enabled her to continue to transmute positive affects into the care she sent home and gave to her employers. In these nodes, she played off *inayan* and *alayan* to sustain her caring self. Thus, as she moved across London, she moved from one extreme to the other, from hostility and aggression to welcome and love.

## Making Space for Care

As we saw in the bus crash, Labanet transmuted positive affect into care in the way she cultivated herself in her daily life. This work was also made material, and visible, in her shared flat. When I visited a few days after Christmas, she had a bed in a small front room, overlooking the street, in an area not far from central London. She shared the room with three other Filipino migrants. Two bunk beds took up most of the space, a dining table, two wardrobes, a refrigerator, and two chairs, and many boxes occupied the rest. Labanet's personal space—half of one wardrobe and the top of a chest of drawers—was decorated with two Christmas cards. Both were from families she worked for—her main employer and a part-time one—with greetings from both parents and little sketches from the kids. These cards were given pride of place. On her bed, she had a paperback copy of *Raise Your Child's Social I.Q.*

She explained, watching my gaze fall on the different sections of the room and fixing on the book, "This is helping me advise the kids. You know, when they have problems with making friends or conflicts with their friends. Stuff like that . . . I need to be prepared."

I asked, "Which kids? Your employers'? Or yours?" She laughed:

Both, of course. But mostly here I am speaking with my kids over Skype. It's all online now. Their art, their reports, our communication. You know, if they send photos, it's on my phone, on my Facebook. What's here is the stuff from the kids I care for here in London. They give me paper . . . No more paper from the Philippines. It's rare these days. They're on Skype, or on email, in my pocket, instead!

For my kids, if I advise them, when they open their school problems to me, they don't see the book. They just think I'm wise. But also it's for my employers' kids, mostly. You know, when I get them from school, they'll tell me if they've had problems. Like, if the other kids won't play with them or their friend isn't being kind, even after they've had a play date on the weekend. You know . . . Sometimes they are not so good at . . . going along with others . . . Their pride is so high. Or they don't want to take turns unless they are always first. They insist on things going their own way. So it's good for me to give them some ways to think about what to do. Practical tools, you know, to stop and ask themselves: what's important to me? How would I feel if I was the other child? Like that.

Labanet's bunk was the site of her self-education on early adolescence and emotional intelligence.

Unlike Essex Street, the new flat did not have anywhere to socialize. The kitchen was a long galley setup, with nowhere to sit. During that visit, she was struggling with the internet connection, too. It had been cut off for nonpayment. Labanet had been giving money to the ex-husband of the woman whose place she had taken up in the flat, but the money didn't seem to have been passed on. If it had, the ex-flatmate hadn't paid the subscription. This meant she had to go somewhere else with internet—a nearby café—to e-mail and she couldn't Skype. More than space to socialize, she needed private internet access: "My employer lets me use her wireless, of course. But I don't like her to see how much time I need. And I don't want her to hear—or the kids, either—what I discuss, so no Skype." She solved this problem by investing in a more expensive phone plan.

I queried, "Why don't you just live in? Would that be feasible?" Labanet explained:

> Well, they've asked. . . . The kids really want me to stay! "Can't you sleep here tonight?" they ask me. But it would be not so comfortable. They'd need to convert their home office to a bedroom, like that.
>
> Last week, our neighbors' nanny . . . she was Colombian, she got caught. The younger one was so upset when he heard. You know, that his friends' nanny wasn't coming back anymore, just all of a sudden. He is saying how angry he would be if it happened to me. If they got me! So those feelings are real. And my employer, she's a good friend to me. We've adjusted with each other. We understand each other. She's the one advising me on my father's treatment. She gave me money for Biag's paperwork with his business! They give me £500 ($770) bonus for Christmas, too. And they make me promise to spend it on myself! They care! Really!
>
> When I am calculating my pay by my hours just last month, I notice I am receiving £40 ($62) over. So I tell her. And she says, "Oh, we know that transport is increased. So we will pay for your bus pass now." She thinks about me even without me asking her, you know? I can discuss my problems with her, the ones with my family, supporting my parents, our business. She can advise me—she also has a family with some conflicts, before, and also know about setting up a business. You know? She won't be gossiping to anyone about my plans, but . . . I don't tell her all, of course. It's just enough, that she knows I'm human. That I'm investing the money I'm earning, you know? That we have a plan, there in the Philippines. That it—me, working here—is really changing our lives there.
>
> But for me, it's too much to be with them all the time. I mean, I have only three days with them now. That's what they need for a nanny/housekeeper. They don't need full-time and they can't really afford to pay it. And I can't afford to let my time go without earning. I earn with the rest, right? So I have so many part-time [jobs]: the other family, two and a half days right now; my other babysitting in the evenings maybe three days per week, more if it goes late; Tuesday afternoon I take care of the elderly man; and Friday night, if no babysitting, I'm doing cleaning near Bond Street, right? So they'd be disturbed. I'd need to come in late and leave early.
>
> And they are always telling me not to work so hard, not to send so much money home, to take care of myself. This would let them observe how I really live! And I love the kids, they're great, they love me. But I don't want to be there for them when I'm not being paid, you know? 'Cause maybe they'll get jealous of what time I'm giving my own kids? And how would I see my friends, you know, to send things home, to find out what's happening there or get recommendations for new babysitting, like that? That's also what keeps me going, really. Talking with people who also understand how I live, all the stuff that happens back home!

Labanet had other stories of her UK employers' kindness and their willingness to go out of their way to ensure that she felt cared for and was able to send money home. When we talked at length, though, about what Labanet thought of her employers, it was that they were good people, but stressed and lonely, living in an unsupportive society. The employers she described seem to find Labanet safe to talk to because, they imagined, she wasn't in competition with them and could not really see they were struggling and, perhaps, at risk of failure in their own projects. For example, one of her early employers went bankrupt and left the country: "I could see, you know, that they were scrambling to pay me, day by day. There were so many bills, not opened, by the door. And lots of phone calls . . . but they look at the phone, see the number calling, and don't accept. So I made my plans. It's good I now know what to tell my friends to look for!" Labanet was pleased she had been able to see this coming and found another job, so it was her replacement, not her, who was terminated at short notice. She described households who were over-stretched and too proud of their apparent status to admit problems, households that were themselves elite migrants, but without a reliable safety net. Even though they were earning much higher salaries, it seemed to her that many employers were spending frivolously on maintaining their high status and not, as Labanet herself did, living modestly and saving or investing.

Labanet had been consistently taken aback that UK employers lacked life skills she took for granted. She showed me a text message she had saved from a former employer, sent in the middle of the night, asking Labanet to send Biag to their house immediately. This employer's roof had been leaking and a sudden heavy rainstorm has caused a flood in the upstairs bathroom. Labanet was critical: "Back home, we'd ask the neighbors, our family to come help, even in the middle of the night. Here, they don't have their family, they don't know the neighbors. Who they have is us. We'd be the ones to know what to do!" In another example, Labanet had used her employers' hair dryer after taking the kids swimming. The fuse blew. She had replaced it with a three-amp fuse from a broken lamp they had sitting in the garage and left her employer a note to that effect. "Wow! She was amazed. She was saying to me, 'How did you know what to do? To change the fuse?!' You know, I pity her that she didn't learn. But I'm also glad, because it gives me a job and gives her a good feeling to me." Labanet said this with warm affection. This was, after all, the same employer who had called up the bank that was holding Labanet's remittance payment and pointed out just which UK and EU regulations the bank's activities were contravening. "See, we complement each other here, really!" Labanet described an easy, mutually exposed and interdependent global intimacy that she felt was facilitated by but went beyond the employment relation. She was willing to consider the relationship in some critical depth in our conversations.

I asked if she felt her employer looked down on her and she replied:

> No . . . I don't think so; there isn't that feeling. You know? I'd feel it, if she were thinking like that. And she would not be saying good things. It's me, I'm the

one who goes to the parents' meetings at school, who prepares the kids for the speech day, oversees their homework . . . like that. And she knows . . . we discuss my projects, back home. So she knows I am using my earnings to make a big difference in our life. I don't just scatter it; enjoy my time off in London. That's why she and the kids are always telling me to do something for just myself, buying me gifts like handbags . . . It's not like . . . with some of us Filipinos here, you go to socials, you exchange numbers and they say "friend," then they want to sell you . . . pots and pans, cosmetics. They really make you their business! To me, my employer also cares. It's more than just business. There's care. She is not asking extras with no money. She respects that I have my purpose here—that I'm building my project at home, that I manage my money.

For Labanet, the everyday domestic space of her work transmuted global affect into care. This entailed sustaining exchange and respect across differences in culture and status between people as employer and employee. Not that she felt the exchanges were always even, but she didn't describe them as predatory or extractive. Labanet's critique was directed instead to the false closeness and bonding practices of her fellow Filipinos.

For her, market making in intimate relationships had been more of a problem in her social life than in her employment relations. What had come about with Philippine globalization was the rise of models of doing business that functioned through people's ability to commodify their own intimate relationships without acknowledging this as commodification. So while Labanet's employer was her employer, she had found that too many of her friends in the United Kingdom's Filipino migrant community and in the Philippines now wanted to sell her Tupperware, or Sarah Lee (Avon), or vitamins from various pyramid selling schemes, or funeral plans, education plans, or pension plans, all on commission.[8] Labanet had learned there could be more financial and emotional exploitation in such family or neighbor relations than in her nanny/housekeeper workplace. With her employers, she was self-evidently selling her physical labor and providing a flow of positive affect as care with it, and she felt the exchange was more straightforward. If she had been, for example, offering manicures or selling cosmetics to her flatmates to pay her rent, it would be a case of asking them to ignore their exploitation so she would not lose face. For her, that would generate a bad feeling. Though this kind of practice went on all the time under the discourse of bonding and mutual support, Labanet didn't approve of it.

In London, Labanet found that a new feeling of closeness had arisen from the other side of giving care as part of her work instead.

Sometimes, I think my employer is the one who understands best, here, what I face. We're close. She knows my projects, my hopes and plans. She sees me feeling big, feeling small. She's not jealous, you know? Because she is also making a life here. Not like my friends, sometimes . . . She's not worried how it will seem to her [she won't compare herself to Labanet] if we get a big lot in

Baguio or if our kid is the valedictorian, you know? Mostly, she will listen, 'cause she cares, too. Overtime, when I stay longer, I can just ask it, you know? And sometimes I don't have to ask. She sees it, and she's the one who does something or says something.

Labanet described herself as feeling "adjusted to," "cared for," and "close" to her employer, but did not often disclose her emotional states to her employer. Instead, she reported that they had a relationship in which she offered practical services and asked for practical advice in return. Both of them, the way they were living in London, had found such services and advice were in short supply. For Labanet, *inayan*, as an ethic, insisted on a sacred space of human connection here beyond her informal employment contract. Thus there was something here beyond commodification of her care that she had to honor: "For me, I'd like to stay until my projects are secured, of course. But also to see the kids I care for grow until they don't need me so much, for the parents' work to be more stable for their hours. *Inayan*. Like her mother-in-law says, I'm like family now, after six years. . . . There'll soon be a better time for all of us to make a change."

There are good, political economic reasons to analyze Labanet's situation as exploitation. But Labanet did not feel her employer was personally exploiting her any more than she, the employer herself, was being exploited by her own employment circumstances and her lack of work-life balance in her job, the fact that her partner's work and her own had required them to move far away from their families, and so on. Within the relationship with her long-term employer Labanet said, "There's a lot of good feeling."

## Coping with Chaotic Lives

*Alayan*—help and care—for others and for herself was what Labanet practiced in her time off. Much of this help and care involved assisting other Filipinos, mostly fellow Kankanaeys, in their own mobility strategies.

The limits of the space in the flat meant it didn't matter so much that it wasn't heated for most of the day. "We all go out each morning," she explained. She did not feel so close to her flatmates now, and she felt comfortable with the distance. Instead, her closest connections to other Filipinos, including former flatmates and relatives, were online or arranged meet-ups. Maintaining physical distance was a key tactic in staying secure in her relationships, so she avoided spending too much face-to-face time with close kin: "Because I am now T&T, *inayan*, if I am caught, they might get to my accommodation. What more if I am sharing with my cousin or my sister-in-law? If I'm the one caught, ok. But with that, she could lose her projects also. It would be a disaster for our families. But, if it's just me, she can still help." Without papers, Labanet's strategies for creating and sustaining lateral connections were directed in a one-on-one, personal way, largely toward visa-holders and permanent residents. At the same time, she had to cope with the exposure created by her ties to fellow irregular migrants.

Labanet no longer attended church, as she was equally concerned that any association with advocacy groups might attract immigration enforcement. Instead, she did a lot more small group and one-on-one socializing, attending big community center events only occasionally. She marked her friends' birthdays by taking them out to dinner and posting their pictures on Facebook. In her time off, Labanet also bought her groceries, did her laundry at the laundromat, and visited her Kankanaey neighbors, one road over, to play with their kids. She invested much of her free time babysitting their two babies. The parents were working in low-paid or casual jobs and struggling to organize child care around their hours.

I joined her on an impromptu Saturday afternoon babysitting excursion. She explained this often happened. Kittay, the mum on child care duty, had received a call asking her to do last-minute cleaning work. Kittay didn't want to turn down the hours or discourage her employer from calling again, so she took the opportunity. Ringing the neighbor to come around was her first option. Labanet was happy to oblige, because she loved babies: "It's not like with my employers' kids— they're older already. You know, you have to correct their behaviors, advise them on settling quarrels with their brother or sister, share their toys, get them to pick up their things—or do it yourself. All that. But these little ones, they just need some play and you hold them. Give them their bottle. Find them something to see. And hold them. . . . It's a good feeling, you know?" Did she mind spending her day off babysitting? She continued, "For me, it's ok. It's part of my community work, like . . . *Inayan*, it would be me. I'm happy to help out. I love babies. And the mum's desperate to earn. She might give me £10 or £15 as a thank you. But she's earning less than the per-hour for babysitting doing cleaning, really. So I can't take it. Because how will she buy her food for the evening, you know?"

Kittay's flat was, like Labanet's, a two bedroom, with electric heat kept on off or low. There was a combined kitchen/dining/living area. The bathroom was unheated and moldy. One baby had a head cold and the other had a persistent viral chest infection—he'd already been taken to the doctor three times. The flat was not designed for six people, and the damp and mold seemed to have hindered the child's recovery. Kittay's husband had Indefinite Leave to Remain in the United Kingdom and was on track to apply for citizenship, while she had permission to work on a spousal visa. Despite that, they could not keep their child well fed and healthy while living close to central London. Working shifts for the NHS and casual cleaning didn't allow them to offer their child consistent presence, visits to green space, or much stimulation or socializing. They needed their two irregular flatmates to support them, and their roster of Kankanaey friends who stepped in as babysitters. Labanet was one. She posted a sweet photograph herself on Facebook, taken by Kittay, showing her asleep, with Kittay's sleeping child in her arms, stretched out on the couch.

Several months later, she told me Kittay and her husband had taken her advice. They had taken their now year-old child back to the Philippines to be raised by his grandparents and aunts and uncles. On Facebook, I saw Labanet commenting regularly on the shots Kittay posted from their daily Skype sessions and photographs taken by Kittay's husband's family. In the Philippines, the child had what Labanet and other friends and relatives considered a better life. On Facebook, Kittay and her husband had amassed documentary evidence in photographs, showing how their low-wage jobs in central London in a period of austerity offered poor circumstances in which to parent. Their photos showed exhaustion etched on faces after overnight duty on the NHS for extra money; doing cleaning work with an infant held in an *oban* (shawl) on mum's back; limited public park space; grey crowded streets; and equally crowded, cold, dark accommodation. From the Philippines, the received photos showed their child not only beaming into the camera on Skype, but also seeking sensory stimulation in nature, walking on grass in fresh air, exploring rocks and mud, and being safe on a quiet road under the supervision of grandparents, aunts, and uncles. These portrait-type photos contrasted with previous images of a chronically ill, lonely, understimulated, and housebound child. The comments Labanet made offered evidence of this transformation in the child's happiness, and her own relief, commenting on health, toys, and space available. But the most commented-on photos were those of this child with stepsiblings, cousins, and other playmates. Comments here suggested London living simply did not facilitate what people saw as optimal socialization for children, because they lacked safe access to their peer groups and thus opportunities to engage in unstructured play with others.

Labanet explained:

To raise children here is the hardest thing. There's simply not enough here in London . . . Enough time, enough money. . . . Even for those with papers who have professional work. If you live where it's not so expensive, the schools are terrible. Awful behavior. Bullying. And the city, it's not good for the kids' health. Even with my employers' kids, I see that. They struggle to find places to go. So I am relieved we couldn't try to bring our kids, ever. With me earning and Biag back home, our kids . . . they're better off. That's the thing here. Even if you have your papers and your profession, like nursing, you will be just struggling here. Like your idea of what it would be is . . . a fake. Here, you earn what you think will be a very good salary, but you can't afford anything. Not babysitting, not transport, not clothes for the child. If you want to go to a play center, you pay. If you want to eat out, you pay again—for junk food. So it is sad for the mum and dad to be away, but better for the child to be home with the grandparents. There's so much more the mum and dad can give them there than here . . .

Me, I think my way . . . I'm not the one paying taxes and I can't become a permanent [resident] here. God willing, I won't go back before my projects are finished back home. But I can go back to something I've built and see people I've helped, you know? Here, even if you have a profession, you will struggle. Maybe not so much your kids when they're grown if you came earlier, but now, those coming, they struggle, and they will struggle more, even their kids. It's a false improvement in your life, to think you can stay.

And Kittay commented, "You see all the photos on Facebook, all our events? Well, we're really the ones showing how hard it is here. It's not all money and parties . . . You struggle to raise a healthy child. You sacrifice so much for them, but it's never what you want for your child. People are convinced it's good here, but it's really very hard . . . to make it."

The struggles of settled and still-settling migrants also played out in Labanet's own flat, giving her additional headaches while she was building new bridges with neighbors. It became her own chaotic housemates who posed the biggest threat to Labanet's stay in the United Kingdom. First, she coped with her friend Yapeng's depression after the death of her employer. Yapeng had been Labanet's first contact in the new flat, after she had left the first sublet she had shared with Biag when he went home. Shortly after Labanet moved in, the older person whom Yapeng had been caring for died in her care. Yapeng was still owed a month's wages, but the family employing her was in turmoil, commuting in from outside London and trying to settle the estate. Not only was Yapeng out of pocket, she was out of work. The bereaved children of her employer could not offer recommendations for more work of the same kind. Yapeng had overstayed on a tourist visa, so did not have the right to work. This was less of a problem than her lack of networks and marketable skills. Labanet attempted to find her a job with some difficulty.

It's hard to find an employer now. Used to be you could just ask yours if they had any friends, you know, who needed a worker . . . Now, with the new immigration regulations, or maybe it's the recession, the work is harder to find. Employers, they don't know any, or they don't like to say, to recommend, maybe because we are often undocumented. But for *Manang* [older sister] Yapeng, it's very hard. It's not even the documents, really. It's that she is already caring for an elderly person for almost five years. And she is somewhat older, already, herself, late fifties. So when she is having an interview for nanny/housekeeper, she is too quiet. As if she won't have the energy for the kids, to have fun with them and keep up. She just feels so heavy and small to them, I think . . . The employers are afraid their kids won't have fun. Like she'll just clean and cook and take them wherever, but not really enjoy . . . You know, when someone we are caring for dies, that's the hardest. You are sad, you are mourning them. And there's no other work waiting. You have to spring back, very fast. I sent her for one interview, recommended. But Yapeng, she is already feeling . . . small . . . and cold. As if she cannot warm up to them.

Labanet realized Yapeng was deeply depressed. While in London, and caring for her elderly employer, she was rumored to have had a brief affair with a fellow Filipino, both of them having spouses in the Philippines. Whether true or not, the rumors had estranged Yapeng from most of her Kankanaey networks in the United Kingdom. As Yapeng's savings ran out, and she stopped remitting to support her children's college fees, Labanet scrambled to find her some part-time babysitting work and booked her a ticket back home.

> I had to help her to go home. She is too depressed. I will just have to shoulder her share of the rent, to brace it, for a while. Yes, it's a big problem. But an even bigger problem is . . . What more if she becomes unstable? You see, I am already paying her rent, her food, giving her some money for transport, setting up interviews. And she is too . . . small inside to take on any . . . So it's all to me. I can't let this problem grow any bigger. It can't be escaped, either. If I come in, she's there in her bed, crying. If it's getting worse, then I'll be affected too. She'll be the one to be stopped by the Immigration, on the bus somehow, or the Tube. And the feeling in the flat, it's heavy. She says she has nothing at home, no way of earning. Well, maybe. But she has fixed her house, her husband is working, her kids are there. It's better than just . . . being here, like that.

Labanet found a replacement for Yapeng in the flat, Alicia. At the same time, their landlord rented out the other room in the flat to a new Filipino flatmate from outside Labanet's networks. This woman had moved in with her girlfriend. This was the most chaotic situation Labanet had encountered. The chaos arose in part because the new flatmate, Fely, unlike all the others, had Indefinite Leave to Remain in the United Kingdom: full papers. Fely did not need Labanet's advice or her networks, did not want her help to find babysitting jobs, or have much respect for Labanet or her projects.

Fely had secured ILR by converting her work visa several years earlier. She had been working as a senior care assistant in nursing homes. Labanet thought Fely was now working part-time, but she wasn't sure. Fely had met Mina, her girlfriend, at a Filipino social event. She had convinced Mina to leave an abusive employer after she had arrived in the United Kingdom on a domestic worker visa. With the help of an NGO, Mina had made a claim for protected status (asylum) and was seeking back pay and a settlement to compensate for the abuse she had suffered. As this process played out, Fely was supporting both of them. Fely had also claimed Housing Benefit from a previous period when she was out of work and had renewed her claim. Fely's sexuality, immigration status, and financial history didn't pose problems for Labanet. Instead, the threat came from Fely's management of her own social networks.

Fely gambled as one of her leisure activities. When she didn't repay a gambling debt, her gambling creditors threatened to report her for fraud because Fely was still claiming Housing Benefit even though she was working. If Fely's creditors convinced the local council that she was falsifying her claim, they would send workers to the flat. The creditors thus applied pressure to Labanet to settle Fely's debts with her own money, figuring she might wish to avoid such a visit. Fely diverted money from their rent to repay some of her gambling debts. Being late with the rent was also a problem, but easier to deal with than the intrusion of government authority into the flat. However, Fely needed to show the local authority a signed tenancy agreement to support her claim for Housing Benefit. Their joint landlord did not want to issue any formal tenancy agreements, particularly because she would now have to record the visa details of all the flat's occupants, who she knew would turn out to be predominantly irregular. Fely sought advice from the Citizens Advice Bureau, a charity supporting people in dealing with the government, and refused to pay any more rent until she had such a contract. Fely also refused to move out. This situation put huge stress on the other occupants of the flat; they were concerned that the landlord would evict all of them. Fely and her girlfriend Mina began fighting at night, waking the whole flat with screaming matches and objects thrown against walls.

In the end, Labanet was obliged to move, again. The landlord had decided to sell the property. Labanet did not want to remain in Fely's orbit, fearing she would bring the local council's attention to the flat. Labanet said of the impasse:

> I cannot even speak to her—to Fely. You know?! As if it's pointless. She has such a bad feeling. Shouting, throwing things . . . all that bad feeling going to her girlfriend . . . and us, too. She just insists on her own. What she wants. Her rights. You know, Citizens Advice is for citizens, right?! Well, that means her rights are more than mine and all the others' rights here. So we need to find another flat. Also close by work and also cheap. I don't think it is so hard with the restrictions on landlords now. They will just charge more, like always, because they have also a risk of being caught. But, if I stay, I could lose my projects and my work here, so easily . . .
>
> For me, if I'm stressed at my accommodation, then I'll be stressed also at work. And I'll get a bad feeling, you know, if there's some small problem with my employer. Or when I Skype my kids, things back home . . . you know, as if I am already not able to absorb it. It's not worth it, taking the risk. I need my time off to be, you know, giving me a good feeling, going smoothly, so that I help people and they help me.
>
> To me . . . It's like this: if it makes you crazy, being a permanent, or you have kids here, but have to send them home, why? Why would I want that? To work for that, to spend for that? Then what?! Who wants the life of a citizen, if that's what it is? There are so many who think it's better to go with papers. No, if you can manage yourself, keep your feeling strong, you can make ways and means to earn. And you'll have something to go back to.

Sustaining herself to care for employers and for her family meant sustaining her social networks and ensuring that those networks sustained her. These lateral connections were both the source of her strength and the biggest threats to her continuing abilities to care, to work, and to provide. So her networks required continual renewal, extension, and cutting to maintain them in good health. Labanet evaluated her networks not so much on their financial possibilities or demands on her time as on their affective impacts. She tried to focus on maximizing the moments of positive affect, support, and recognition to strengthen her in her sojourn. To do so, to keep herself safe and sane, she was, again, on the move across London, seeking another place to live, using all the contacts she had to assist her.

## Against Deportability

Labanet knew her vulnerability to being identified as a potential irregular migrant, stopped, intimidated into revealing her status, and eventually deported was about affect and performance as much as regulation. She had seen almost immediately how Yapeng's depression made her flatmates vulnerable. She had realized that repeatedly exposing herself to the authorities at Lunar House made her more vulnerable, too. She chose to babysit to restore her affective equilibrium. She had avoided confrontation with Fely and instead moved on. Her strategy was to move toward and engage with those affective nodes sustaining her, cutting out those draining her, to counter her own deportability.

Deportability is the sociospatial condition produced by irregular migration as migration regulation, work, and social networks come together.[9] Labanet's deportability was produced not only by the decision of the tribunal to reject Biag's application, but also by the "coup of charisma" in the confrontation with immigration officers at the Tube station and the "low, harsh voice" of the UKBA officer behind the desk at Lunar House. This deportability came about because Labanet experienced affective flows as being transmitted, mobile, and more or less contagious. So she distanced herself from those whose distress and anger might have influenced her own security. She instead sought out the affirming, positive affects, whether caring for a child, or building a bond with her employer, or having lunch with a friend. She countered affect with affect, firm in the belief that sustaining herself would enable her to continue to be confident and thus go unnoticed in the crowds, as she did during the bus accident. Hiding in plain sight, performing prosthetic citizenship, meant it was unlikely she would be the first to be discovered and deported.

Labanet thus consciously built up her own confidence in her performance. She invested in work and travel clothes and frames for her glasses that she saw as part of a uniform of entitlement—portraying the role of an outdoorsy-but-educated nanny to wholesome middle-class British kids. But Labanet knew her gait, her demeanor, her vocal tone and timbre all mattered too, and perhaps even more. Feeling and thus being confident and networked was paramount in her strategy to avoid being deported. At this point in Labanet's stay, the ironies of her employment relations came to the forefront. Here she was, struggling to look the part while putting together a deposit to take on a new flat-share with a permanent resident and she had a whole £500 ($770) stack of gift cards in her purse. These were all from stores selling goods unsuited to her performance of prosthetic citizenship.

The gift cards covered purchases at High Street stores and were her birthday, Christmas, and bonus gifts from part-time employers, but she hadn't been able to use them. Employers had given her the cards so she could treat herself, she explained, but the clothing and footwear at the stores she visited was almost always unsuitable.

> See, I even have £200 in gift cards . . . for Urban Outfitters . . . But there's nothing there I would use. It's all for teenagers, going to parties. Not even for my daughter in the Philippines—I wouldn't have her wearing THAT! Mostly the clothes would be destroyed if you washed it like they do back home, by hand, in the bucket. Or even here in the laundromat! So I know they think this will be nice for me, my employers, but they just don't understand my project. I'm not here for shopping, to show myself off, to be trendy. It's see-through. Or it's lace. Or just . . . flimsy, and short. Not suitable for my work at all, cleaning and babysitting, or even for socials.
>
> I'm here to work, for my projects back home. That's my purpose. So why can they not give me something . . . showing they understand that? If they want to make me a gift, ok, but make it something useful for me, that I can be the one to decide. Don't make it a requirement to spend here, in London. With gift cards, they aren't treating me to something nice; it's just . . . useless! Yes, it makes it look like I'm really part of this here, in the UK, like I belong, with all the trends, but that's not what I need.

In the plastic card, the gift of potential of material things was being used by her employers as a way to establish control over flows of value. Employers apparently hoped this would intensify their own one-to-one caring relationship with Labanet as employee. Labanet had switched part-time employers quite often, always looking for combinations yielding extra hours and extra money, so it sounded like these employers gave her these gifts to show they wanted to hold on to her and show her she was valued. But as much as employers wanted to show their care for her as an individual, their attempts to control the flow of value in the exchange and fix it to Labanet's person frustrated her own sense of herself. In echoes of the boxes sent home, Labanet found the stuff all wrong for her purposes.

Labanet was who she was and could care for them because she cared for others, elsewhere. Honoring those commitments through the work relationship was how she wanted to be shown respect and consideration—to be cared about.

Because the cards had cash amounts attached to them, it made them less of a gift, as Biag described it earlier, and more of a cash bonus. But that bonus was limited by being redirected to some inappropriate High Street chain store. To address this problem, Labanet and I visited Urban Outfitters. We determined that there was nothing in the store that suited her, but she found a couple of things that more or less suited me. I bought the cards from her, in cash, and spent them at the till. Afterward we sat in the park, eating snacks under a tree, deferring our walk back to the bus and underground to enjoy the sunshine. Labanet reflected on what had sustained her in the United Kingdom and her relations with employers and non-Filipino migrants.

> When I first came here, you know, I thought I should be worried about . . . white people. That they might have some racism . . . That they would discrimi-nate . . . or be angry with me because I am working without papers . . . But what I've found . . . it's that they aren't so worried. When I show a bankcard for my ID, they say nothing. It's not them who shows me bad feeling, it's the other migrants. You know, if they're here and they are not *kababayans* [fellow Filipi-nos], they know I am the one without papers, so they aren't always so nice . . .
>
> They are then the ones I want to avoid, the other migrants. That we should have unity? No, there's a competition. Maybe it's as if they know I am the one taking a job that might go to their family member? But for my employers, they don't see it the same . . . Their kids, their in-laws—all their relatives—they would not be working as cleaners or nannies or carers or babysitting here in London. So it's like there's no thought that I am having any competition with them.
>
> And, for me . . . it's better even not to be permanent here. Those ones who are, they are even more struggling with their life. If you hear that a Filipino is committing abuses . . . against employers or the ones they are caring for, it's usu-ally a permanent, isn't it? It's having projects back home—something to go back to—that keeps you from feeling yourself small, so you can swallow your feeling.
>
> For me, it's really been staying strong in our Kankanaey customs that I can keep sane here. Being able to send money for a ritual, when there's a death in the family or someone in hospital, and to support the kids, it really makes me bear up. For all the other *kailians* [covillagers, meaning fellow Kankanaey speakers], too, it's the same. Even if sometimes I'm not the one for socials, it's friends who really help you stay here. Kittay, she's found me my new flat. She understands what I'm carrying . . . So I can keep going here . . . You know, it's as if our first project with the contracting is a taster. We earned little, after expenses, but we have almost 4 million [Philippine pesos] of equipment now! That's how I can go on, when I will get on the bus and go to work. I am feel-ing strong then, that I know we have these projects, that my friends care for me, that I have something to go back to . . . when I will go home and that we Kankanaeys are supporting each other, here.

Through the gift card gift, employers attempted to shape a one-to-one rela-tionship between individuals as having a kind of affective equity and containment to it. They did not want this relationship to involve recognition of all these other people and their demands on Labanet and her obligations to them. But this global network of demands and obligations, care and chaos, made Labanet who she was and enabled her to offer the care she provided. Such global links are what her friends understand, without having to have it explained to them. Labanet herself found that the way she felt and thought about herself in the world was spread out, globally, through all these affective nodes. She dwelt within this archipelago of care and found herself—in the "we" she had slipped into in the quote, above— distributed across this global space. What countered deportability came from her feeling of global belonging: she was, herself, the archipelago of care.

Labanet's story shows us how culture helps her resist deportability. Her ability to persist and sustain herself here is how London's shatter zone extends the global one. For her, persistence is possible because her sense of herself and being in the world is located across the archipelago of care and not limited to who she is or what work she does in London. As one of perhaps a million migrants inhabiting this shatter zone space, Labanet is difficult to locate within the overall statistics describing the impact of migrants on the economy and quality of life in the United Kingdom or in London. She works in jobs not formally listed, except, perhaps fleetingly, on Gumtree.com. Mostly these positions are filled by word-of-mouth, paid cash-in-hand, offer no benefits, and are unregulated in terms of hours or conditions. Likewise, the flats she shares are not advertised and either no tenancy agreements are signed or she is not added to the lease as a tenant. The space she inhabits lies both beyond and beneath the United Kingdom's regulatory framework and statistical radar. Instead, she dwells in an affective, physic space of global networks, and this space shapes her sense of self as mobile, archipelagic, and global.

With this sense of self and her social networks, Labanet is able to circumvent much of the regulatory squeeze on irregular working implemented by the authorities. She does not need a driver's license in London; she uses public transportation as flexibly and anonymously as possible. She no longer rents in her own name. Instead she sublets from a friend who has Indefinite Leave to Remain and steady, professional work. Working cash-in-hand, she can live without access to a bank account. Though she has borrowed a bankcard from a friend, it's for identification—prosthetic citizenship only—instead of actual banking. Labanet remits her cash to the Philippines at least once each month across the counter of a high street bank. Moving house several times and not providing a forwarding address enabled her to evade contact from Capita as part of the attempt to force those in the migration refusal pool to leave the United Kingdom. She kept herself going with a mixed portfolio of work. She had a steady, mainstay, housekeeping job and rotated among shorter-term cleaning, property management, babysitting, and elder care work. When we last talked about earnings, Labanet was averaging

£700–£730 ($1,078–$1,124) per week. If she had been earning this amount as a formal economy salary or self-employment wages, she would have taken home about £27,839 ($42,872) per year or £535 ($824) per week. In 2014, Labanet was earning about £36,400 ($56,056) cash-in-hand each year, saving £8,603 ($13,248) in tax and £4,231 ($6,516) in National Insurance—which covers payments into the public health care and benefits systems as well as state pension. These tax savings made her take-home earnings equivalent to a salary of £48,600 ($74,844) or £930 ($1,432) per week. She was still remitting £1,400 most months with extra amounts going home for Biag's business needs, including interest and repayments on their loans, and her children's school fees. She now owned several multimillion peso pieces of road-paving equipment. Her own costs in London, covering rent, utilities, transport, food, sundries, and social activities, had almost doubled from our first interview in 2009, increasing to over £1,100 ($1,694) per month. For all of this, she depended on her friends to sustain her.

It was being careful in her movements, in her friendships, and in her feelings that kept her safe. Recognizing the ironies of this position made her laugh with relief, and she told me about her last interaction with the Home Office at Lunar House.

> I explained to the man at the window that I was staying with friends, that they were supporting me. And that I was working, just casual babysitting, only just enough to pay my food. Then the man at the window, he told me that, well, something like, "Nobody's friends care for them like that! Just letting them stay . . . You're lying. You are working." And I say, "No, it's true. My friends do!!"
>
> And I'm laughing inside . . . This happening at the time when I am the one who is sending Yapeng home! I'm finding her the babysitting, organizing her ticket, loaning her the money to pay for it, paying her rent, paying her food and transport . . . Oh, Lord! Nobody's friends?! I'm that friend now!
>
> But what I observed with Yapeng's problems . . . is it's very risky just to have one employer or to just care for an older person. There's not so much that you can find, right away, after they will die. So, I'm trying to make sure my part-time [jobs] are many, and really paying. And now, it's my friend who is accommodating me, with renting . . . and also the one who loaned me her bankcard. They're Kankanaey, yes, but I didn't know them, back home. It's that I met them both here, in London, at our socials. Our bonding, it works!

With that, she turned back toward the bus stop, toward the anonymity of public transport. Her phone was in her pocket, ready for her next Skype call on her way to her next several hours work. She would clean the flat of an older man and do his grocery shopping in the afternoon, then take another bus to clean an office in central London in the evening, and, finally, travel back to her flat again to rest.

# Notes

1. Prime Minister David Cameron, quoted in Anonymous, 2015b.
2. Legislation currently passing through the UK Parliament. See http://services.parliament
.uk/bills/2013-14/immigration/documents.html.
3. Anonymous, 2014.
4. Williams, 2014.
5. HM Government, 2006.
6. Found at http://blogs.telegraph.co.uk/news/iainmartin1/100258799/mark-harper-had-to
-resign-he-was-the-immigration-minister-who-took-no-prisoners/.
7. Syal and Travis, 2014.
8. Wilson, 2004.
9. De Genova, 2002, p. 440.

# Conclusion
## *Care's Archipelago*

WHAT IS CARE? Here, I have shown the simple answer is a flow of affect made through line dancing, picnics, socials, excursions, birthday celebrations, anniversaries, Facebook, Skype, phone calls, text messages, boxes of gifts, foundation days, saints' feasts, demonstrations, campaigns, shared flats, house moves, and shared meals. Through these sites and activities, migrants sustained their care by expanding their networks through conjugation. Migrants joined up with "friends of friends" in friendship and newly discovered or intensified extended kinship. Migrants also pruned their networks, cutting people out and cutting off groups of kin or former friends, refusing to renew or extend connections. A deeper answer is that care originates through the affective flows and underlying ethics and norms channeling affect in these nodes. Within each node, particular strategies of conjugation and cutting shape and sustain care. Migrants doing care work draw on flows of affect across several nodes—connecting spaces in the United Kingdom, in the Philippines, and elsewhere—in order to deliver to their employers the felt experience of being cared for. The way migrants' own sense of self was embedded in these networks—both being in and feeling as an archipelago of care—made the care they delivered global. Features of specific nodes turned up in others, seeping into each other and blending nodes together. Church was on Facebook, Skype was at work and home in the Philippines, and it was all there, the whole archipelago accessible through the open channel on the phone in Labanet's pocket, when she was on the bus in London.

Each chapter revealed affect flowing between people and across spaces as energy—both positive and negative, and even as spiritual potency. Affect moved through images, words, expressions, things, and value. In the chapter on the church, people stood to sing, swaying in unison, arms around each other's waists, incorporating new arrivals into the practices of bonding. Yet after the same service, friends would fall out over gossip. In the chapter on the community center, the performance of culture enabled caring exchanges but also exclusions. People needed to produce and perform their ethnicity to be affirmed and supported by others and to extend their networks. The networks forged through seemingly more frivolous "socials" sustained migrants to a much greater extent than more overtly political projects that attempted to negotiate routes to formal citizenship. Not all networking was smooth! Not only were faces slapped in church because of gossip shared back in the Philippines, but rows also broke out on Facebook. People were excluded from online photos taken of events, and former housemates no longer recognized each other in public—in fact, they couldn't even sit in the same pew or at the same table. The chapter on Facebook showed how social media enabled people to bring expectations from back home to church and community center and to bring family, virtually, into their workplace. The images and comments that comprised social media feeds mediated affect, carrying care, censure, support, and haunting around the world. All of these flows were conjugated, in different ways and with varying norms and obligations, in rented houses, back home in the Philippines, and in migrants' movements across the city. Mediation carried affect from one node to the next, causing each node to bleed into all the others, so migrants' sense of themselves was that they inhabited one archipelagic space—and that this space had made them who they were. The final chapter on transiting London revealed how skills in channeling and managing affect and holding in or expressing the resulting emotions enabled migrants to sustain their connections with others. Migrants recognized how, fundamentally, all people need to feel love and belonging, to feel the good feeling others have for them. Because they recognized how affective flows sustained their ability to care and their sense of self, they were able to work and live in conditions of global precarity.

In global social networks, peer-to-peer connections were migrants' most fraught relationships. My respondents reported comparatively few acrimonious divorces or irreparable ruptures with children or siblings back home. Over five years, I knew of only two of my sixty-one respondents who separated or divorced. No parents lost touch with their children and no siblings stopped speaking to each other. Like Conyap and Rachel, some have tense relationships but remain in contact, others have become even closer. Former flatmates and fellow congregants, on the other hand, are still accusing each other of various misdemeanors and failing to recognise each other in public. Back in the Philippines, chaotic lives and unstable families are now frequently seen as a consequence of financial instability resulting from the failure to access the benefits offered by migration, rather than by migration itself.[1] In London, while migrants changed employers fairly frequently, only in a handful of instances was the termination of employment charged with ill feeling. Griping about employers—and family expectations—was consigned to mutually supportive domestic spaces in rented homes and Facebook. I only saw—and heard about—harsh words and physical violence emerging within peer relations. Flows of affect between housemates, coworkers, neighbors, former classmates or village-mates, and more distant kin—those beyond second or third cousin—were the most unstable. People were continually using culture—the idea of *inayan*—to frustrate and remake obligations and norms for exchange and support, cutting and conjugating networks as a result. Scholars have considered these friendship and neighbor relations "weak ties" but my respondents used affective nodes to strengthen them. Making their lateral networks stronger then let them circumvent immigration regulation in the United Kingdom and secure investments at home. However, these ties often couldn't bear the strain of expectation and obligation; peer relationships were repeatedly stressed by the reciprocity demanded in Kankanaey culture. In London, people shifted best friends and housemates frequently. They complained most vociferously about their perceived exploitation by friends and distant kin who were not meeting their "proper" obligations to them. This cutting, the shadow side of bonding, happened in the same physical and virtual spaces where bonding occurred. The results saw intense affective flows constantly rearranging my respondents' social networks, meaning they spent much time "in transit" between houses, congregations, and friendship groups.

Each chapter also revealed how its particular affective node was structured by different concepts, rituals, exchanges, and practices of mediation. The church and the community center were nodes shaped by public ritual and performance. Migrants' houses and investments back home were shaped by norms for kinship, friendship, and intimacy. Facebook and lives in transit blended both these themes. In London, migrants used faith to help them renegotiate ideas of debt, *inayan*, and kinship through their church congregations. On Facebook, they reinvented rituals of socializing and exchange, generating new kinds of belonging and strategies to cope with surveillance. When the new norms and obligations they created were iterated back through the space of the community center and social media, they shaped practices of prosthetic citizenship for migrants and subversive citizenship for host nationals. At migrants' houses and back home, networks were cut and conjugated through the materiality of objects, both as gifts and as expressions of control. Back home even the most apparently durable material things—houses and roads—took shape through global relationships, as did government administration and police recruiting. As these affective nodes connected, dissolved, and reconnected global networks, their mediating work was done through digital fora. Skype and Facebook were central in migrants' everyday lives. Meanwhile the global shatter zone in London was held open by migrants and subversive citizens through face-to face encounters that facilitated real and symbolic exchanges: money for work, recognition for care.

The affective nodes mapped by these chapters were sequential focal points shaping migrants' feelings about the world and their places within it during their sojourns in London. Church typically served as the initial node for networking, but it was quickly supplemented and then replaced by Facebook, community center events, and domestic arrangements, followed by politics and investments back home and navigating precarity in the city. By attenuating their investments of time and energy into particular nodes and transferring them into others, irregular migrants minimized their deportability while maximizing investments in their future back home. They recruited their employers to these investment projects. Employers apparently identified with and rewarded migrants' desires for future security and social mobility. For migrants, "home" was thus where they imagined they could feel and be recognized by others as middle-class—with all the stability and security they thought that status ought to entail. They competed with others to attain this status, considering it success.

Flows of affect consoled migrants and assuaged their guilt over their irregular statuses. Simultaneously, affect enabled employers practicing subversive citizenship to gesture to globality itself to justify employing irregular workers. These subversive citizens expressed their disgust at the outcomes of globalization by refusing to take on the government's outsourced border checks. In a situation in which all citizens were being made over into proxy border police, they subverted attempts to expand the regulatory apparatus governing migration beyond the state's formal borders. Faced with the demand that citizenship's boundaries would have to be policed by citizens themselves, subversive citizens were globally angry. Where the neoliberal, outsourced state was not just operationalized in private companies, like Capita, holding contracts to track irregular migrants, but also by employment regulations that required employers to check visas and documents, subversive citizens would not play their role. Instead, they refused to embody the border on both ethical and administrative grounds. Because they cared about a global world, they rejected the requirement that they treat migrants differently from other employees. Some circumvented their obligations by choosing to ignore possible substitutions of documents. Other subversive citizens campaigned to make migrants feel welcome and to be recognized for their work, while trying to open up routes to formal citizenship for them. Subversive citizens made the care migrants delivered visible to a wider public. Connecting, affectively, with subversive citizens enabled migrants to counter the negative effects of surveillance, policing, and migration regulation. These intercultural connections also sustained migrants' spatial and temporal strategies of affective self-management, so that their performances of prosthetic citizenship were convincing. Reciprocal care, from their employers and these wider British social networks, helped migrants to look and feel as if they belonged in the United Kingdom and avoid being apprehended. Migrants' affective strategies were conjugated with subversive citizen's anger at the unethical outcomes of globalization in Britain to create and hold open the global shatter zone.

Though this global shatter zone is found inside British borders, it is a social space beneath and beyond migration regulation and state governance. It is produced by affects conjugating networks of very different actors: employers, activists, church congregants, banks, *karbut* sellers, remittance agents, and migrants themselves. Managing affect here enabled migrants to navigate London with mobile employment, residential, and spiritual strategies, and to connect what happened here to events and flows in the Philippines. Tracing affective flows across the shatter zone located care's origins in the particularities of culture and explained why this version of globalization needs the shatter zone to give it its distinctive shape.

## Care As Global Particular

My respondents located their capacity to care—to manage these affective flows to sustain selves who can cope with making unreciprocated donations of positive affect—in a culture of exchange. People who found their reciprocal obligations to peers most problematic were those people most aware of the intensity of affect now flowing through cultural exchanges and life-course events. Across the affective nodes, people understood open reciprocity as a spiritual good—governed by *inayan*—and this understanding then justified attaching a spiritual value to an enduring a lack of reciprocity. People who did not share and would not give then deserved what fate delivered to them. Those who helped others—even non-Kankanaey others—were entitled to community and family care and support. As a cultural ethic, *inayan* made it risky not to care, to give, to loan, or to forgive.

*Inayan* attached a spiritual advantage to those who donated care in open, generalized, long timescale and global exchanges. The concept explained how a personal capacity to care relied on collective norms and shared expectations for respect, sustenance, exchange, and security. Thus all donations of care should come back to the donor through other means, including global ones. Belief in *inayan* sustained migrants by conjugating their everyday care work with their deeper Kankanaey cultural notions of debt and obligation, futures, and the shape of Kankanaey selves. Migrants deployed *inayan* to reconcile the different standards of reciprocity they expected from friends and distant relatives as compared to employers and close family. *Inayan* promised to compensate them for what were largely one-way affective flows. Thus migrants' capacities to care depended on culture, but also the economic arrangements and colonial histories that had shaped their migration. Their cultural construction of care through *inayan* made their care global, but also particular, locating it in cultural histories shaped by colonial encounters in their sending region in the Philippines.

Care in London thus depended on the cultural ethics of the not yet entirely capitalist global periphery in the Philippines. Migrant caregivers were the insurgent edge this periphery, part of a nation where the middle class was still expanding. The care they provided to employers was not so much extracted in the Philippines and delivered in Britain but generated through flows of affect, differentiated and uneven, across global networks. Being able to tap into these global flows of feeling offered migrants an advantage largely unavailable to workers at the bottom of the United Kingdom's formal labor market. Migrants' cultural difference was not simply their coping strategy for the structural violence inflicted on them by the regulations shaping migration regimes. Instead, their culture offered far more than mere coping; it gave them a global strategy for accumulation and expansion. It was their culture that gave my respondents a facility for managing affect and joining together affective nodes that saw them recognized by host nationals as superb communicators and excellent caregivers. Their skills in understanding and responding to affective messages, not naming English emotions, were what my respondents relied on.[2] Their comparative success revealed how the expanding international market for migrants' caring labor depends on these global affective flows.

My respondents did not subscribe to the neoliberal belief that every individual could become what he or she wanted to be, regardless of circumstance or starting point. Instead of self-determining individuals, their culture produced extended persons whose sense of self was distributed across social networks. Thus migrants felt that they were, themselves, affective nodes in the archipelago of care they inhabited. Migration did not make them bounded individuals, or locate them within a bounded Kankanaey ethnic enclave per se. Instead, they built broader social and networked solidarity to sustain care: for selves, for others, for family, for subversive citizens and for UK employers. Not being strongly individuated by their migration experiences meant that their global orientation remained more neotribal than neoliberal. So their global care emerged from within the older, different, and adaptive cultural politics that underpinned their neotribal approach to the world. Though Kankanaey migrants had moved into a nation where governments increasingly approach their population as data generators or clients—a resource to be sold off—their culture meant that their care remained resistant to complete commodification. Their sojourns in London saw them transform and intensify ritual celebrations, performances, and gifting, all strategies directed to navigating the global shatter zone and producing multiple versions of good citizenship simultaneously.

In London, the roll back of government services meant the lawless frontier of the eighteenth- and nineteenth-century colony was now being replicated in the internal spaces created through migrant sojourns. New, mediated forms of belonging and citizenship—substantive citizenship and pathways to formal citizenship—proliferated in this UK shatter zone. This space was connected to similar spaces in other countries by almost instantaneous flows of affect. While state regulations produced weak fixities—visa categories, fixed abode, formal citizenship—people in the shatter zone deployed global, mobile strategies of living and connecting to subvert state attempts to control them. The affective links between national shatter zones accreted into a global shatter zone composed of intimate and intercultural connections. Thus the global shatter zone emerged in particular places as the constitutive shadow side of corporate, capitalist globalization.

Across this space, people used collective and collaborative intercultural action to limit or defer the effects of regulatory regimes, institutions, and implementation strategies for migration management. Kankanaey migrants arrived in London already English speakers and from a nonstate society, so were used to relying on their own culture and personal networks to subvert, repress, evade, and avoid the state. Simultaneously, the United Kingdom benefitted from having them in its large shadow workforce, particularly for the care supporting highly mobile, global professional elites and a growing population of infirm, older retirees. Though migrants were unable to depend on the state benefits of flowing from formal citizenship or legitimate residence and work, both employers and employees deployed their affective connections to hold the UK's shatter zone open and make it global.

In the UK, it seemed even elite London employers somehow felt they were at risk. They feared loss of jobs, status, security, and the impositions of work, even if these impositions "only" meant being suddenly redeployed to Geneva, New York, or Singapore, or switching from one well-remunerated job to another. The shatter zone's informal spaces of migrant work supported employers at the top end of the British labor market—government ministers—as well as those closer to the "squeezed middle" of the salary scale who perhaps had greater reason to be afraid. "Squeezed middle" employers identified with middle-class, professional Filipino migrants because they shared the migrants' imagined future of security and family social mobility. These employers, however, felt themselves at risk of Sassen's expulsion, rather than their employee's more proximate fear of being instantly deported. Such employers sought to escape still life by shifting their relationships with migrants toward the social networks, patron-client relations and informal hiring that had characterized Britain before the welfare state was created. Employers operating in this social space were willing to recognize obligations to reciprocate extending beyond the informal, cash-in-hand contract, into reciprocating care for their employees. Enacting the role of patrons gave employers a sense of shoring up their class position against a precarious future. London's global shatter zone was thus shaped by ongoing debts and exchanges and recognition of mutual exposure between employers and migrants. Networks of exchange and interpersonal obligation which my respondents established via their employers extended to the wider community and protected them from being reported to the authorities. Though a weak form of security—finding a good private employer—this seemed to my respondents to be tacitly sanctioned as a route to substantive belonging. As migrants, they belonged because they cared for those important British families and communities to whom the United Kingdom could not reliably deliver the flexible, affordable care the nation's economy and society required.

Beyond their employers, other subversive citizens—activists and civil society groups—also reciprocated migrants' care. Activist and civil society groups tried to trade services and support for migrants' participation in their projects and campaigns, but these exchanges tended to falter. Migrants' participation required a visibility running against their interests in sustaining their earning power. Migrants, meanwhile, performed prosthetic citizenship, having success appended to them through others' readings of their actions. Such performances of prosthetic citizenship materialized the neoliberal discourse of citizenship— showing self-perfecting participant-citizens "worthy" of the United Kingdom. They presented themselves as the kind of migrants activists wished to claim as deserving of public recognition. But migrants' performances were largely in-tended to convince others in their Filipino and local-citizen networks of their reliability and stability. It was initially incidental that their performances could be seen as evidence of the good works required for substantive citizenship. While grateful to employers, activists, and NGOs for holding the shatter zone open, most irregular migrants were not seeking formal citizenship.

Rather than relying on the efforts of subversive citizens to generate belong-ing in Britain, migrants depended on digital technologies to shape new forms of belonging across the global shatter zone. Social media let migrants fold affective nodes into each other through global exchanges of affect and information. But this folding of nodes had some subtle and surprising outcomes for the global. It undid the purported power of globalization to homogenize plural cultures and places into a singular "global." Instead, the particularities of the networks extending through the global shatter zone reshaped the ways migrants could belong. Via social media, migrants could now perform a version of prosthetic citizenship that was simultaneously digital, subnational, and global. Though polymedia did shift users' perceptions of the self and reveal how tensions be-tween individuality and extended personhood were always being renegotiated, it was deployed to strengthen culture. Migrants used polymedia to reinvent and intensify Kankanaey ritual and exchange. They were compelled to do so by a sense of self now distributed across the affective nodes of the global archipelago of care that defined them.

## Insights for Migration Policy

A qualitative study of a small group of workers in a particular global niche, my research highlights further questions for migration policy. Policy makers would want such questions to be answered by research with a much wider scope and much more extensive quantitative data. But this project has made key questions visible: Who are these employers who hire irregular migrants as cash-in-hand care workers—who, why, where, when, and how much? To what extent does a wider informal economy of casual, cash-in-hand care work also sustain low-wage or state-supported residents of the United Kingdom? Do irregular migrants in the informal economy of care work effectively suppress wages or prevent care sector and related jobs from opening up for citizens and residents across the United Kingdom, or does London's social geography make it an exceptional case?

Returning to the three popular assumptions about migration outlined in the introduction, my findings show what can be gained from nuancing them. Firstly, the irregular migrants I've studied were middle-class professionals in their sending countries. They were not the increasingly mobile poor but from emergent middle classes whose aspirations could not be met by opportunities at home. Though they came from less than politically stable places, they were unlikely to meet the requirements to be formally recognized as refugees. These people were what migration managers call "mixed flows" even at the level of their individual histories: they simultaneously sought security and economic opportunity. Their migration had improved standards of living but was not necessarily making conditions in their sending country more stable or less precarious. Secondly, these migrants did not always wish to become citizens of their receiving nations. In the United Kingdom, contradictions at the bottom of the labor market meant caregiving work done without a work visa was far more attractive than with a work visa or citizenship. The way the global shatter zone was configured in the United Kingdom meant irregular migrants could find an occupational niche not available to them if they had "papers"—a space where they could enjoy better pay and working conditions. These migrants knew they were better off being irregular, despite paying lip service to the ideal of attaining eventual citizenship. Circular migration schemes and formal access arrangements for labor-sending countries may help to protect workers' rights and long-term interests here. Migrants doing informal work may have been happy with their earnings, but they were possibly losing out on health care, pension savings and education while insecure and vulnerable to exploitation.

Finally, migrants in all categories drew others to the United Kingdom and helped to sustain co-ethnics in London and in their global networks during their stay. Migrants moving to the United Kingdom were not necessarily best understood through the initial visa categories that regulated their migration. Instead, migrants' trajectories were shaped by their networks. Migrants were not only domestic workers when they held that specific visa. I found migrants from all visa categories doing domestic work, often as part of a portfolio of casual employment. Though migrants who had arrived as legitimate students, tourists, or family visitors might have become overstayers, they had typically worked in domestic work or as caregivers throughout their sojourn. Similarly, qualified nurses who had arrived on work visas as National Health Service care assistants could also vanish into the informal care economy. In London, irregular migrants' work sustained the networks that supported not only care workers, but the broader Filipino community. The economic situation in the city meant that other Filipinos needed irregular migrants' earnings to pay their rent or their mortgages, even if they held work visas or already had residency or citizenship themselves.

Rather than allowing overstayers to be apprehended and deported by the authorities, community members worked together to return irregular migrants who were no longer earning sufficient wages to the Philippines. Working with settled communities to better support routes home for overstayers could reduce the burden on the United Kingdom's asylum and deportation regimes. Regularizing migrants doing private care work, at least by offering shorter-term visas, if not a formal visa scheme, might be a viable option to meet London's care needs.

If the United Kingdom envisions a future of home-based care where families hire "nannies for grannies," that future is already here in London's informal care economy. Predictions suggest irregular migrants will continue to find work. Plans to raise the United Kingdom's minimum wage will strain the formal system of state-funded or subsidized nursing homes and domiciliary care over the next few years. At the same time, demographic changes will see demand for care work expand. Increasing costs and expanding demand along with government-funded personal care budgets for older people will push more employers to seek out cash-in-hand, private arrangements. Meanwhile, the government has returned nursing jobs to the Shortage Occupation List, reopening the British labor market to Filipino nurses. However, the salary requirements for converting nurses' temporary work permits to Indefinite Leave to Remain have not been lowered. More Filipino nurses will be recruited to work in lower-rank nursing positions, but then fail to earn enough to qualify for permanent residency. The government's intention seems to be to create circular migration: these migrant nurses should leave the United Kingdom after their work visa expires. Given the history and circumstances in the Filipino community, it seems likely that this change will only increase the number of people who overstay to work in the informal care economy. At the same time as the informal care economy is expanding, low salaries for migrant nurses will make it difficult for new arrivals to recoup the costs of their education and travel, and to repay any loans they've taken out to get to Britain. Migrants who feel they have lost their imagined future in Britain may then try their luck as "T&T" in order to build up the savings that would make returning home seem feasible. Responding to that outcome with increased enforcement, more regulations, and additional deportations will be costly and unpleasant. If Britain wished to discourage overstaying to take up care work as a migration strategy, it needed to reinstate exit controls. The UK government did this, phasing in controls starting in April 2015. The regulatory squeeze on irregular migrants' access to formal housing, banking, and health care has continued with the introduction of new control and reporting requirements effectively delegated to bank tellers, landlords, and front-line health care staff.

If the United Kingdom deems the kind of informal economy care work Filipinos have been doing desirable and it could be shown not to undermine local workers, at least in particular labor markets and regions, it should be formalized with short-term contracts, regulatory protection for working conditions, and clear contract terms. The United Kingdom could look to the lessons learned from caregiver migration schemes in Israel and Canada.[3] Such schemes have costs and frustrations for migrants and their families and are by no means a perfect solution, but they do make migration trajectories—and thus family and financial plans—somewhat more predictable and secure and enable people to access health care and contribute to pensions.

Despite the demand for non-EU care workers, British migration policy has instead been sourcing domestic workers from Europe. The United Kingdom had deregulated its au pair scheme in an attempt to move European Union migrants into what were traditionally positions as mother's helpers. Since 2008, this scheme has been opened up to become one covering generalized domestic work, but not specifically care for older or disabled people.[4] Notwithstanding the change in migration policy, it appears that au pairs from the EU have not edged out Filipino migrants with professional backgrounds working as nannies, housekeepers, and caregivers in the London labor market. EU migrants' are less able to compete, not because of EU migrants' comparatively higher expectations for wages and working conditions per se, but because of their comparatively weaker global networks.[5] EU migrants seem to find themselves both less able to channel affect into care and more alienated in the United Kingdom, as compared to the dense and dynamic global networks sustaining Filipinos. Resolving the tension between offering formal access to EU citizens versus the informal non-EU migrant workers depends on the United Kingdom's negotiation of migration regulations within the European Union. Since the United Kingdom has just voted to leave the European Union, the future of the au pair scheme is uncertain. At the same time, the resulting fall in value of the pound and the possible departure of elite financial service workers from London mean Britain will be less attractive to Filipino migrants intending to overstay for work in the informal economy of care, regardless of regulatory changes.

Here, my results suggest that the cultural and global origins of migrant care mean that low-cost, high quality care provided by these irregular migrants cannot be easily and fully substituted by care work from local workers, at least within current economic conditions and social histories. Global care is a valuable contribution to British society and much needed, particularly by older people and families with workers in long-hours or flexible-time roles. If the United Kingdom requires people to perform this work but cannot afford to offer much above minimum wage remuneration relative to local costs, it makes sense to offer the work to qualified people for whom these wages will make a real difference—in futures to be lived elsewhere.

## Notes

1. Katigbak, 2013.
2. Yoo, Matsumoto, and LeRoux, 2006.
3. Liebelt, 2011; Pratt, 2012; Stasiulis and Bakan, 2005.
4. Busch, 2013; Williams and Myerson, 2014.
5. Busch, 2013; Miller and Búriková, 2010.

# Bibliography

Abinales, Patricio, and Donna Amoroso. 2005. *State and Society in the Philippines.* Manila: Anvil.

Aguilar, Filomeno V. Jr. 1998. *Clash of Spirits: The History of Power and Sugar Planter Hegemony on a Visayan Island.* Honolulu: University of Hawai'i Press.

Allen, John. 2002. *Lost Geographies of Power.* Oxford, UK: Blackwell.

Anderson, Ben. 2014. *Encountering Affect.* Farnham: Ashgate.

Andersson, Ruben. 2014. *Illegality, Inc.* Berkeley: University of California Press.

Anonymous. 2014. "Mark Harper Resignation Letter in Full." BBC News online. February 8.

———. 2015a. "175,000 Migrants 'Missing,' says National Audit Office." BBC News online. July 22.

———. 2015b. "Calais Crisis: Cameron Pledges to Deport More People to End 'Swarm' of Migrants." *The Guardian* online. July 30.

Appadurai, Arjun. 1990. "Disjuncture and Difference in the Global Cultural Economy." *Public Culture* 2(2): 1–24.

Ashcroft, Bill. 2001. *Postcolonial Transformation.* London: Routledge.

Bartley, Emma. 2015. "Doing it All: My 10 Worst Moments as a Working Mum." *Get The Gloss* online. March 1.

Basu, Paul, and Simon Coleman. 2008. "Introduction: Migrant Worlds, Material Cultures." *Mobilities* 3(3): 313–30.

Busch, Nicky. 2013. "The Employment of Migrant Nannies in the UK: Negotiating Social Class in an Open Market for Commoditized In-Home Care." *Social and Cultural Geography* 14(5): 541–57.

Cangiano, Alessio, Isabel Shutes, Sarah Spencer, and George Leeson. 2009. *Migrant Care Workers in Ageing Societies: Research Findings in the United Kingdom.* Oxford: Centre on Migration, Policy and Society (COMPAS).

Cannell, Fennella. 2006. "Reading as Gift and Writing as Theft." In *The Anthropology of Christianity,* edited by Fennella Cannell, 134–62. Durham, NC: Duke University Press.

Coleman, Simon. 2006. "Materializing the Self: Words and Gifts in the Construction of Charismatic Protestant Identity." In *The Anthropology of Christianity,* edited by Fennella Cannell, 163–84. Durham, NC: Duke University Press.

Colombo, Jesse. 2013. "Here's Why the Philippines Economic Miracle Is Really a Bubble in Disguise." *Forbes* online. November 21.

Constable, Nicole. 1997. *Maid to Order in Hong Kong.* Ithaca, NY: Cornell University Press.

———. 1999. "At Home but Not at Home: Filipina Narratives of Ambivalent Returns." *Cultural Anthropology* 14(2): 203–28.

———. 2014. *Born Out of Place.* Berkeley: University of California Press.

Cooper, Jacquie, Stewart Campbell, Dhiren Patel, and Jon Simmons. 2014. *The Reason for Migration and Labor Market Characteristics of UK Residents Born Abroad.* Home Office Occasional Paper 110. London: UK Home Office.

Costa, Elisabetta, Nell Haynes, Tom McDonald, Danny Miller, Razvan Nicolescu, Jolynna Sinanan, Juliano Spyer, Shriram Venkataraman, and Xinyuan Wang. 2016. *How the World Changed Social Media.* London: University College London Press.

Dalsgaard, Steffen. 2008. "Facework on Facebook: The Presentation of Self in Virtual Life and Its Role in the US Elections." *Anthropology Today* 24(6): 8–12.

Das, Veena, and Deborah Poole. 2004. "State and Its Margins: Comparative Ethnographies." In *Anthropology in the Margins of the State*, edited by Veena Das and Deborah Poole, 3–33. Santa Fe, NM: School of American Research Press.

Datta, Kavita, Cathy McIlwaine, Yara Evans, Joanna Herbert, Jon May, and Jane Wills. 2010. "A Migrant Ethic of Care?: Negotiating Care and Caring Among Migrant Workers in London's Low-Pay Economy." *Feminist Review* 94: 93–116.

De Coppet, Daniel. 1981. "The Life-giving Death." In *Mortality and Immortality*, edited by Sarah Humphreys and Helen King, 175–204. London: King, Academic Press.

De Genova, Nicholas. 2002. "Migrant 'Illegality' and Deportability in Everyday Life." *Annual Review of Anthropology* 31: 419–47.

Derrida, Jacques. 1992. "Force of Law: The 'Mystical Foundations of Authority.'" In *Deconstruction and the Possibility of Justice*, edited by Drusilla Cornell, Michael Rosenfeld, and David Gray Carlson, 3–67. New York: Routledge.

Dorling, Kamena. 2013. Government Reforms Threaten Migrants. *The Guardian* online. September 4.

Eggan, Fred. 1960. "The Sagada Igorots of Northern Luzon." In *Social Structures in Southeast Asia*, edited by George Peter Murdock, 24–50. Chicago: Quadrangle Books.

Faier, Lieba. 2009. *Intimate Encounters.* Berkeley: University of California Press.

———. 2013. "Affective Investments in the Manila Region: Filipina Migrants in Rural Japan and Transnational Urban Development in the Philippines." *Transactions of the Institute of British Geographers* 38: 376–90.

Feldman, Gregory. 2012. *The Migration Apparatus.* Stanford: Stanford University Press.

Fumanti, Mattia. 2010. "Virtuous Citizenship, Ethnicity and Encapsulation Among Akan Speaking Ghanaian Methodists in London." *African Diaspora* 3(1): 12–41.

George, Kenneth. 2007. "Art and Identity Politics: Nation, Religion, Ethnicity, Elsewhere." In *Asian and Pacific Cosmopolitans: Self and Subject in Motion*, edited by Kathryn Robinson, 37–59. New York: Palgrave.

Gibson, Katherine, Lisa Law, and Deirdre McKay. 2001. "Beyond Heroes and Victims: Filipina Contract Migrants, Activism and Class Transformations." *International Feminist Journal of Politics* 3(3): 365–86.

Gordon, Avery. 1997. *Ghostly Matters.* Minneapolis: University of Minnesota Press.

Gregson, Nicky, Mike Crang, Jennifer Laws, Tamlyn Fleetwood, and Helen Holmes. 2013. "Moving Up the Waste Hierarchy: Car Boot Sales, Reuse Exchange, and the Challenges of Consumer Culture to Waste Prevention. *Resources, Conservation, and Recycling* 77: 97–107.

Gregson, Nicky, and Louise Crewe. 1997. "The Bargain, the Knowledge, and the Spectacle: Making Sense of Consumption in the Space of the Car-Boot Sale." *Environment and Planning D: Society and Space* 15(1): 87–112.

Gregson, Nicky, Louise Crewe, and Beth Longstaff. 1997. "Excluded Spaces of Regulation: Car-Boot Sales as an Enterprise Culture Out of Control?" *Environment and Planning A* 29: 1717–37.

Hage, Ghassan. 2002. "The Differential Intensities of Social Reality: Migration, Participation, and Guilt." In *Arab-Australians Today*, edited by Ghassan Hage, 192–205. Melbourne: University of Melbourne Press.

Harvey, Rachel. 2014. "The Particular." In *Framing the Global*, edited by Hilary Kahn. 182–205. Bloomington: Indiana University Press.

HM Government, 2006. *Work and Families Act 2006*, chapter 18. Available at http://www.legislation.gov.uk/ukpga/2006/18/pdfs/ukpga_20060018_en.pdf.

Holston, James. 2008. *Insurgent Citizenship*. Princeton: Princeton University Press.

Johnson, Mark, Claudia Liebelt, Deirdre McKay, Alicia Pingol, and Pnina Werbner. 2010. "Sacred Journeys, Diasporic Lives: Sociality and the Religious Imagination Among Filipinos in the Middle East." In *Diasporas: Concepts, Identities, Intersections*, edited by Kim Knott and Sean McLoughlin, 217–22. London: Zed Books.

Johnson, Mark, and Deirdre McKay. 2011. "Introduction: Mediated Diasporas: Material Translations of the Philippines in a Globalized World." *Southeast Asia Research* 19(2): 181–96.

Jowit, Juliette. 2014. "Reality Check: Is Migration Good or Bad for British Jobs?" *The Guardian* online. March 5.

Katigbak, Evangeline. 2013. "The Emotional Economic Geographies of Translocalities: The Philippines 'Little Italy.'" PhD diss., National University of Singapore.

Kelly, David, and Anthony Reid, eds. 1998. *Asian Freedoms*. Cambridge: Cambridge University Press.

Kelly, Philip. 2000. *Landscapes of Globalization*. Routledge: New York.

Lazar, Sian. 2013. "Citizenship, Political Agency and Technologies of the Self in Argentinean Trade Unions." *Critique of Anthropology* 33(1): 110–28.

Levinson, Amanda. 2005. *The Regularization of Unauthorized Migrants*. Oxford: Centre on Migration Policy and Society, Oxford University.

Liebelt, Claudia. 2011. *Caring for the Holy Land*. Oxford: Berghan Books.

Longboan, Liezel. 2011. "E-gorots: Exploring Indigenous Identity in Translocal Spaces." *South East Asia Research* 19(2): 319–41.

Lury, Celia. 1998. *Prosthetic Culture*. London: Routledge.

Lusis, Tom, and Philip Kelly. 2006. "Migration and the Transnational Habitus: Evidence from Canada and the Philippines." *Environment and Planning A* 38: 831–47.

Madianou, Mirca, and Daniel Miller. 2012. *Migration and the New Media*. London: Routledge.

———. 2013. "Polymedia: Towards a New Theory of Digital Media in Interpersonal Communication." *International Journal of Cultural Studies* 16(2): 169–87.

Manalansan, Martin. 2010. "Servicing the World." In *Political Emotions*, edited by Janet Staiger, Ann Cvetkovich, and Ann Reynolds, 215–28. New York: Routledge.

McKay, Deirdre. 2004. "Performing Identities, Creating Cultures of Circulation: Filipina Migrants between Home and Abroad." In *Asia Examined*, edited by Robert Cribb, online. Canberra: Asian Studies Association of Australia and the Australian National University.

———. 2005. "Translocal Circulation: Place and Subjectivity in an Extended Filipino Community." *The Asia Pacific Journal of Anthropology*, 7(3): 265–78.

———. 2007a. "Identities in a Culture of Circulation: Performing Selves in Filipina Migration." In *Self and Subject in Motion*, edited by Kathryn Robinson. London: Palgrave.

———. 2007b. "'Sending Dollars Shows Feeling'—Emotions and Economies in Filipino Migration." *Mobilities* 2(2): 175–94.

———. 2010. "On the Face of Facebook: Historical Images and Personhood in Filipino Social Networking." *History and Anthropology* 21(4): 483–502.

———. 2012. *Global Filipinos*. Bloomington: Indiana University Press.

———. 2014. "Affect." In *Framing the Global*, edited by Hilary Kahn, 18–36. Bloomington: Indiana University Press.

McKay, Steven. 2006. *Satanic Mills or Silicon Islands?* Ithaca, NY: ILR.

Migration Advisory Committee. 2015. *Partial Review of the Shortage Occupation Lists for the UK and for Scotland*. London: Migration Advisory Committee, UK Home Office.

Migrationwatch UK. *An Amnesty for Illegal Immigrants? Migrationwatch Response to the GLA Paper*. Briefing Paper 11/7. Available at http://www.migrationwatchuk.org/briefingpaper/document/166. Last accessed September 15, 2015.

Miller, Daniel. 2007. "What Is a relationship? Is Kinship Negotiated Experience?" *Ethnos* 72(4): 535–54.

———. 2011. *Tales from Facebook*. Oxford: Polity.

———. 2016. *Social Media in an English Village*. London: University College London Press.

Miller, Daniel, and Don Slater. 2001. *The Internet*. Oxford: Berg.

Miller, Daniel, and Zsuzana Búriková. 2010. *Au Pair*. Cambridge: Polity.

Moore, Henrietta. 2011. *Still Life*. Oxford: Polity.

Nickell, Stephen, and Jumana Saleheen. 2008. *The Impact of Immigration on Occupational Wages: Evidence from Britain*. Working Paper 08-6, Federal Reserve Bank of Boston.

Pain, Rachel. 2009. "Globalized Fear? Towards an Emotional Geopolitics." *Progress in Human Geography* 33(4): 466–86.

Parreñas, Rhacel Salazar. 2001. *Servants of Globalization*. Stanford: Stanford University Press.

———. 2005. *Children of Global Migration*. Stanford: Stanford University Press.

———. 2011. *Illicit Flirtations*. Stanford: Stanford University Press.

Pattacini, Eleonora, and Yves Zenou. 2012. *Ethnic Networks and Employment Outcomes*. CReAM Discussion Paper Series, CDP No 02/12. Centre for Research and Analysis of Migration, University of London.

Pertierra, Raoul, ed. 1992. *Remittances and Returnees*. Quezon City: New Day.

———. 2002. *The Work of Culture*. Manila: De La Salle University Press.

Pingol, Alicia. 2001. *Remaking Masculinities*. Quezon City: University of the Philippines–University Center for Women's Studies.

Pratt, Geraldine. 2012. *Families Apart*. Minneapolis: University of Minnesota Press.

Rafael, Vicente. 1988. *Contracting Colonialism*. Ithaca, NY: Cornell University Press.

Raghuram, Parvati, Clare Madge, and Pat Noxolo. 2009. "Rethinking Responsibility and Care for a Postcolonial World." *Geoforum* 40(1): 5–13.

Raghuram, Parvati, Leroi Henry, and Joanna Bornat. 2010. "Difference and Distinction? Non-Migrant and Migrant Networks." *Sociology* 44(4): 623–41.

Raghuram, Parvati. 2012. "Global Care, Local Configurations—Challenges to Conceptualizations of Care." *Global Networks* 12(2): 155–74.

Reid, Anthony. 1993. *Southeast Asia in the Age of Commerce, 1450–1680*. New Haven: Yale University Press.

Rodriguez, Robyn. 2010. *Migrants for Export*. Minneapolis: University of Minnesota Press.

Rutten, Roseanne, ed. 2008. *Brokering a Revolution*. Manila: Ateneo de Manila University Press.

Sassen, Saskia. 1991. *The Global City*. Princeton: Princeton University Press.

———. 2006. *Territory, Authority, Rights*. Princeton: Princeton University Press.

———. 2014. *Expulsions*. London: Belknap/Harvard University Press.

Scott, James C. 2009. *The Art of Not Being Governed*. New Haven: Yale University Press.

Scott, William Henry. 1983. "*Oripun* and *Alipin* in the Philippines." In *Slavery, Bondage and Dependency in Southeast Asia*, edited by Anthony Reid, 138–55. New York: St. Martin's.

Schneider, Friedrich, and Colin Williams. 2013. *The Shadow Economy*. London: Institute of Economic Affairs.

Strathern, Marilyn. 1988. *The Gender of the Gift*. Berkeley: University of California Press.

———. 1992. "Parts and Wholes: Refiguring Relationships in a Post-Plural World." In *Conceptualizing Society*, edited by Adam Kuper, 75–104. London: Routledge.

———. 1996. "Cutting the Network." *Journal of the Royal Anthropological Institute* 2: 517–35.

Stasiulis, Daiva, and Abigail Bakan. 2005. *Negotiating Citizenship*. Toronto: University of Toronto Press.

Syal, Rajeev, and Alan Travis. 2014. "Britain's Immigration System in Chaos, MPs' Report Reveals." *The Guardian* online. October 29.

Szanton-Blanc, Cristina. 1996. "'Balikbayan: A Filipino Extension of the National Imaginary and of State Boundaries." *Philippine Sociological Review* 44(1–4): 178–93.

Tan, Michael. 2012. "TNT Dreams." *The Philippine Daily Inquirer* online. January 26.

Travis, Alan. 2009. "Skilled Jobs for Migrants Cut by 300,000." *The Guardian* online. April 29.

UNISON. *A Time To Care*—A UNISON Report into Homecare. Available at https://www.unison.org.uk/content/uploads/2013/11/On-line-Catalogue220152.pdf. Last accessed October 10, 2015.

Van Schendel, Willem. 2002. "Geographies of Knowing, Geographies of Ignorance: Jumping Scale in Southeast Asia." *Environment and Planning D: Society and Space* 20: 647–68.

Vine, John. 2012. *An Inspection of the UK Border Agency's Handling of Legacy Asylum and Migration Cases*. London: Independent Chief Inspector of Borders and Immigration, London.

Voida, Amy, and Elizabeth Mynatt. 2005. "Six Themes of the Communicative Appropriation of Photographic Images." Proceedings of the ACM Conference on Human Factors in Computing Systems, 171–80. New York.

Weiner, James. 1992. "Anthropology *contra* Heidegger: Part II: The Limit of Relationship." *Critique of Anthropology* 13: 285–381.

Wiegele, Katherine. 2005. *Investing in Miracles*. Honolulu: University of Hawai'i Press.

Williams, Rachel. 2014. "Isabella Acevedo: The Immigration Minister's Cleaner Stuck in Yarl's Wood." *The Guardian* online. July 23.

Williams, Zoe, and Julie Myerson. 2014. "Au Pairs on a Pittance." *The Guardian* online. October 18.

Wilson, Ara. 2004. *The Intimate Economies of Bangkok*. Berkeley: University of California Press.

Yoo, Seung Hee, David Matsumoto, and Jeffrey LeRoux. 2006. "The Influence of Emotion Recognition and Emotion Regulation on Intercultural Adjustment." *International Journal of Intercultural Relations* 30: 345–63.

# Index

refusal pool, 22–23, 114–115, 143, 157; as preference, 18–19, 25–26, 89, 153, 156; regular/irregu-
lar migrant relations, 29–30, 39, 82–83, 86–87,
152–153; return migration, 118–131; stories
of overstaying: after student visas, 99–100,
102–103, 108–110; after temporary work visas,
111–113 (*See also* Labanet and Biag); after tourist visas, 1, 15, 17, 47–48, 105; Labanet and Biag,
15, 29, 93–94, 114–115, 136–138, 142–143, 153–155,
157–158. *See also* asylum

Jewish families, and kinship, 40
*John* 15:4–5, 42
Johnson, Boris, 88

Kankanaey people, region of origin, 4, 10–11
*karbut* (car boot sales), 101, 104–105, 115
Kelly, Philip, 7
kickbacks and bribery, 117, 118, 125–126, 130, 131, 132
kinship, 37–39, 40–41, 119–124

Labanet: in bus accident, 136–139; career/work
of, 18–19, 100, 114, 156, 158; church of, 48–49;
demands on from home, 99, 108–110; employers of, 19, 67–68, 145–148, 155–159; homes of,
96–101, 114–115, 143–145, 153; investments and
return planning, 18–19, 117–118, 124–131, 138,
156; migration of, 15, 29, 35; migration status
issues, 15, 29, 114–115, 136–138, 142–143, 153–
155, 157–158; networks with other migrants,
70–71, 72–73, 96–101, 108–113, 147, 148–154, 158;
online motherhood, 51, 53, 144; social media
use of, 51, 52–53, 56–58, 65–66, 92–94, 150
land disputes, 117, 128
landlords, delegation of policing responsibility
to, 94, 139, 153, 170
language requirements, 112
lending and borrowing, 46, 70–71

McKay, Steven, 7
methodology of fieldwork, 15–18
middle classes: in Asia, 9–10; in Philippines, 10,
130–131, 133, 164, 169; in United Kingdom, 9,
21, 23
migrants (Filipino), numbers and profile of, 27, 29
migration (general), impact on United Kingdom,
23–26
migration refusal pool, 22–23, 114–115, 143, 157
Moore, Henrietta, 9
mothers as migrants, 26–27, 52–53, 56–57,
149–151

narratives about Filipino migrants, 26–27
neoliberalism, 166–168
netizenship, 83–85, 87
networks: among British people, perceived lack of,
146; *balikbayan* boxes as, 101–107; at churches,
15, 39, 41; at community centers, 70–74; employers, caring relationships with, 19, 37–38,
145–148, 164; via Facebook, 51–54, 56–57, 61,
80–82, 98–99; to find or offer work, 47, 65–66,
70, 151; at homes of migrants, 97–98, 99–100,
108–116; migration status, and management of,
148–149, 151–154; between peers, as challenge,
162–163; regional nature of, 36; regular/irregu-
lar migrant relations, 29–30, 39, 82–83, 86–87,
152–153; as sustaining sources, 147–148, 153–154,
156, 157. *See also* cutting; debt and obligation
New People's Army (NPA), 76–77, 128–130
NGOs and activists, 73–76, 77–78, 84–86, 87–89,
129–130, 167–168
nurses, 3, 30–31, 102, 112, 170
nursing homes, 25, 110–111, 121

Oedma: on care and *inayan*, 38; community
performances of, 98; digital haunting of, 38;
employment of, 99–100, 110, 111–112 116 102;
flatmate troubles of, 108–109; gifts sent home
by, 102–103, 105, 107
older people, care of. *See* elder care
overstaying. *See* irregular immigration

pagan rituals, 36
parenting and migration, 26–27, 52–53, 56–57,
149–151
Parreñas, Rhacel, 7
permanent residency. *See* Indefinite Leave to
Remain (ILR)
photos. *See* Facebook
policing. *See* UKBA (UK Border Agency)
political scandals, 139–142
polymedia, 51–68. *See also* Facebook; Skype
precarity, 131–135, 167–168
presents: *balikbayan* boxes, 101–107; from
employers, 47, 102, 145, 155–156
private equity firms, 25
privatization: of irregular immigrant tracking,
22–23; of nursing homes, 25
property ownership, back home, 118–124, 128,
132–133, 134
public transport: bus accident (Labanet's), 136–
139; bus ads (anti-immigrant), 87–88, 140; stop
and search on, 47, 75, 76–77, 78, 87, 90–92, 94

DEIRDRE McKAY is Senior Lecturer in Social Geography and Environmental Politics at Keele University. She is author of *Global Filipinos: Migrants' Lives in the Virtual Village* (IUP) and a Framing the Global fellow.